Classroom Companion: Economics

The Classroom Companion series in Economics includes undergraduate and graduate textbooks alike. It welcomes fundamental textbooks aimed at introducing students to the core concepts, empirical methods, theories and tools of the field, as well as advanced textbooks written for students at the Master and PhD level seeking a deeper understanding of economic theory, mathematical tools and quantitative methods.

Keijiro Otsuka

A Primer on Development Economics

Towards Zero Hunger and No Poverty

Springer

Keijiro Otsuka
Distinguished Honorary Professor
of Kobe University
Kobe, Japan

ISSN 2662-2882 ISSN 2662-2890 (electronic)
Classroom Companion: Economics
ISBN 978-981-95-5396-9 ISBN 978-981-95-5397-6 (eBook)
https://doi.org/10.1007/978-981-95-5397-6

The original submitted manuscript has been translated into English. The translation was done using artificial intelligence. A subsequent revision was performed by the author(s) to further refine the work and to ensure that the translation is appropriate concerning content and scientific correctness. It may, however, read stylistically different from a conventional translation.

Translation from the Japanese language edition: "Naze mazushii kuni wa nakunaranainoka? Tadashī kaihatsu senryaku wo kangaeru" by Keijiro Otsuka, © Nikkei Business Publications, Inc. 2020. Published by Nikkei Business Publications, Inc. . All Rights Reserved.

Nikkei Business Publications, Inc.

This Springer imprint is published by the registered company Springer Nature Singapore Pte Ltd.
The registered company address is: 152 Beach Road, #21-01/04 Gateway East, Singapore 189721, Singapore

To Tomoko Hashino

Foreword

Keijiro Otsuka stands among Asia's most respected and influential economists. This new book is another testament to his enduring scholarship and influence.

Getting to know and collaborate with Keijiro, whom friends and colleagues fondly call "Kei," has been an experience that has profoundly shaped my own journey as a scholar and policymaker. I first met him in the late 1980s, when I was just beginning my academic career at the University of the Philippines. At the time, he was working with my graduate school mentor, Cristina C. David, on a major comparative study examining the income distribution effects of the Green Revolution—modern rice technology—in Asia.

That pioneering research became a touchstone for understanding how agricultural technologies transform lives in developing countries. It set the standard for empirical studies linking innovation and equity, and its influence continues to be felt in agricultural and rural development policy across Asia and beyond.

Over the years, I have followed Kei's remarkable intellectual journey as he ventured into new areas of development—spanning technology transfer, innovation, industrialization, environmental management, climate change, and international development cooperation. His work reflects a rare blend of theoretical depth, rigorous field-based research, and an intuitive grasp of how policies shape real-world outcomes. His insights, drawn from decades of fieldwork across many countries in Asia and Africa, are enriched by his leadership in global research institutions and professional associations.

Kei's contributions to advancing economic development in low- and middle-income countries have been both exceptional and enduring. His studies on the rice Green Revolution in Sub-Saharan Africa (SSA) have been instrumental in addressing food insecurity and poverty in the region. As Chairman of IRRI's Board of Trustees, he spearheaded collaborative rice research between IRRI and AfricaRice and inspired the creation of the Coalition for African Rice Development (CARD), which helped double rice production in SSA from 2008 to 2018. Kei has always emphasized that lasting agricultural transformation requires more than just better seeds and fertilizers—it demands strong extension systems to teach crucial management practices such as land leveling, water control, and weeding.

Beyond agriculture, Kei turned his attention to the challenges of industrial development in SSA, advocating for the adaptation of East Asia's cluster-based growth model and the use of the *kaizen* approach to improve productivity and entrepreneurship. His lifelong work has deepened global understanding of how technology transfer, institutional learning, and human capacity development drive inclusive and sustainable growth. Kei's career stands as a powerful testament to how academic excellence and practical impact can go hand in hand.

I have had the privilege of working with Kei in many capacities—seeking his advice, inviting him to speak, and collaborating in conferences and forums on agricultural and rural development. These moments, particularly during my years as the director and chief executive of the Southeast Asian Regional Centre for Graduate Study and Research in Agriculture (SEARCA) and as the founding editor of the *Asian Journal of Agriculture and Development*, remain among the highlights of my professional life.

Kei's scholarship has profoundly shaped the way I view my own work. His theories and field-based insights have deepened my understanding of what truly drives rural transformation, poverty reduction, and sustainable growth. They have also guided me throughout my career—as both an academic and a policymaker—including my tenure as economic secretary (minister) under two Philippine administrations and as founding chairperson of the Philippine Competition Commission. I was deeply honored when Kei contributed a chapter to the festschrift volume published by ISEAS (Singapore) in my name—a piece that reflects not only his intellectual depth but also his enduring commitment to understanding the real-world dynamics of development. Reading his contribution reminded me once again how his ideas have intersected with, and enriched, my own journey in both research and policy.

Kei's new book, *A Primer on Development Economics: Towards Zero Hunger and No Poverty*, is a timely and inspiring contribution. It distills decades of research and experience into an accessible, engaging guide to the forces that shape development success—and failure. Though designed as an introductory text for students of economic development, it offers rich insights for seasoned practitioners and newcomers alike, especially those engaged in development work across Asia and Africa. Policymakers and professionals in development assistance organizations will find it equally valuable for its practical wisdom and clarity of thought.

What sets this book apart is its clarity, relevance, and compassion. It is not only *A Primer on Development Economics* but also a reflection of Kei's lifelong commitment to making research serve people—to ensuring that economic growth is not just faster, but fairer. It is, without doubt, a must-read for anyone dedicated to the pursuit of shared prosperity, rural transformation, and sustainable development.

Arsenio M. Balisacan
Department of Economy, Planning, and Development
Manila, Republic of the Philippines

Preface

This book is an introductory text for those who may not wish to study economics in-depth but are interested in learning about *development economics*. It is written with such readers in mind. They may be students considering a future career in international development or those who eventually wish to study development economics more seriously, government officials involved in official development assistance (ODA), and nongovernment organization (NGO) members working on poverty alleviation and women's empowerment in developing countries. I aim to explain development economics as I understand it, in the simplest terms possible.

The few available textbooks are often intended for graduate students already well-versed in economics or focus narrowly on specific subfields. To understand these, one must first learn the basics of economics. Moreover, economic theory is often mathematical and difficult to grasp, and much of it is unrelated to development issues, making the effort required disproportionate to the practical benefit. Nevertheless, there are many people involved in ODA or working in the field of development who wish to learn at least the fundamentals of development economics. Many students are also interested in this area. Despite this, introductory texts on development economics remain rare. Why is this the case?

I believe the reason is that development issues are so diverse that it is not easy for a single researcher or a small group to write an introductory book or textbook on the subject. For example, in the context of advanced economies, there are specialists in each field—such as public finance, industrial organization, labor, economic history, education, agriculture, trade, regulation, energy, healthcare, welfare, and others—each writing separate textbooks. Developing countries are numerous, and the range of important economic issues is correspondingly broad. Within each country, there are issues similar to those in advanced countries, such as public finance, industrial organization, and so forth. Therefore, it is quite challenging to write an introductory book on development economics that covers the various fields relevant to all developing countries.

However, the current lack of communication among researchers, policymakers, practitioners, and students is highly undesirable. There is much that researchers can learn from practitioners, and vice versa. Furthermore, researchers must foster the next generation of scholars and experts through communication with young people.

In an effort to address this situation, I have drawn on my limited knowledge to write this book. As I discuss within these pages, economics is a discipline that *systematizes common sense*, and I firmly believe that topics which may appear difficult at first glance can, in fact, be explained in simple terms. I encourage readers to test this belief by reading this book and judging for themselves whether my approach is effective.

Like all works in economics, this book frequently uses concepts such as income and gross domestic product (GDP). This is because *income* is closely related not only to living standards but also to education, health, life expectancy, and other aspects of *quality of life*. Some may question whether economic development is truly desirable for developing countries, but to such readers, I recommend visiting these countries in person. Experiencing firsthand the harsh realities of low income and poverty will provide a deeper understanding of their severity.

For example, in early November 2013, a major typhoon (called Haiyan) struck the Philippines, particularly Leyte Island, resulting in thousands of casualties due to storm surges. I urge you to consider the people who live in such hazardous areas. When water and food are desperately needed, why did the news reports state that there were only four helicopters available in the Philippines to deliver relief supplies? Many lives could have been saved if adequate emergency aid had been available. Increasing income is crucial for avoiding such situations and enhancing the quality of life.

I have conducted extensive field-based research on both agriculture and manufacturing across Asia and Africa. The countries and regions where I have carried out empirical case studies include Japan, China, Taiwan, Vietnam, the Philippines, Thailand, Indonesia, Bangladesh, India, Nepal, Sri Lanka, Senegal, Ghana, Côte d'Ivoire, Ethiopia, Kenya, Uganda, Tanzania, Malawi, Mozambique, and South Africa. In addition to the development of agriculture and industry, my research interests have also encompassed environmental issues, the role of the state, and gender. As a development economist, I take pride in the breadth of both the regions and topics I cover. Nevertheless, I am acutely aware that what I understand represents only a small fraction of the broader issues in development. Therefore, I would like readers to recognize that this book differs from conventional textbooks or introductory works that provide comprehensive explanations of established theories.

This book is, above all, an *introductory text* centered on what I know, and as such, the topics covered are inevitably limited in scope and subject to my own biases. Furthermore, on topics that remain under debate, I may have presented arguments that are mistaken due to my own misunderstanding. Yet, I would like to emphasize that this book focuses on the first two goals of the United Nations Sustainable Development Goals (i.e., zero hunger and no poverty).

This book is grounded in the results of my own research in development economics over the past 40 years. In that sense, it may be described as a scholarly work that reflects the culmination of my career as a researcher. Looking back, I owe a great debt to many individuals who have supported me along the way. First and foremost, I wish to express my gratitude to the late Professor Yujiro Hayami, who guided me during my graduate studies at Tokyo Metropolitan University from 1972 to 1974. Although his guidance was extremely rigorous, I would not be who I am today without his heartfelt mentorship. Through our joint research and co-authored publications, I learned countless invaluable lessons. I am also deeply grateful to the late Professor Theodore W. Schultz, who had a decisive influence on my decision to pursue an academic career during my graduate school years, personally funded my first-year scholarship at the University of Chicago, and continued to encourage my research thereafter. These two individuals, in my opinion, are among the most respected development economists, and I consider myself fortunate to have received direct guidance from such giants in the field.

I am heavily indebted to my wife, Tomoko Hashino, for preparing this book manuscript. As an economic historian, this book naturally pays due attention to the historical development of currently developed countries. She carefully reviewed the first draft of the book manuscript, and we discussed the book intensively. Therefore, I would like to dedicate this book to her.

I have published 150 articles in internationally renowned journals; 29 authored, coauthored, or coedited books in English; and 12 books in Japanese. I was extremely fortunate to collaborate with more than 100 competent and dedicated colleagues. Without them, it would not have been possible to publish so many articles and books. Their influences on my thoughts and ideas are enormous, and, hence, the contents of this book are undoubtedly and deeply affected by them.

They are so numerous that I cannot thank them all here. I am particularly thankful to coauthors and coeditors of my books: the late Gustav Ranis and Gary Saxonhouse, Cristina C. David, Deqiang Liu, Naoki Murakami, Frank Place, Agnes R. Quisumbing, Jonna P. Estudillo, Tetsushi Sonobe, Kaliappa Kalirajan, Stein H. Holden, Yasuyuki Sawada, Takashi Yamano, Koichi Hamada, Ken Togo, Donald F. Larson, Tomoko Hashino, Kimiaki Jin, Shenggen Fan, Yukichi Mano, and Kazushi Takahashi. I have also learned great deal from my former colleagues: Peter Hazell, Masakatsu Akino, Masao Kikuchi, Yoshihisa Godo, Masayoshi Honma, Jikun Huang, Xiaobo Zhang, Kei Kajisa, S. Suyanto, Thom Jayne, and Futoshi Yamauchi. I also would like to thank my former students who read the earlier version of the book manuscript and gave useful comments: Yoko Kijima, Tomoya Matsumoto, Yukichi Mano, Eiji Yamamura, John Akoten, Kazushi Takahashi, Shingo Kimura, Yuko Nakano, Rie Muraoka, and Aiko Kikkawa.

Finally, I would like to express my appreciation to Maki Nakajima and Fumiyo Aburatani for their significant contributions to the preparation of figures and other aspects of this book's publication. I am also deeply indebted to Avril Adrianne D. Madrid for her assistance with the English editing. My thanks go to Juno Kawakami at Springer for her support in bringing this book to publication. I would like to take this opportunity to extend my sincere gratitude to all. Finally, I am grateful for the financial support of JSPS KAKENHI Grant Number 25K00633.

Keijiro Otsuka
Kobe, Japan

Contents

II What is Happening?

III What Must and Must not be Done?

About the Author

Keijiro Otsuka is a distinguished honorary professor at Kobe University and a fellow of the Asian Development Bank Institute in Tokyo. He received a PhD in economics from the University of Chicago in 1979. Before joining Kobe University, he was a Professor at the National Graduate Institute for Policy Studies from 2001 to 2016. Previously, he served as Chairman of the Board of Trustees of the International Rice Research Institute from 2004 to 2007, President of the International Association of Agricultural Economists (IAAE) from 2009 to 2012, and President of the Japanese Association for Development Economics from 2019 to 2024. He is an honorary life member of IAAE, a fellow of the Agricultural and Applied Economics Association, a distinguished fellow of the African Association of Agricultural Economists and the Asian Society of Agricultural Economists, and a fellow of the Japanese Society of Agricultural Economics. He received the Purple Ribbon Medal in 2010 and the Orders of the Sacred Treasure, Gold and Silver Star in 2021 from the Japanese government and became a member of the Japan Academy in 2018. He has conducted numerous case studies on agricultural and industrial development in Asia and Sub-Saharan Africa over the last 40 years.

List of Abbreviations

AGRA	Alliance for a Green Revolution in Africa
ASEAN	Association of Southeast Asian Nations
CARD	Coalition for African Rice Development
CDM	Clean Development Mechanism
CIMMYT	International Maize and Wheat Improvement Center
COP	Conference of the Parties
DAC	OECD Development Assistance Committee
EU	European Union
FAO	Food and Agriculture Organization of the United Nations
FDI	Foreign direct investment
GDP	Gross domestic product
GHG	Greenhouse gas
GNI	Gross national income
GPS	Global positioning system
GRIPS	National Graduate Institute for Policy Studies
IT	Information technology
ICT	Information and communication technology
IFPRI	International Food Policy Research Institute
IMF	International Monetary Fund
IPCC	Intergovernmental Panel on Climate Change
IRRI	International Rice Research Institute
JICA	Japan International Cooperation Agency
JPY	Japanese yen
MDG	Millennium Development Goals
MV	Modern variety
NGO	Nongovernment organization
ODA	Official development assistance
OECD	Organisation for Economic Co-operation and Development
PISA	Programme for International Student Assessment
PPP	Purchasing power parity
RCT	Randomized controlled trials
SDG	Sustainable Development Goals
UN	United Nations
US	United States
USD	US dollars
WIPO	World Intellectual Property Organization

List of Figures

List of Tables

What are the Issues?

What Is Development Economics?

Contents

K. Otsuka, *A Primer on Development Economics*,
Classroom Companion: Economics, https://doi.org/10.1007/978-981-95-5397-6_1

1.1 Let's Start With a Definition

As is the case in any field of research, it is often difficult to answer the question, *What is the study of development economics?* In the case of development economics, the subject matter is highly diverse, and the field continues to expand and deepen as it evolves, making it even harder to define. Perhaps for these reasons, there is still no universally accepted definition of development economics.

I would like to define *development economics* as *the academic discipline that studies strategies to reduce poverty in poor developing countries*. However, many development economists may not agree with this definition. For example, some may argue that development economics is not solely concerned with poverty reduction, but also addresses important issues such as how middle-income countries can join the ranks of advanced economies. Others may point out that it is also important to study how countries like Japan, which was a poor developing country in the early Meiji period, managed to become an advanced economy.

Indeed, Japan's experience is valuable, and the rapid development of emerging economies such as China and India—countries that, despite overall growth, still face significant poverty—remains an important topic. However, from an academic perspective, this is not a fundamental distinction. This is because, in principle, there are many commonalities between strategies to raise the incomes of the poor and those to help middle-income individuals become high-income earners. Similarly, the question of why the growth rate of advanced economies like Japan has slowed can also be analyzed from the perspective of development economics.

Furthermore, in middle-income countries with significant income disparities, poverty can remain a serious issue even if average incomes are high. China, where rural inland areas lag behind in development, and India, where caste-based discrimination leads to pronounced income inequality, are prime examples. Therefore, if we adopt a broader definition, development economics can be described as *the study of development strategies and poverty reductionstrategies for developing countries in general, including emerging economies*.

There is also a closely related field known as *the theory of economic development*. In English, both are referred to as development economics. However, the former tends to emphasize the formulation of policies to promote economic development, while the latter places more importance on endogenous economic growth—though the distinction is subtle. Similarly, the terms *developing country* and *less developed country* are essentially synonymous. In this book, I will use the former.

A more fundamental objection may be raised regarding the term *strategy*. When development economics emerged in the 1950s and 1960s and was still in its infancy through the 1970s, researchers in this field were primarily concerned with constructing strategies aimed at *poverty reduction* or *raising the incomes of the poor*. Subsequently, it became clear that most development theories proposed at the time were, unfortunately, unrealistic, and they gradually faded from prominence (see ► Box 1.1). The problem is that, along with this, interest in formulating development *strategies* also waned. Today, it seems that most researchers who identify as development economists, even those interested in analyzing poverty, often show little interest in constructing strategies for poverty reduction.

Box 1.1 No Silver Bullet for Development

When development economics emerged in the 1950s and 1960s, most economists regarded people in developing countries as fundamentally different from themselves, with distinct ways of thinking. A prominent example is Arthur Lewis, who was awarded the Nobel Prize in Economics in 1979.

Lewis (1954) argued that farmers in developing countries are engaged in unproductive agricultural work and do not earn income in accordance with their work. Since they are performing unproductive tasks that make little difference whether done or not, if their income were determined by productivity, it would be so low that survival would be impossible. Therefore, he claimed, such farmers receive only a bare minimum *subsistence level* income necessary for survival. According to this view, if farmers engaged in unproductive work are shifted to productive non-agricultural employment, the economy will develop. However, if the subsistence level truly determines farmers' incomes, then most farmers should have similar incomes. Yet, there is no evidence to support this. For example, in Africa, as in rural Asia, significant income disparities exist among farming households (Otsuka et al. 2009).

Harris and Todaro (1970) posed the question of why, in developing countries, many rural migrants to cities often end up unemployed and idle, and they sought to provide a theoretical explanation for this phenomenon. According to their analysis, creating productive jobs and providing employment for the unemployed is the key to economic development. While job creation is important, in reality, very few urban poor in developing countries are truly unemployed and idle. Most cannot afford such a luxury and are instead engaged in low-income activities such as garbage collection or street vending.

The problem is not the absence of jobs, but rather that many are compelled to take low-paying work due to factors such as a lack of education. Therefore, even if high-wage, skilled jobs are created, the likelihood that poor workers could obtain such positions is extremely low. Fortunately, arguments like those of Lewis and Harris and Todaro, which can be considered speculative, are gradually being forgotten over time. The prevailing view today, as first advocated by Schultz (1964), who, like Lewis, was awarded the Nobel Prize in Economics in 1979, is that people in developing countries are rational economic agents. Their poverty is attributed to low levels of education and the lack of dissemination of high-productivity technologies. In other words, there is no magic bullet for development; rather, steady investment in education and technological improvement is the fundamental condition for economic growth. This argument applies not only to developing countries but also to advanced economies.

Just as doctors diagnose and treat based on their findings, many development economists conduct analysis (diagnosis) and propose policy recommendations (treatment). Still, few seem to consider fundamental development strategies that would promote growth (i.e., economic development). I became acutely aware of this when I participated as a core member in the writing of the World Bank's World Development Report 2013: Jobs (World Bank 2012) in 2011–12. The World Bank is renowned as a global center of expertise on development issues. In the field of development economics, it is considered the world's leading institution, surpassing even the economics departments of the prestigious Ivy League universities. Yet, to my surprise, the World Bank showed little inclination to formulate effective development strategies. Its basic stance was that each country has its own circumstances, and therefore, effective development strategies will also differ.[1] While it is true that each country has unique circumstances and that effective development strategies may differ in some respects, is there not a common core? The mission of academic inquiry is precisely to identify such commonalities or universal principles. I was greatly disappointed by the World Bank's attitude in this regard. I will revisit this issue in ► Chap. 3.

To avoid any misunderstanding, I would like to state in advance that my interest in poverty reduction in developing countries does not imply indifference to the development of countries that have escaped poverty or to that of wealthy, advanced economies. On the contrary, learning from past success stories is extremely important for understanding the secrets of development. In the early 1980s, I conducted research on the development of the cotton spinning industry in prewar Japan, which was still a poor country at the time.[2] After the mid-1980s, I shifted my research focus for a time to the development of Asian countries,[3] and from the mid-1990s, I began conducting comparative studies between Asia and Africa,[4] eventually centering my research on African development.[5]

By chance, this proved to be a stroke of luck. There is much to learn from Japanese history when considering the development of emerging economies in Asia. Understanding how Taiwan and China have developed became critically important when I considered development strategies for other Asian and African countries. Furthermore, my research on Japan's rapid postwar growth and subsequent prolonged stagnation, from a development economics perspective, was also an invaluable experience.[6]

---

1 This World Development Report (World Bank 2012) discusses eight distinct types of economic development, arguing that appropriate development strategies fundamentally differ among them. However, it also notes that there are some similarities.

2 This was published as Otsuka et al. (1988).

3 I conducted research on agricultural development (Hayami and Otsuka 1993; David and Otsuka 1994), and on industrial development (Otsuka et al.1998; Sonobe and Otsuka 2006, 2011, 2014).

4 I published a number of journal articles on this. To take advantage of the complementarity of these articles, I published a number of books, including Otsuka and Place (2001); Quisumbing et al. (2004); Otsuka et al. (2009); Sonobe and Otsuka (2011, 2014); Holden et al. (2013); Otsuka and Shiraishi (2014); and Otsuka and Sugihara (2019).

5 See Holden et al. (2009); Yamano et al. (2011); Otsuka and Larson (2013, 2016); Otsuka et al. (2023); and Otsuka et al. (2018).

6 Hamada et al. (2011). In addition, there is Otsuka (2024), which provides a comprehensive review of my previous studies since the early 1980s.

Before concluding the discussion on definitions, I would like to briefly address the more fundamental question: *What is economics?* When you look at newspapers and magazines, you see terms like exchange rates, inflation, interest rates, and fiscal deficits. Many people, therefore, think that economics is the study of such issues. However, these are the domain of macroeconomics, while my own expertise, like that of most development economists, lies in microeconomics. In fact, across the discipline, there are far more microeconomists than macroeconomists. So, what is microeconomics? The details are complex, but in essence, microeconomics analyzes the behavior of economic agents such as consumers, firms, workers, farmers, and the self-employed family workers. By summing up analyses of the behavior of individuals and organizations, we can then examine the development of industries, agriculture, and ultimately the economy as a whole.

To date, I have conducted questionnaire-based surveys on the behavior of farmers and firms in many countries across Asia and Africa, collecting and analyzing original data. To conduct robust surveys, a solid understanding of local realities is essential, so I have listened to the stories of countless farmers and entrepreneurs. Throughout this book, you will find *economic* discussions based on the results of my field research, often presented in plain language that may not seem like economics at first glance. If readers can sense a flavor of microeconomics from this book, I would be most grateful.

1.2 International Comparison of Income

Economists are quick to talk about income, but some readers may feel, "There's more to life than just income." I completely agree. However, when income is low, life can indeed be harsh, and it becomes difficult to cope with unexpected events, such as crop failures or illness. On the other hand, higher income allows people to accumulate assets, which brings greater security and more choices in life. Some readers may remain unconvinced, but I ask for your patience as we proceed with this discussion. Later in this chapter, I hope to present indicators that will convince you of the importance of income.

The first basic statistics we should examine are the disparities and changes in average per capita income across countries. To do this, we first divide each country's GDP by its population to obtain per capita GDP. However, since this is expressed in each country's own currency, it cannot be directly compared across countries. Therefore, we use exchange rates to convert these figures into US dollars (USD) for comparison. Yet, because price levels differ between countries and fluctuate over time, direct comparison is still not meaningful. For example, a haircut in Japan often costs more than 4,000 Japanese yen (JPY), which is USD 30, while in many developing countries it can be less than JPY 400.

To address this, economists use per capita real GDP adjusted for purchasing power parity (PPP), which takes price differences into account, to compare incomes across countries. However, a major issue arises in choosing which goods and services to use for price comparisons. Despite such statistical challenges, it is

1

broadly possible to compare living standards and their changes across countries using income figures adjusted for price differences. In addition, we must also account for year-to-year changes in prices. Here, too, we use price indices to adjust for inflation and employ real GDP figures that reflect these changes.[7] ◘ Table 1.1 presents the values for several countries for the years 1990, 2000, and 2020.[8]

The figures are based on 2021 international dollar prices; however, the final column displays the price ratio for 2015. According to this, prices in Japan are 15% lower than the international dollar, while prices in Ethiopia are only 39% of that level. Intuitively, this means that having 39 cents in Ethiopia allows one to purchase roughly the same amount of goods and services as having one dollar in the US.

Looking at 1990, the average per capita GDP of the four East Asian countries selected here was just under 4% of that of the four high-income economies, while South Asia and Africa (more precisely, Sub-Saharan Africa, but hereafter referred to as Africa) were only about 1.7%–3.4% of that. Even after adjusting for price differences, when the annual income of a Japanese person was about USD 30,000, Ethiopia—one of the poorest countries—had an income of USD 278, and Nepal and Bangladesh were around USD 400–500. This illustrates the unimaginably low-income levels in these three countries.

Here, East Asia refers to the entire region, encompassing Northeast Asia (including Japan, South Korea, and China) and Southeast Asia (including Myanmar). East Asia, driven by China's growth, experienced rapid economic expansion, and by 2020, income levels had risen to approximately 20% of those in advanced economies. The average annual growth rate in East Asia exceeded 7% in both the 1990s and 2000s; a 7% growth rate means that income doubles in ten years with compound growth.

Compared to East Asia, South Asia's growth has been slower. Nevertheless, the average annual growth rate accelerated from 3.0% in the 1990s to 5.6% after 2000. In particular, the acceleration of India, often referred to as the "sleeping giant," has been remarkable. In contrast, Africa has lagged behind Asia, with slow growth. The silver lining is that growth rates have increased since the 2000s. However, income levels remain extremely low. It is therefore understandable that the focus of development economics has shifted significantly from Asia to Africa.

Although income levels in South America are high, growth has been sluggish, and it appears likely that East Asia will overtake the region in the near future. It may be hard to believe, but in the 1930s, Argentina was wealthier than the United States. In the long term, South America's stagnation is striking. This may be because, satisfied with past achievements, the region failed to pursue reforms aimed

7 For example, if annual income increases from JPY 1 million to JPY 3 million, but prices rise by 50%, real income would change from JPY 1 million to JPY 2 million (300 /1.5).

8 Deciding which countries' data to present in this book was a difficult task. Including data from too many countries would make the tables overly large and hard to interpret, while too few would undermine generalizability. Furthermore, for many African countries, historical data are unavailable. Readers should understand that the selection of countries shown in the tables represents a certain compromise—a balance between data availability and generalizability.

Table 1.1 Comparison of real GDP (PPP-adjusted) per capita among selected countries and regions (based on USD in 2015)[a] (World Bank's World Development Indicators various years)

	1990	2000	2020	Average annual growth rate, 1990–2000 (%)	Average annual growth rate, 2000–2020 (%)	Comparison of price level with the US in 2015
High-income countries	34,165	41,645	49,529	2.00	1.16	0.97
Japan	28,422	31,431	34,651	1.0	0.7	0.85
US	39,200	48,616	59,493	2.2	1.4	1.00
UK	30,876	38,922	42,216	2.3	0.5	1.06
France	27,993	33,255	35,709	1.7	0.5	0.90
East Asia	1,301	2,634	9,784	7.3	9.1	0.53
Indonesia	1,471	1,828	3,739	2.2	4.9	0.30
China	905	2,194	10,358	9.3	10.9	0.56
Thailand	2,632	3,515	6,035	2.9	3.7	0.36
S. Korea	9,367	16,996	31,378	6.1	4.2	0.76
South Asia	573	773	1,740	3.0	5.6	0.27
Bangladesh	473	621	1,605	2.7	6.5	0.36
Pakistan	951	1,050	1,526	1.0	2.5	0.28
India	538	757	1,807	3.5	6.0	0.26
Nepal	423	547	1,032	2.6	4.3	0.30
Sub-Saharan Africa	1,174	1,041	1,764	−1.2	3.6	0.44
Ethiopia	278	257	799	−0.8	7.8	0.39
Nigeria	1,577	1,422	2,338	−1.0	3.4	0.45
Kenya	1,329	1,195	1,609	−1.1	2.0	0.45
South America	6,094	7,020	8,603	1.4	1.4	0.57
Peru	2,707	3,286	5,832	2.0	3.9	0.48
Brazil	6,150	6,818	8,435	1.0	1.4	0.56
Argentina	8,115	10,632	11,393	2.7	0.5	0.67

[a] Group averages are weighted averages, where the weight is the population ratio

at further progress, falling into the so-called middle-income trap. The East Asian countries that have enjoyed robust development so far could also fall into this trap if they become complacent and neglect further efforts toward development.

1.3 Income as an Indicator of "Quality of Life"

About 15 years ago, I visited a rural village in western Kenya that appeared extremely poor. As shown in ◘ Table 1.1, Kenya is not among the poorest countries in Africa, so this village was not exceptionally poor by African standards. However, the corn in the village fields was sparse and poorly developed. The unpaved roads of red soil had deep holes, likely made by trucks, making them impassable for ordinary vehicles. The houses were also very modest.

I asked the villagers, "How many times a day do you eat?" To my surprise, the answer was "once." However, they added, "In the morning, we drink a cup of milk." Even for me, who has visited many poor villages, this was a shocking response.

Under such conditions, people are likely to feel hungry throughout the day and experience a lack of energy. They are likely more susceptible to illness, but with no money and no clinic nearby, even if they become seriously ill, they may not be able to see a doctor. Infants and young children, who are physically vulnerable, may not survive. Moreover, even if parents want to send their children to school, the demands of daily life may force them to prioritize farm work instead.

◘ Table 1.2 presents the infant mortality rate up to age one and the average life expectancy at birth—that is, the expected lifespan—for the same countries listed in ◘ Table 1.1. The focus on infant mortality stems from the belief that nothing is more painful for parents than the loss of a young child. While it cannot be said unequivocally that longer life expectancy is always better—since, as in Japan, China, and S. Korea, an aging society brings various challenges such as the need for long-term care—it is nonetheless tragic when many people die young. The key point is that these indicators of quality of life are closely linked to per capita income. Several important facts can be discerned from ◘ Table 1.2.

First, infant mortality rates are low in high-income countries and extremely high in low-income countries, while life expectancy is long in the former and short in the latter. The most dire situation is found in Nigeria, where the number of infant deaths per 1,000 live births was 124 in 1990 and still as high as 72 in 2020. This is an alarmingly high figure. The average life expectancy in Nigeria is also around 50 years, which is exceedingly short. Since Nigeria is not among the poorest countries, it is likely that factors other than average income, such as income inequality, have a significant impact on infant mortality and life expectancy.

Nevertheless, the general trend evident in the table is a strong negative correlation between income and infant mortality, as well as a positive correlation between income and life expectancy. Second, in East Asia, where income has grown rapidly, infant mortality rates have declined substantially from 1990 to 2020, and life expectancy has increased markedly over the same period. In South Asia, al-

Table 1.2 Comparison of infant mortality rates and life expectancy among selected countries and regions[a] (World Bank's World Development Indicators various years)

	Infant mortality rate per 1,000		Life expectancy (years)	
	1990	**2020**	**1990**	**2020**
High-income countries	7.8	4.3	76.4	79.6
Japan	4.6	1.8	78.8	84.6
US	9.4	5.5	75.2	77.0
UK	7.9	3.7	75.9	80.4
France	7.3	3.3	76.6	82.2
East Asia	43.9	7.6	67.6	76.9
Indonesia	61.7	19.4	63.2	68.8
China	42.8	5.5	68.0	78.1
Thailand	30.3	7.4	70.4	79.3
S. Korea	13.5	2.6	71.6	83.4
South Asia	88.6	31.2	58.5	69.8
Bangladesh	101.1	25.7	56.0	72.0
Pakistan	106.9	54.1	60.1	66.3
India	84.4	28.1	58.7	70.2
Nepal	96.3	24.9	54.8	69.2
Sub-Saharan Africa	115.1	55.6	47.3	58.1
Ethiopia	120.5	36.1	44.6	65.4
Nigeria	124.4	72.3	46.0	52.9
Kenya	64.4	31.8	58.6	62.7
South America	48.6	12.3	66.8	74.3
Peru	56.8	12.2	65.1	73.7
Brazil	52.5	13.0	66.0	74.0
Argentina	25.4	8.9	71.8	75.9

[a]Group averages are weighted averages, where the weight is the population ratio

though not to the same extent as East Asia, conditions have also improved. Thus, rising income can be seen as reducing infant mortality and increasing life expectancy. It is important to emphasize here that per capita income is related not only to material well-being but also to health and medical standards. Readers should understand that income is closely tied to the quality of life.

Table 1.3 shows the enrollment rates for primary and lower secondary school children. The numerator represents the number of school-age children who are enrolled (excluding those who have exceeded the school age due to

1

Table 1.3 Comparison of primary and lower secondary school attendance ratios among selected countries and regions in 2019[a] (World Bank's World Development Indicators various years)

	Primary	Lower secondary
High-income countries	96	92
Japan	99	99
US	95	92
UK	99	97
France	99	95
East Asia	96	80
Indonesia	93	79
China	99	n/a
Thailand	98	77
S. Korea	97	98
South Asia	90	60
Bangladesh	91	67
Pakistan	68	37
India	92	62
Nepal	96	62
Sub-Saharan Africa	77	35
Ethiopia	85	31
Nigeria	64	26
Kenya	80	48
South America	93	77
Peru	96	89
Brazil	96	82
Argentina	99	91

[a] In countries where 2019 data are not available, the data from the most recent years are used. Group average data are directly taken from the data source
n/a indicates data is not available

grade repetition), and the denominator represents the total population of school-age children. Because enrollment data are incomplete and it is difficult to obtain historical figures, only data from 2019 or the most recent year available are presented. It is a universal phenomenon that, without education, people cannot obtain the jobs they desire; education is the most important determinant of income (Otsuka, Estudillo, and Sawada 2009). Therefore, whether or not education is available is a matter of great concern not only for people in developing countries but also for practitioners, bureaucrats, politicians, and researchers interested in development issues. According to this table, primary school enrollment rates are close to 100% in high-income countries, East Asia, and South America, but only 90% in South Asia and just 77% in Africa. Although the data are incomplete, there is even greater variation among countries in lower secondary school enrollment rates. Nevertheless, it is clear that countries and regions with lower incomes tend to have lower enrollment rates. Because there is a bidirectional relationship—income affects investment in education, and the results of educational investment affect income—the causal relationship is not clear. However, there is no doubt that income is closely related to children's education. Here again, income can be seen as an indicator of certain aspects of quality of life.

1.4 Income and Poverty

When considering the standard of living of an individual or household, it is preferable to use consumption data rather than income data. This is because income can fluctuate significantly due to factors such as poor harvests caused by adverse weather conditions, illness or accidents that prevent people of working age from working, or unemployment, whereas consumption tends to be more stable.

For example, even if the primary earner in a household loses their job, the family may be able to draw on savings or borrow money from relatives or friends based on expected future income. In other words, while consumption is related to the household's long-term income level, annual income can fluctuate due to unforeseen events. Therefore, it is inappropriate to use a single year's low income as a measure of poverty. However, it is also true that consumption data are often difficult to obtain, so income data are frequently used instead. At the national level, individual or household-level luck tends to cancel out, so using income data as an indicator of living standards is generally not problematic.

How, then, should poverty be defined and measured? The fundamental perspective is to determine the cost required to obtain the minimum calories and nutrition necessary for life. However, as the phrase *food, clothing, and shelter* suggests, life is not just about eating. Therefore, the poverty line is defined as the income needed to cover the minimum food expenses plus a modest amount for other basic necessities. Since the modest amount involves subjective judgment, the poverty line cannot be defined entirely objectively.

Despite these issues, the basic approach is to consider people whose income falls below this poverty line as poor (Haughton and Khandker 2009). In line with this, many developing countries have established their own poverty lines. However, this makes international comparisons difficult, so the World Bank has adopted an international poverty line of USD 1.25 per day (adjusted for PPP).[9]

9 Previously, one dollar a day was used as the poverty line, but due to rising prices, 1.25 dollars a day was considered more appropriate in 2005 (Ravallion et al. 2009), and more recently, 2.15 dollars a day has been adopted.

1

Table 1.4 Comparison of poverty ratio among selected countries and regions around 1990 and 2020[a] (World Bank's World Development Indicators various years)

	Around 1990[b]		Around 2020[c]	
East Asia	68.3		0.4	
Indonesia	61.8	(1990)	2.8	(2020)
China	72.0	(1990)	0.0	(2020)
Thailand	12.3	(1990)	0.1	(2019)
South Asia	48.2		13.0	
Bangladesh	41.9	(1991)	5.0	(2022)
Pakistan	65.1	(1990)	4.9	(2018)
India	48.0	(1993)	15.5	(2020)
Nepal	55.2	(1995)	0.4	(2022)
Sub-Saharan Africa	54.2		30.4	
Ethiopia	69.2	(1995)	27.0	(2015)
Nigeria	52.4	(1992)	30.9	(2018)
Kenya	26.4	(1992)	35.0	(2020)
South America	19.8		2.3	
Peru	19.8	(1997)	5.8	(2020)
Brazil	24.0	(1990)	2.0	(2020)
Argentina	1.0	(1991)	1.2	(2020)

[a] Poverty line is USD 2.15 per day. Group averages are weighted averages, where the weight is the population ratio.
[b] The numbers in parentheses are years in which data closest to 1990 are available.
[c] The numbers in parentheses are years in which data closest to 2020 are available.

While the appropriateness of this amount is open to debate, this poverty line has been widely adopted globally as a standard measure. This book also uses this criterion to attempt international comparisons of poverty ratio (the number of poor people as a proportion of the country's population) (see Table 1.4).[10]

Even if a country's average income is high, if income distribution is skewed, it is possible for a small number of wealthy individuals to coexist with a large number of poor people. In regions such as South America and the Philippines, large estates were established during the colonial era, and the resulting disparities have persisted across generations. Income distribution remains highly unequal. In recent years, it has been said that income inequality in China has reached levels

10 This is an indicator known as the poverty headcount ratio. In addition, there are indicators such as the poverty gap ratio and the squared poverty gap ratio, which take into account not only the number of poor but also the depth of poverty.

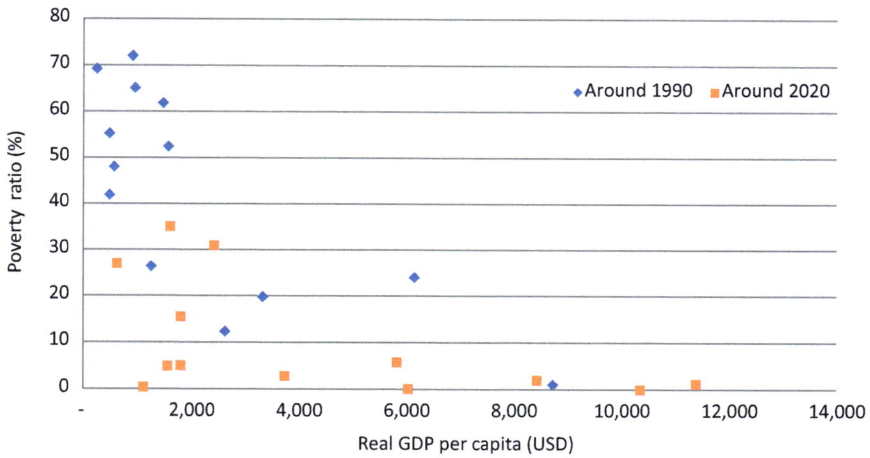

Fig. 1.1 Correlation between real GDP per capita (USD, horizontal axis) and poverty ratio (vertical axis) around 1990 and 2020 (World Bank's World Development Indicators various years)

comparable to those in South America. The gap between wealthy cities and poor rural areas, as well as between the prosperous coastal regions and the stagnant inland areas, has widened the disparity between the rich and the poor. In Japan, farmers in the suburbs of cities are relatively affluent, but in China, where land is state-owned, those who have successfully obtained urban land use rights have become very wealthy by collecting building rents and other means. In such situations, even if the average income is high, the poverty ratio may remain high. This issue will be revisited in ▶ Chap. 2.

According to Tables 1.4 and 1.1, despite differences in income distribution among countries, there is a very clear and strong negative correlation between GDP per capita and poverty ratios, which is clearly illustrated by Fig. 1.1. Both in 1990 and in 2020, there is a stable negative relationship between real GDP per capita and poverty ratio This suggests that it is difficult to eradicate poverty without economic development and raising average income levels.

Why is this the case? To use a simple analogy, suppose a worker in New York City earns USD 10,000 per month, while in a regional city, let us suppose the monthly income is USD 5,000. This represents a significant disparity. However, would such a situation persist for long? Some workers from regional cities would likely attempt to move to New York. As a result, the regions would gradually experience labor shortages, while New York would see an increase in its labor supply. Consequently, wages in the regions would rise, while those in New York would tend to decline. In addition, companies with factories near New York might relocate their facilities to regional areas in search of cheaper labor. This would lead to a surplus of labor in New York and a shortage in the regions, thereby equalizing incomes. While other factors may also play a role, it appears that labor mobility and factory relocation in both the United States and Japan have contributed to the equalization of regional incomes. Traveling across various parts of the United States or Japan, one is often struck by the remarkable similarity in residential architecture.

In general, labor income for the same type of work does not vary greatly within a single country. In other words, when one part of a country develops and workers' incomes rise, incomes in other regions also tend to increase. This mechanism likely explains the strong correlation between average income and the poverty ratio. However, inequality in non-labor income, such as returns on assets, is more difficult to resolve.

Of course, this is not to suggest that income inequality should be ignored, but I believe that raising incomes is an essential condition for reducing poverty. Therefore, it is crucial to promote industrial development to create employment opportunities for those living in poverty. While the details will be discussed in later chapters, what I wish to emphasize here is the importance of income growth. Without an increase in income, it is practically impossible to reduce infant mortality rates or extend life expectancy. Moreover, improvements in education and reductions in poverty are extremely difficult to achieve without income growth.

1.5 Fundamental Perspectives and the Structure of This Book

A term closely related to *economic development* is *economic growth*. While the two share many similarities, economic growth primarily concerns the increase in income, whereas economic development emphasizes structural changes in the economy. For example, in poor economies, agriculture is the main sector; in middle-income countries, manufacturing becomes more prominent; and in advanced economies, the service sector dominates. Development economics seeks to understand why such structural changes occur and how they can be promoted.

In practice, there is a close relationship between per capita income and economic structure. Typically, as economies develop, the leading sector shifts from agriculture to industry and then to services. ◘ Table 1.5 illustrates the relationship between income levels and industrial structure across countries. It can be seen that the lower a country's income, the greater the importance of agriculture; conversely, the higher the income, the more significant the service sector becomes.

Why does this happen? Looking back on history, even today's advanced economies were once agricultural societies, with most people engaged in farming. A key point is that, even as societies become wealthier, the demand for agricultural products does not increase substantially. Although rising incomes may lead to a shift from lower-quality to higher-quality foods, the capacity of the human stomach is limited, so the increase in demand for agricultural products is gradual. This is the main reason why the relative importance of agriculture declines as economies develop.

As incomes rise, demand for industrial goods such as electrical appliances also increases. In Japan, during the late 1960s, color televisions, air conditioners, and automobiles were referred to as the "new three sacred treasures." As demand for such products grew, the manufacturing sector developed accordingly. With fur-

Table 1.5 Comparison of industrial structures among selected countries and regions in terms of proportion of GDP (%)[a]

	1990			2000			2020		
	Agriculture[b]	Industry[c]	Service	Agriculture[b]	Industry[c]	Service	Agriculture[b]	Industry[c]	Service
High-income countries	2.3	30.9	66.8	1.4	25.7	72.9	1.0	19.7	74.2
Japan	2.1	37.5	60.4	1.5	31.1	67.4	1.1	29.1	69.5
US	2.1	27.9	70.1	1.2	23.4	75.4	0.9	17.3	77.1
UK	1.8	34.1	64.1	1.0	27.3	71.7	0.7	17.4	72.1
France	4.2	27.1	68.7	2.8	22.9	74.2	1.5	16.3	71.0
East Asia	25.0	40.9	34.1	14.6	45.5	39.9	8.5	37.5	53.2
Indonesia	19.4	39.1	41.5	15.6	45.9	38.5	13.7	38.2	44.4
China	27.1	41.3	31.5	15.1	45.9	39.0	7.7	37.8	54.5
Thailand	12.5	37.2	50.3	9.0	42.0	49.0	8.7	33.3	58.0
S. Korea	8.9	41.6	49.5	4.6	38.1	57.3	1.8	32.5	57.0
South Asia	30.3	29.3	40.4	24.0	25.7	50.4	18.6	24.8	49.1
Bangladesh	30.3	21.5	48.3	25.5	25.3	49.2	12.0	32.9	51.5
Pakistan	26.0	25.2	48.8	25.9	23.3	50.7	21.9	18.6	53.7
India	30.4	31.0	38.6	23.1	26.1	50.8	18.7	25.1	47.9
Nepal	51.6	16.2	32.1	40.8	22.1	37.0	22.2	12.0	53.9
Sub-Saharan Africa	31.9	25.8	42.2	31.4	25.1	43.5	27.5	25.3	44.5
Ethiopia	54.3	11.1	34.5	49.9	12.4	37.8	35.6	23.1	36.8

(continued)

Table 1.5 (continued)

	1990			2000			2020		
	Agriculture[b]	Industry[c]	Service	Agriculture[b]	Industry[c]	Service	Agriculture[b]	Industry[c]	Service
Nigeria	21.2	34.9	43.9	21.4	33.9	44.7	24.1	28.2	46.4
Kenya	29.5	19.0	51.4	32.4	16.9	50.7	22.7	18.5	54.0
South America	8.2	37.1	54.8	5.8	27.9	66.2	6.0	21.2	59.6
Peru	8.5	27.4	64.1	8.5	29.9	61.6	7.7	30.3	54.2
Brazil	8.1	38.7	53.2	5.6	27.7	66.7	5.7	19.5	61.4
Argentina	8.1	36.0	55.9	5.0	27.6	67.4	6.4	22.4	54.9

[a] Group averages are weighted averages, where the weight is the population ratio
[b] Agriculture includes fisheries and forestry
[c] Industry includes manufacturing, mining, construction, electricity, water supply, and city gas

ther increases in wealth, people desire more comfortable homes, better education for their children, improved healthcare, and opportunities to travel, all of which drive demand for services. Thus, in advanced economies, the service sector flourishes.

At the same time, while a high level of education is not particularly important for agricultural work, its significance increases in manufacturing and becomes crucial in service industries that require advanced computer skills. This is another reason why industrial structure and per capita income are closely related.

So, if we were to ignore agriculture and manufacturing and focus solely on promoting the development of the service sector, would the economy grow, and would people become more prosperous? Is it possible to take a shortcut from agriculture directly to the service sector? Observing the recent economic development in countries like India and the Philippines, one might think that a development path from agriculture to services is indeed possible. But is this truly feasible, and even if it is, would it actually lead to poverty reduction? These are major questions in the field of development economics.

Let us now return to the discussion of impoverished rural areas in Kenya. Such severe poverty arises because some part of the economic system is "malfunctioning." For example, there may be no improved maize varieties available, fertilizers may be too expensive, or the lack of education makes it difficult for villagers to find good jobs outside their communities, among other issues. What, then, should be done? One possible set of approaches is to pave roads to reduce transportation costs, enable farmers to easily access job information via mobile phones, provide fertilizer subsidies, establish legal frameworks so that poor farmers can borrow money from banks at low interest rates, and build not only primary but also secondary schools in villages to make it easier for children to attend school. While this is one possible solution, it is questionable whether it is truly the most desirable course of action. These are precisely the kinds of issues that constitute important research topics in development economics. If there were an abundance of budget and personnel for development, it might be possible to implement a variety of measures. However, the reality is that both budget and human resources are limited, and it is not possible to implement every policy that seems desirable. To prioritize and implement development policies, the first step is to accurately assess the current situation in developing countries and understand the fundamental causes of poverty. Although I do not have perfect answers myself, as a general principle, resources should be allocated to objectives that yield the greatest benefits (or returns) relative to their costs, while also considering income equality. So, should priority be given to paving roads, expanding mobile phone access, subsidizing fertilizers, improving access to bank loans, or building schools? Easier said than done—rigorous cost–benefit analysis is not so simple. In particular, when investments in one area stimulate further investments elsewhere, creating spillover effects, it becomes even more challenging to accurately measure cost-effectiveness. This can be seen, for example, when paving roads reduces transportation costs, which in turn lowers fertilizer prices, increases fertilizer use, raises farmers' incomes, and boosts the incomes of fertilizer merchants; yet it remains difficult to quantify these benefits. Nevertheless, the fact that cost–benefit analysis is rarely conducted remains a significant problem. I will discuss this further in ▶ Chap. 3.

While I have not always conducted cost–benefit analyses in my own research, I have always kept such considerations in mind. In ▶ Chaps. 4 through 7 of this book, I aim to explore development policies and strategies that are highly effective relative to their costs. ▶ Chapter 4 analyzes the characteristics and current state of agricultural development, while ▶ Chap. 5 examines the realities of industrialization. ▶ Chapter 6 discusses development policies that should absolutely be avoided or are undesirable, and ▶ Chap. 7 presents economic development strategies that I am convinced are effective. Although the central theme of this book is escaping poverty, ▶ Chapter 8 will address the "middle-income trap" and why many countries that have escaped poverty remain stuck at middle-income levels. Finally, in ▶ Chap. 9, I will discuss, from the perspective of development economics, the greatest challenge of our time: how to achieve sustainable development in developing countries while mitigating climate change.

Before that, in ▶ Chap. 2, I will examine where poor people are located, who they are, and how their numbers have changed, in order to clarify the target of poverty reduction. In ▶ Chap. 3, I will also consider the most fundamental question: why has humanity been unable to eradicate poverty? At this point, some readers may find themselves wondering: Even if we understand what constitutes an economically rational, effective, and sustainable development strategy, in many poor countries, power is held by corrupt and undemocratic governments. Would such countries ever truly adopt effective development strategies, and, ultimately, is economic development even possible under these circumstances? I do not entirely dismiss this concern, but I am also reluctant to fully endorse it. Readers interested in this issue should refer to the discussion in ▶ Box 1.2.

Box 1.2 The Role of the State and Development Economics

There is an argument that, no matter how hard people strive for economic development, in countries where the state is corrupt, social conditions are unstable, and sound development policies are not adopted, the economy will not develop. Indeed, in situations of rampant hyperinflation or where the government could be overthrown at any moment, it is difficult to make forward-looking investments. Thus, economic development is unlikely to occur. Furthermore, even if infrastructure investments such as roads are planned, in societies where politicians take large kickbacks, infrastructure construction will not progress. However, I believe that the claim that economies cannot develop in corrupt or undemocratic states lacks sufficient empirical support.

It is unrealistic to expect poor countries to establish clean, corruption-free, and democratic states from the outset. Rather, it is more appropriate to view the relationship between the formation of states capable of achieving sustainable economic development and economic development itself as mutually interdependent (Otsuka and Shiraishi 2014). For example, the Meiji government in Japan was not democratic, nor did it possess the capacity to implement effective economic policies, yet the Japanese economy developed steadily, albeit at a moderate pace. In Indonesia, Thailand, and Malaysia, the state remained undemocratic and corrupt until the 1990s. Still, the governments understood that economic development was crucial for political stability, and their economies developed quite rapidly. More recently, democratization and economic development have progressed in tandem in countries like Indonesia and the Philippines. While the relationship between state-building and economic development is complex, if the state understands effective development strategies and implements them as policy, a virtuous cycle may emerge: effective development policy → economic development → construction of a democratic state. However, a review of the historical trajectories of today's democratic states makes it clear that this path is by no means smooth (Otsuka and Shiraishi 2014).

On the other hand, if the state can stabilize politics, thereby stabilizing the economy, and at the same time fulfill basic roles such as promoting education and building infrastructure, some degree of growth is possible. The aim of development economics, as I see it, is to consider effective development strategies that can further accelerate this growth. Moreover, when a neighboring country succeeds in economic development, there is a tendency for surrounding countries to follow suit. In this respect, Japan has played a significant role in East Asia. Hong Kong, Singapore, Taiwan, South Korea, and China all looked to Japan's economic success as a reference. In stark contrast, there have been very few success stories in Africa. However, if a few countries in Africa achieve development, a chain reaction may occur. Based on the Asian experience, it seems reasonable to conclude that the circumstances of neighboring countries greatly influence the relationship between the quality of the state and economic development.

1.6 Summary

Finally, let us review the key points of this chapter.

- I would like to define *development economics* as the academic field that studies strategies to reduce poverty in poor developing countries. However, to this end, it is also important to study the experiences of advanced and middle-income countries.
- Per capita income is not only an indicator of economic wealth, but is also closely related to indicators of quality of life, such as infant mortality, life expectancy, and educational attainment.
- Per capita income is closely correlated with the proportion of people living in poverty.
- To promote economic development, raise per capita income, and reduce poverty, it is essential to devise *strategies* for the effective utilization of limited resources. The purpose of this book is to explore such strategies.

Questions

1. Since it is desirable to improve agricultural technology, road systems, schooling, and bank lending to the poor in poor villages, should the government improve all of them immediately and simultaneously?
2. Since income fluctuates due to unexpected events, is consumption a better indicator of living standards over extended periods?
3. Since average income per capita is closely and negatively correlated with the incidence of poverty, is it appropriate to implement policy measures to increase income without considering the impacts on income distribution?
4. Can the use of income per capita as an indicator of living standard be justified, partly because it is positively related to the quality of life, and partly because the income data are relatively easy to collect compared with consumption and assets data?

References

Chen, S., & Ravallion, M. (2010). The developing world is poorer than we thought, but no less successful in the fight against poverty. *Quarterly Journal of Economics, 125*(4), 1577–1625.

David, C.C., & Otsuka, K. (Eds.). (1994). *Modern rice technology and income distribution in Asia.* Lynne Rienner.

Hamada, K., Otsuka, K., Ranis, G., & Togo, K. (Eds.). (2011). *Miraculous growth and stagnation: Lessons from the experience of postwar Japanese economic development.* Routledge.

Harris, J.R., & Todaro, M.P. (1970). Migration, employment and development: A two-sector analysis. *American Economic Review, 60*(1), 126–142.

Haughton, J., & Khandker, S. (2009). *Handbook on poverty and inequality*. World Bank.

Hayami, Y., & Otsuka, K. (1993). *The economics of contract choice: An agrarian perspective*. Clarendon Press.

Holden, S.T., Otsuka, K., & Deininger, K. (Eds.). (2013). *Land tenure reforms in Asia and Africa: Assessing impacts on poverty and natural resource management.* Palgrave Macmillan.

Holden, S.T., Otsuka, K., & Place, F. (Eds.) (2009). *The emergence of land markets in Africa: Assessing the impacts on poverty, equity, and efficiency*. Resources for the Future.

Lewis, A.W. (1954). Economic development with unlimited supplies of labor. *Manchester School of Economic and Social Studies, 22*(2), 139–191.

Otsuka, K. (2007). Efficiency and equity effects of land markets. In R. E. Evenson & P. Pingali (Eds.), *Handbook of agricultural economics, Volume III*. Elsevier.

Otsuka, K. (2024). *Transforming poor economies: Effective development strategies for agriculture and industry*. Edward Elgar.

Otsuka, K., & Larson, D. (Eds). (2013). *An African Green Revolution: Finding ways to boost productivity on small farms.* Springer.

Otsuka, K., & Larson, D.F. (Eds). (2016). *In pursuit of an African Green Revolution: Views from rice and maize farmers' fields.* Springer.

Otsuka, K., & Place, F. (Eds.). (2001). *Land tenure and natural resource management: A comparative study of agrarian communities in Asia and Africa*. Johns Hopkins University Press.

Otsuka, K., & Shiraishi, T. (Eds). (2014). *State building and development*. Routledge.

Otsuka K., & Sugihara, K. (Eds). (2019). *Paths to the emerging state in Asia and Africa*. Springer.

Otsuka, K., Estudillo, J.P., & Sawada, Y. (Eds.). (2009). *Rural poverty and income dynamics in Asia and Africa*. Routledge.

Otsuka, K., Jin, K., & Sonobe, T. (Eds.). (2018). *Applying the kaizen in Africa: A new avenue for industrial development.* Palgrave Macmillan.

Otsuka, K., Liu, D., & Murakami, N. (1998). *Industrial reform in China: Past performance and future prospects.* Clarendon Press.

Otsuka, K., Mano, Y., & Takahashi, K. (2023). *Rice Green Revolution in Sub-Saharan Africa.* Springer.

Otsuka K., Ranis, G., & Saxonhouse, G. (1988). *Comparative technology choice in development: The Indian and Japanese cotton textile industries.* Macmillan Press.

Quisumbing, A.R., Estudillo, J.P., & Otsuka, K. (2004). *Land and schooling: Transferring wealth across generations.* Johns Hopkins University Press.

Ravallion, M., Chen, S., & Sanguraula, P. (2009). Dollar a day revisited. *World Bank Economic Review, 23*(2): 163–184.

Schultz, T.W. (1964). *Transforming traditional agriculture.* Yale University Press.

Sonobe, T., & Otsuka, K. (2006). *Cluster-based industrial development: An East Asian model.* Palgrave Macmillan.

Sonobe, T., & Otsuka, K. (2011). *Cluster-based industrial development: A comparative study of Asia and Africa.* Palgrave Macmillan.

Sonobe, T., & Otsuka, K. (2014). *Cluster-based industrial developments: Kaizen management for MSE Growth in developing countries.* Palgrave Macmillan.

World Bank. (2012). *World Development Report 2013: Jobs.* World Bank.

World Bank. (various years). *World development indicators.* World Bank DataBank.

Yamano, T., Otsuka, K., & Place, F. (Eds.). (2011). *Emerging development of agriculture in East Africa: Markets, soil, and innovations.* Springer

Is Poverty Declining?

Contents

K. Otsuka, *A Primer on Development Economics*,
Classroom Companion: Economics, https://doi.org/10.1007/978-981-95-5397-6_2

2.1 Introduction

Poverty reduction is one of the most important goals of economic development and is a matter of global concern. The direct impetus for this movement was the adoption of the United Nations Millennium Declaration at the UN Millennium Summit in September 2000, and the subsequent formulation of the Millennium Development Goals (MDGs). The international community set forth eight goals to be achieved, the first and arguably most important of which was to "halve, by 2015, the proportion of people living on less than USD 1 a day (now USD 2.15) compared to the 1990 level."[1]

At the UN General Assembly in September 2015, the Sustainable Development Goals (SDGs) were established, setting out 17 global goals and 169 targets for sustainable development. The first of these goals is to eradicate poverty by 2030.

In this chapter, we will first examine whether global poverty is declining in line with this goal. Next, we will provide an overview of the relationship between poverty and factors such as population age structure, industrial employment structure, and income distribution. We will also consider who the poor are in rural areas, where poverty ratios are particularly high.

2.2 How Many Poor People Are There and Where Do They Live?

The poverty ratio was already discussed in ▶ Chap. 1, so here, using ◘ Table 2.1, we will examine differences and changes in the absolute number of poor people across developing countries. Since data are lacking for many countries, we will focus not on the world as a whole, but only on the major developing countries listed in the table. The total population of the countries included in ◘ Table 2.1 was approximately 3.61 billion in 2020, while the world population was around 8 billion, accounting for about 45% of the global total.

According to this table, there were as many as 1.6 billion poor people around 1990. About half of them, or roughly 800 million, were in East Asia, with nearly 700 million residing in China alone. Although China initiated economic reforms in 1978, poverty persisted even in 1990 due to the inefficiencies of socialist economic management. South Asia also had over 600 million people living in poverty, with 440 million of them residing in India. Africa, with a smaller total population, had 100 million poor people in the three countries shown in the table.

By around 2020, the total number of poor people had fallen to 360 million, representing a reduction of 23% of the 1990 figure. During this period, the world population increased from about 5.3 billion to about 8 billion, so the poverty ratio declined dramatically. As a result of this trend, by 2020, the absolute number

1 Other goals include universal primary education, gender equality, reduction of infant mortality, improvement of maternal health, strengthened responses to AIDS and malaria, achievement of environmental sustainability, and establishment of a global partnership for development. See Ministry of Foreign Affairs Japan (▶ http://www.mofa.go.jp/mofaj/gaiko/oda/doukou/mdgs.html#goal).

Table 2.1 Comparison of population below poverty line among selected developing countries (million people) around 1990 and 2020[a] (World Bank's World Development Indicators various years)

	Population below the poverty line				Ratio (%)
	Around 1990		Around 2020		XXX
	XXX		XXX		
East Asia[b]	788.0		7.8		1.0
Indonesia	99.6	(1990)	7.7	(2020)	7.7
China	683.2	(1990)	0.0	(2020)	0.0
Thailand	6.3	(1990)	0.1	(2019)	1.1
South Asia[b]	658.5		237.1		36.0
Bangladesh	47.7	(1991)	8.5	(2022)	17.8
Pakistan	75.6	(1990)	11.1	(2018)	14.7
India	442.6	(1993)	217.4	(2020)	49.1
Nepal	12.3	(1995)	0.1	(2022)	1.0
Sub-Saharan Africa[b]	107.4		109.6		102.1
Ethiopia	39.8	(1995)	28.0	(2015)	70.4
Nigeria	53.6	(1992)	63.3	(2018)	118.1
Kenya	6.4	(1992)	18.3	(2020)	283.9
South America[b]	29.2		6.6		22.7
Peru	5.0	(1997)	1.9	(2020)	38.1
Brazil	35.8	(1990)	4.2	(2020)	11.7
Argentina	0.3	(1991)	0.5	(2020)	163.2
Total[c]	1583.1		361.1		22.8
Total population	2939.7	(1990)	4233.8	(2020)	144.0

[a] Poverty line is USD 2.15 per day. Numbers in parentheses indicate the years for which data closest to 1990 or 2020 are available
[b] Weighted averages with weights being population ratios
[c] Total refers to the sum of sampled countries

of poor people had dropped to about one-quarter of its previous level. In other words, the first MDG target was almost certainly achieved, which is undoubtedly a major accomplishment.[2]

China has seen a remarkable reduction in the number of people living in poverty. According to the table, the total number of people in poverty decreased by

2 This is not a novel finding, but rather a widely recognized fact. See, for example, Chen and Ravallion (2010).

approximately 1.2 billion over 30 years, with China alone accounting for a reduction of 680 million. This suggests that, rather than a global decline in poverty resulting from worldwide development efforts led by the United Nations, it is more accurate to attribute the decrease in poverty primarily to China's economic reforms and subsequent growth. In Indonesia, where the economy has also grown steadily, the number of people in poverty fell from around 100 million in 1990 to about 8 million in 2020. In contrast, in South Asia, where economic development has been sluggish, the reduction in the number of people in poverty has been much less pronounced. As discussed in ◘ Table 1.4, the poverty ratio in South Asia decreased from 48 to 13% over the past 25 years; however, in absolute terms, it is difficult to say that the poverty problem has been fully resolved. Of the 360 million people living in poverty around 2020, as many as 240 million are in South Asia. In Africa, where economic stagnation is even more pronounced than in South Asia, the number of people living in poverty has remained unchanged over the past 30 years. The poverty ratio in Africa remains above 30%, and the lack of progress in addressing poverty in this region is a major concern.

Considering these circumstances, even though the global poverty ratio fell to one-third of its 1990 level by 2020, this is by no means a situation that warrants unreserved celebration. Poverty in South Asia remains severe, and in Africa, there is not even a clear path toward resolving the issue. The MDGs concluded in 2015, but given the current conditions, it is only natural that discussions about the post-MDGs agenda are emerging. I will address this topic further in ▶ Chap. 9.

As shown in ◘ Fig. 2.1, both China and Indonesia have experienced a noticeable decline in the poverty ratio, alongside increases in real GDP per capita. In contrast, Nigeria has seen only sluggish growth in real income, with no significant downward trend in its poverty ratio. It cannot be emphasized enough that income growth is the key to poverty reduction.

2.3 Considering the Structure of Poverty

Economics often makes use of mathematics, but this book will not. However, to facilitate understanding, I will use some simple equations. First, household income can be divided into labor income and asset income.

$$\textit{House hold income} = \textit{Labor income} + \textit{Asset income} \tag{2.1}$$

Since income refers to net earnings after necessary expenses are deducted, in the case of the self-employed or farmers, actual expenditures, such as raw material costs, fertilizer expenses, wage payments, and rent, are subtracted from revenue. Additionally, if a farmer consumes crops harvested for personal use, the market value of those crops is considered income.

Labor income is, as the term suggests, income earned through work. For salaried employees, labor income refers to the wages received from their employer. However, for the self-employed or farmers, no wage is paid for their own labor, so it is not always possible to clearly separate income into labor and asset compo-

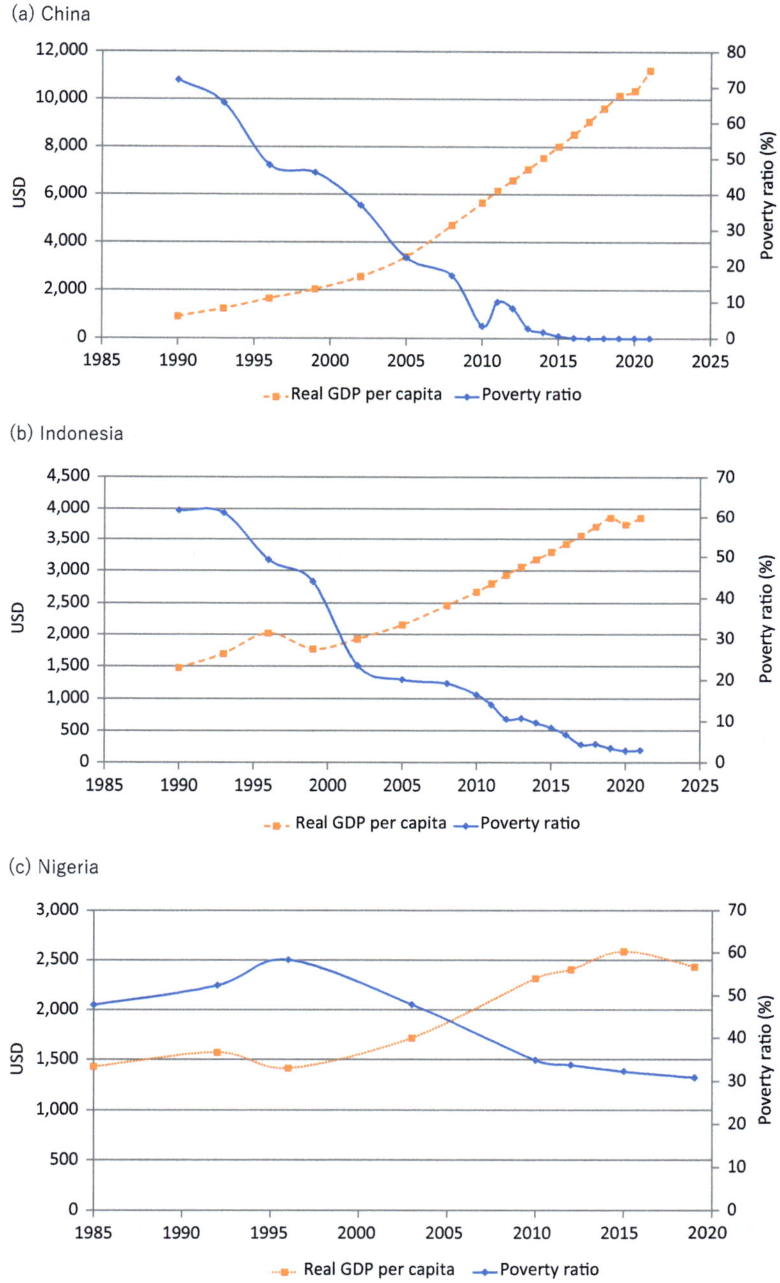

Fig. 2.1 Comparison between long-term changes in real GDP per capita and poverty ratio in China (a), Indonesia (b), and Nigeria (c) (Real GDP is based on 2017 USD, Data are not available after 2020 in Nigeria) (World Bank's World Development Indicators various years)

nents. Nevertheless, conceptually, it is possible to distinguish between the portion of income generated by labor and other sources. If one can estimate how much income a person would have earned doing similar work as an employee elsewhere, that amount approximates labor income. Their assets generate the remainder of the self-employed or farmer's income. Asset income includes earnings from owned land, buildings, and machinery, as well as interest and dividend income. If land or buildings are rented out, rental income is also considered asset income.

Labor income depends on the number of workers in the household and the remuneration each worker receives. If there are several similar workers in a household, the following relationship holds:

$$\textit{Household income} \approxeq \textit{Number of workers} \times \textit{Labor remuneration} + \textit{Asset income} \tag{2.2}$$

If there are multiple workers with different ages, educational backgrounds, experience, or occupations, their labor remuneration will differ, making the equation more complex. However, for the sake of simplicity, such differences are ignored here. Since poverty is related to per capita household income, dividing the above equation by the number of household members yields the following:

$$\begin{aligned}\textit{Per capita income} =& \textit{Household labor force ratio}\\ &\times \textit{Labor compensation per worker}\\ &+ \textit{Per capita asset income}\end{aligned} \tag{2.3}$$

Here, the household labor force ratio refers to the proportion of household members who are actually working. Since the consumption needs of children, the elderly, and young people differ, household size is sometimes calculated using weights, such as counting a child as equivalent to 0.5 of an adult.

Although this is a simple equation, it reveals a great deal. Poverty can be attributed to (1) a low labor force ratio, (2) low per capita labor compensation, and (3) low per capita asset income, or a combination of these factors. Therefore, to reduce poverty, it is necessary to increase the values of these three variables.

Let us consider the first issue. A low household labor force ratio generally indicates a high number of children or elderly members. However, even individuals of working age may not be able to engage in paid employment due to responsibilities such as childbirth, childcare, or caregiving, which also lowers the labor force ratio. Additionally, if children of working age are attending school, this ratio will be lowered. Due to data limitations, it is challenging to make precise international comparisons of labor force ratios; however, the proportion of the working-age population (i.e., the productive-age population) is likely to approximate the labor force ratio. Therefore, in ► Sect. 2.3, we will conduct an international comparison of the working-age population ratio.

Labor compensation, which is the second issue, is determined by the supply and demand for each type of labor. While a rigorous discussion is beyond the scope here, key factors influencing labor compensation include: (a) the quality of the workforce, (b) the quantity and quality of complementary assets such as equipment, machinery, and land, (c) the level of technology, and (d) the scarcity of each type of worker.

The third issue is low asset income. Since poor people cannot afford to save, they seldom accumulate assets and, hence, do not earn sizable asset income. Thus, reducing poverty by increasing asset income for the poor is infeasible.

In economics, the quality of labor is also referred to as human capital. The quantity of human capital is primarily determined by intellectual ability and health status. Individuals who are innately intelligent and healthy possess a larger amount of human capital. However, in practice, abilities acquired through education and on-the-job training are more significant, and health is greatly influenced by exercise and nutrition. Since human capital is an important concept, a supplementary explanation is provided in ► Box 2.1.

Box 2.1 What is Human Capital?

For capital goods such as machinery and buildings, investment (e.g., purchasing new machinery or buildings) increases their quantity. The amount measured at a given point in time, such as the amount of capital, is referred to as a *stock*. The amount of water stored in a reservoir is an example of a stock. In contrast, changes resulting from actions taken over a specific period are referred to as *flows*. Investment is a flow, as is the amount of water flowing into a reservoir. The distinction between stock and flow is important and will be particularly so in the next chapter.

Since machinery wears out over time, the capital stock does not increase by the full amount of investment. The net increase in capital stock is the investment minus depreciation (the amount of wear and tear).

The concept of *human capital* applies this idea to human intellectual ability and health status. Theodore Schultz was the originator of this concept, and Gary Becker (1964) further developed human capital theory into a major field within economics. In this theory, the quality of a worker is assumed to be higher the greater their intellectual ability and health.

Everyone possesses a certain stock of intellectual ability at any given time. Studying and acquiring new knowledge increases this stock, thereby enhancing ability. However, since much knowledge is forgotten over time, the net increase in ability stock is the amount of ability acquired minus the amount lost. In this sense, the discussion is quite similar to investment in machinery. The difference is that most of the cost of investing in human capital is not monetary but rather the cost of time. As the saying goes, "time is money"; if one knows how much income could have been earned by working instead of studying, that amount can be considered the cost of the investment.

Conceptually, the same discussion applies to health status. Health can be considered a stock: engaging in regular exercise, maintaining a balanced diet, moderating alcohol consumption, and getting sufficient sleep all serve to increase this stock of health. Such efforts to improve health can be viewed as investments made for the future enjoyment derived from better health. However, no matter how hard one tries, just as with capital depreciation, the stock of health inevitably declines with age. Therefore, if the rate of decline exceeds the rate of improvement, the stock of health will decrease.

Workers with abundant human capital generally receive high labor compensation. For example, doctors, lawyers, renowned designers, and highly skilled craftsmen typically earn high wages. However, without complementary equipment such as computers or without advances in medicine and other sciences, even individuals with high abilities may not be able to fully realize their potential. Moreover, regardless of how high one's abilities are or how well-equipped the workplace is, if there are many people with similar skills, labor compensation will not be particularly high. For instance, in Japan, lawyers' wages were once remarkably high; however, when the number of those passing the bar exam increased, the scarcity of lawyers diminished, and their compensation dropped sharply. Conversely, jobs such as domestic help do not require special skills or knowledge; however, because there are few applicants, the wages are not low.[3]

International comparisons of labor compensation are difficult due to the lack of comparable data. Therefore, in Sects. 2.4 and 2.5, we will explore avenues for international comparison of labor compensation by examining differences in labor productivity across industries and comparing poverty ratios between urban and rural areas. Asset income, as the term suggests, is the return on owned assets. The poor typically own very few assets, which is the third issue. In rural areas, poverty is found among smallholder farmers who own only tiny plots of land, or among *landless agricultural laborers* who own no land at all and cannot rent in land.

In the Philippines and South Asia, there are many landless laborers. If you visit a rural area and see a particularly modest house, it is almost certainly the home of such individuals. Many believe that *land reform*, which transfers land from large landowners to smallholders and landless laborers, would directly reduce poverty. However, it is not easy to take land away from politically powerful large landowners. According to my research, past land reforms implemented in Asia have, in fact, exacerbated poverty rather than alleviated it. This issue will be revisited in the discussion of "What Developing Countries Must Not Do" in ► Chap. 6.

Urban poor, on the other hand, typically own almost no assets and often live in slums. One might think that imposing progressive income taxes to transfer income from the wealthy to the poor would be a desirable policy. However, in developing countries, where many people work in the informal sector and are not even registered with government offices, it is extremely difficult to collect income taxes. Furthermore, it is not easy to accurately identify who is truly poor. Even in Japan, the incomes of the self-employed and farmers are not accurately captured, making the proper collection of income tax difficult. There have also been issues with individuals who are not in need fraudulently receiving welfare benefits. In developing countries, where the poor are numerous and the wealthy are few, unfortunately, redistributing asset income to eliminate poverty is not a realistic policy option.

---

3 In developing countries, wages for domestic workers (house maids) are surprisingly low.

2.4 Age Structure of the Population and Poverty

The working-age population is generally defined as those aged 15–64 who are capable of engaging in productive employment. In Japan, most young people attend high school, and nearly half go on to university, so it is not entirely appropriate to include those aged 15 to around 22 in the working-age population. However, for the sake of international comparison, we will adopt this definition of working age from 15 to 64 years old. The ratio of the working-age population to the total population can be considered a proxy variable for the labor force ratio. ◘ Table 2.2 shows the working-age population ratios for various countries in 1970, 1990, and 2020.

From this table, several interesting trends can be observed. First, in high-income countries, the proportion of the working-age population is high, around 64%–67%, and remains stable. Second, in Africa, the working-age population ratio is relatively low, at about 55%–65%.[4] However, the difference in the working-age population ratio between high-income countries and Africa is not particularly large, and such a disparity can only partially account for the significant income gap between these regions. Third, in East Asia and South America, the proportion of the working-age population is increasing rapidly. Although not as pronounced, a similar trend is also evident in South Asia. The rise in the working-age population ratio in these regions appears to have made a considerable contribution to improvements in per capita income.

What accounts for the differences and changes in the working-age population ratio among countries? This is related to the population growth rates shown in ◘ Table 2.2. In high-income countries, the population growth rate is low, and the number of children is relatively small, resulting in a high ratio of working-age population. In contrast, in Africa, the population growth rate exceeds 2.5%, resulting in a large number of children and a lower ratio of working-age population. Meanwhile, in East Asia and South America, the working-age population ratio was as low as in Africa around 1970; however, since then, the population growth rate has declined sharply, resulting in a reduction in the number of children and an increase in the working-age population ratio. In South Asia as well, the long-term decline in population growth rate has resulted in a higher working-age population ratio. A population growth rate of approximately 3% represents a rapid rate of increase that can lead to a population explosion (see ► Box 2.2 for details). The decline in population growth rates in many regions is desirable from the perspective of global environmental conservation and the prevention of worldwide food shortages.

Looking at 2020, the proportion of the working-age population in high-income countries is lower than in East Asia or South America. This reflects the rapid aging occurring in high-income countries. As shown in ◘ Fig. 2.2, from 1970 to 2020, the proportion of young people in high-income countries has sharply declined, while the proportion of those aged 65 and over has increased

---

4 This may be related to the spread of AIDS in Africa.

2

Table 2.2 Comparison of proportion of working-age population and population growth rate among selected countries and regions (%)[a] (World Bank's World Development Indicators various years)

	Proportion of working-age population			Average annual population growth rate		
	1970	**1990**	**2020**	**1970–1980**	**1990–2000**	**2010–2020**
High-income countries	63.8	66.7	63.4	1.1	1.2	0.7
Japan	68.8	69.7	58.9	1.1	0.3	-0.1
US	61.8	65.8	65.5	1.0	1.2	0.7
UK	62.9	65.3	63.4	0.1	0.3	0.7
France	62.3	65.9	61.8	0.6	0.4	0.4
East Asia	55.8	65.3	69.3	1.8	1.0	0.5
Indonesia	53.5	59.8	67.6	2.5	1.6	1.1
China	56.4	66.0	69.4	1.8	1.1	0.5
Thailand	52.5	65.3	70.9	2.5	1.0	0.4
S. Korea	54.6	69.4	72.1	1.8	0.9	0.5
South Asia	55.1	57.1	65.0	2.3	1.8	1.2
Bangladesh	51.8	53.8	65.5	2.2	2.1	0.9
Pakistan	53.6	52.5	60.5	3.1	2.6	1.7
India	55.7	58.3	65.7	2.3	1.8	1.2
Nepal	55.6	54.4	62.0	2.2	2.5	0.6
Sub-Saharan Africa	52.9	51.5	55.4	2.7	2.6	2.6
Ethiopia	53.3	52.1	56.5	2.2	3.2	2.8
Nigeria	54.0	52.0	54.2	2.8	2.5	2.5
Kenya	47.5	48.3	57.9	3.8	2.9	2.3
South America	55.5	60.1	68.4	2.4	1.6	0.7
Peru	52.6	57.8	65.8	2.8	1.8	1.2
Brazil	54.2	60.4	69.6	2.4	1.5	0.7
Argentina	63.8	60.4	64.5	1.6	1.2	0.9

[a] Group averages are weighted averages, where the weight is the population ratio. Productive age refers to 15–64 years old

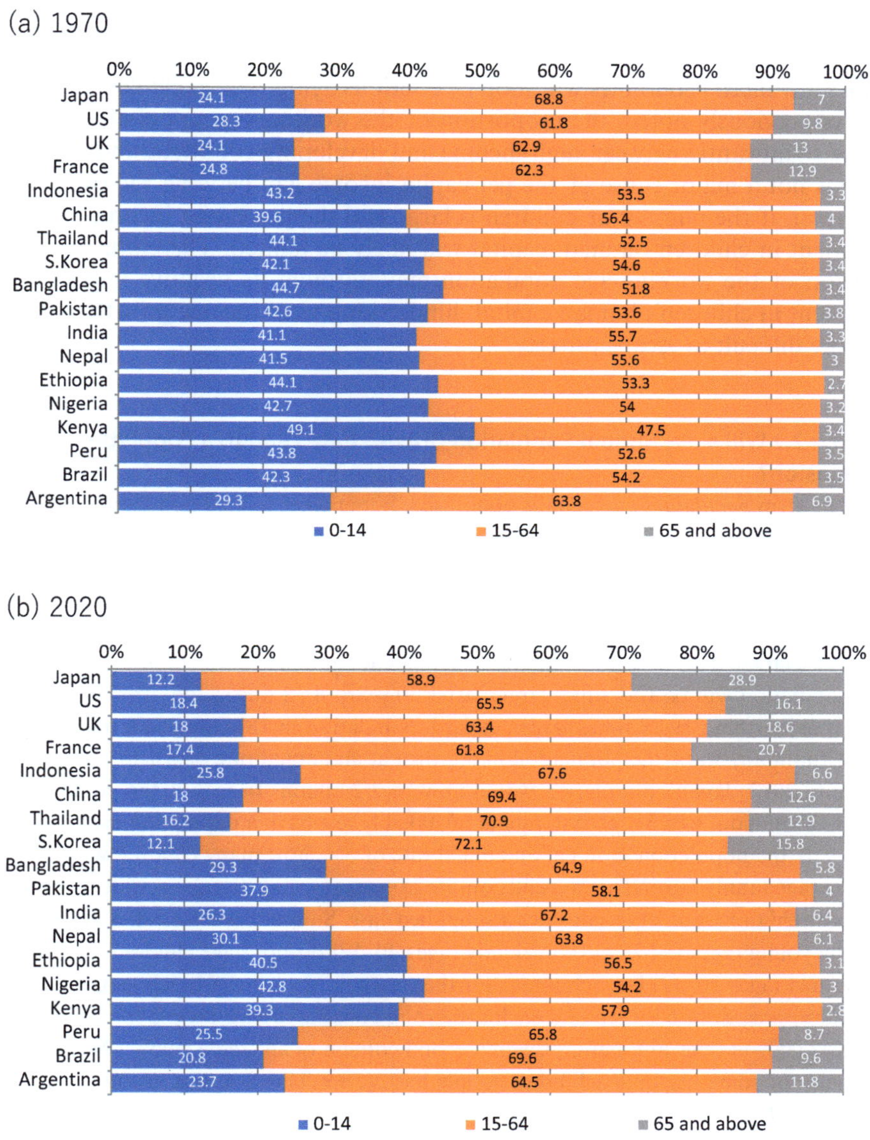

Fig. 2.2 Comparison of age structure of population in 1970 (a) and 2020 (b) among selected countries (World Bank's World Development Indicators various years)

rapidly. Japan is at the forefront of this trend. In East Asia, including South Korea, the proportion of elderly people is on the rise, and it is expected that the region's advanced economies will soon face serious aging-related challenges.[5]

As previously noted, the proportion of the working-age population does not differ significantly between high-income and developing countries, and this difference is not a major cause of the per capita income gap between the two regions. However, if the number of children is large and the per capita income is low, investment in children's human capital will likely be limited. Therefore, a low proportion of the working-age population may, through its negative impact on investment in children's human capital, hinder long-term income growth and make it more difficult to escape poverty.

Box 2.2 Will a 3% Annual Population Growth Rate Lead to a Population Explosion?

The term *population explosion* is often used, but at what annual population growth rate do readers think a *population explosion* occurs? A 3% population growth rate is quite high even among developing countries (see ◘ Table 2.2), and it indeed leads directly to a population explosion. Let me explain why. An annual growth rate of 3% means that in 10 years, the population will be 1.03 to the 10th power, or 1.34 times larger. This may not seem like a significant figure. However, after 20 years, the population will be 1.81 times larger; after 50 years, 4.38 times; and after 100 years, an astonishing 19.22 times larger. Japan's population in 1872 was 34.8 million. If, without any wars, the population had grown at an annual rate of 3% for 140 years until 2012, Japan's population would now be 2.2 billion. In reality, the population is 130 million, so a 3% growth rate unmistakably results in a population explosion.

If the population grows at an annual rate of 3%, how many children would the average family have? This depends on life expectancy and the age at which women bear children, but let us consider a simplified case. Suppose everyone dies at age 59, the young (ages 0–19) and the elderly (ages 40–59) do not have children, and only adults (ages 20–39) bear children. Further, assume that at the baseline, the population growth rate is zero and each age group consists of two people (or 2 million, or 2,000—it does not matter; see the second column of the table below). Now, suppose for some reason, each adult couple has $2(1+x)$ children. For example, if x is 0.5, each couple has three children. After 20 years, the population of the young cohort will be $2(1+x)$ (see the third column). Repeating this process, after 60 years, the population in each age group will be $(1+x)$ times larger than it will be 40 years later. Thus, the total population increases by a factor of $(1+x)$ every 20 years.

5 In China, which has implemented a one-child policy, population aging has become a serious issue. In this context, it is crucial to raise the productivity of the working-age population, which requires effective development strategies.

Age range	Base year	20 years later	40 years later	60 years later
Old (40–59)	2	2	2	$2(1+x)$
Adult (20–39)	2	2	$2(1+x)$	$2(1+x)^2$
Young (0–19)	2	$2(1+x)$	$2(1+x)^2$	$2(1+x)^3$
Total population	6	$6+2x$	$6+3x+2x^2$	....

As described above, a 3% annual population growth rate means that the population increases by 1.81 times in 20 years. This means x is 0.81, so the average number of children per couple is $2(1+0.81)=3.62$. In other words, in developing countries where it is common for families to have nearly four children, a population explosion is occurring.

2.5 Employment Structure and Poverty

As examined in ■ Table 1.5, with economic development, the GDP share of agriculture (which includes forestry and fisheries) continues to decline, while the share of industry rises. As the economy continues to develop, the share of the service sector increases, resulting in a corresponding decrease in the share of the industrial sector. Correspondingly, the employment share in agriculture, forestry, and fisheries continues to fall, while the share in the service sector continues to rise. This is illustrated in ■ Table 2.3. It should be noted that the employment ratios shown in this table are classified based on "main occupation," so members of part-time farming households who also work in non-agricultural sectors are still classified under "agriculture, forestry, and fisheries."

In high-income countries, the employment share in agriculture, forestry, and fisheries was already extremely low by 1995, and it had declined further by 2020. At the same time, the employment share in industry has also decreased considerably over the past 25 years. On the other hand, the employment share in the service sector was already overwhelmingly high in 1995 and has continued to increase by 2020. Similar trends can be observed in South Korea, where income levels are already quite high. Why does this occur? It is likely because income per worker is lowest in agriculture, forestry, and fisheries, higher in industry, and highest in the service sector. However, many service industries in high-income countries—such as finance, insurance, and computer software—are generally knowledge-intensive or require significant human capital. Therefore, not everyone can engage in the service sector and earn a high income.

Corresponding to the existence of income disparities between sectors, in rapidly developing East Asia, the employment share in agriculture, forestry, and fisheries has dropped significantly from 1995 to 2020. The employment share in industry has increased in some countries, such as Indonesia, China, and Thailand, while it has decreased in others, such as South Korea. However, in all countries, the share of employment in the service sector shows a consistent upward trend.

2

Table 2.3 Comparison of employment structure among selected countries and regions in terms of proportion of employment (%)[a] (World Bank's World Development Indicators various years)

	1995			2020		
	Agriculture[a]	Industry[b]	Service	Agriculture[a]	Industry[b]	Service
High-income countries						
Japan	5.7	33.7	60.6	3.1	24.0	72.8
US	2.8	23.4	73.8	1.7	19.4	78.8
UK	2.1	27.4	70.5	1.0	18.1	80.9
France	4.9	26.9	68.2	2.4	20.0	77.7
East Asia						
Indonesia	44.0	18.4	37.6	29.6	21.5	48.9
China	52.2	23.0	24.8	23.6	31.4	45.0
Thailand	54.0	20.5	25.5	31.4	22.6	46.0
S. Korea	11.8	33.4	54.8	5.4	24.6	70.0
South Asia						
Bangladesh	63.4	10.0	26.6	38.0	20.5	41.5
Pakistan	43.9	21.5	34.6	37.9	24.9	37.2
India	62.3	15.1	22.7	44.7	23.7	31.6
Nepal	76.1	9.7	14.2	62.1	17.4	20.6
Sub-Saharan Africa						
Ethiopia	76.9	6.5	16.6	64.4	6.6	29.0
Nigeria	51.6	11.4	37.1	38.0	14.9	47.1
Kenya	47.4	13.4	39.2	33.6	15.3	51.0
South America						
Peru	39.2	16.6	44.2	33.7	15.9	50.5
Brazil	17.0	23.5	59.5	9.3	20.3	70.4
Argentina	1.2	26.9	71.9	0.6	22.6	76.8

[a] Agriculture includes fisheries and forestry
[b] Industry includes manufacturing, mining, construction, electricity, water supply, and city gas

In South Asia, the employment share in agriculture, forestry, and fisheries is much higher than in East Asia, but it is also declining, similar to the trend in East Asia. The employment share in industry in South Asia is generally lower than in East Asia, but is on the rise. This indicates that, although South Asia has not achieved industrialization to the same extent as East Asia, it is nonetheless making progress in this direction. In Bangladesh, in particular, where industrialization is advancing with the development of the apparel industry as a core, the employment share in industry has increased significantly from 10% in 1995 to about 20% in 2020. The employment share in the service sector has also increased. This includes both modern service industries, such as call centers and software development, which utilize computers, as well as traditional commerce and transportation; however, the breakdown is unknown. Needless to say, in the latter case, labor compensation is not high.

In the case of Africa, the proportion of workers employed in agriculture, forestry, and fisheries is particularly high, though it is showing a certain decline. The share of employment in industry remains at a low level. These characteristics strongly suggest that Africa's failure to industrialize has hindered the resolution of poverty issues. By using data on GDP by industry and the number of workers by industry, it is possible to estimate GDP per worker for each sector. However, as previously noted, many people engaged in agriculture, forestry, and fisheries are also involved in other occupations, so the estimated GDP per worker in these sectors tends to underestimate total household income. For example, in Japan, the proportion of farm household income derived from non-farming activities exceeds 80%, and it is nearly 50% even in other countries in East Asia (Otsuka et al. 2009). Of course, GDP is not generated solely by labor; it is also generated by the use of equipment such as machinery and computers, as well as buildings, so not all of GDP is distributed to workers. For many workers whose primary source of income is labor, their actual income is likely to be significantly smaller than the GDP per capita. Bearing this in mind, let us examine the GDP per worker by industry as shown in ◘ Table 2.4.

It should be noted that data deficiencies increase the further back in time one goes, so only data for 2020 are presented here. In 2020, the GDP per worker in the industrial sector in Pakistan, India, and Nepal was significantly lower than in the service sector. This is likely because the service sector includes modern industries, whereas modernization in the industrial sector has lagged behind. Another notable point is that GDP per worker in agriculture, forestry, and fisheries is markedly lower than in the industrial and service sectors. The primary reason for this is likely the high proportion of nonfarm income; however, factors such as aging populations in rural areas and lower educational attainment among rural workers are also likely contributing factors. When considering total income, including nonfarm earnings, the income gap between those engaged in agriculture and those in industry should not be significant. In Japan, farm households are actually wealthier than urban households.

In high-income countries, as well as in Brazil and Argentina, the GDP per worker in the service and industrial sectors is quite similar, likely due to a certain degree of labor mobility between these sectors. In East Asia, there is a large disparity in GDP per worker between agriculture and industry, with the latter being three to six times higher. The presence of nonfarm income among farm households and a lower price level in rural areas are important factors contributing to this disparity, but even taking these into account, a considerable income gap still appears to exist between rural and urban households.

2

Table 2.4 Comparison of GDP per capita by industry in 2020 in 2021 USD[a] (World Bank's World Development Indicators various years)

	Agriculture[b]	Industry[c]	Service
High-income countries			
Japan	19,004	80,104	61,984
US[d]	66,666	111,666	119,022
UK	51,794	91,005	75,336
France	49,673	72,294	79,130
East Asia			
Indonesia	3,514	13,849	7,181
China	6,399	25,127	24,802
Thailand	3,003	16,442	13,487
S. Korea	18,991	81,568	48,035
South Asia			
Bangladesh	1,338	5,870	5,076
Pakistan	2,908	3,824	7,309
India	1,992	5,831	7,811
Nepal	1,740	3,395	10,520
Sub-Saharan Africa			
Ethiopia	955	7,068	2,835
Nigeria	3,276	6,467	6,482
Kenya	2,300	5,066	4,753
South America			
Peru	2,988	22,056	13,409
Brazil	11,102	18,396	18,158
Argentina	280,024[e]	28,817	22,285

[a] Group averages are weighted averages with weight being population ratio
[b] Agriculture includes fisheries and forestry
[c] Industry includes manufacturing, mining, construction, electricity, water supply, and city gas
[d] Data pertain to 2015, which are the latest available data
[e] This seems to be abnormal

Unlike high-income countries and China, in other East Asian countries, GDP per worker is significantly higher in the industry sector than in the service sector. This is probably because the service sector includes traditional retail and similar service activities. In South Asia, the disparity in GDP per worker between the industries and service sectors is at most about threefold. These observations suggest that in low-income countries, income disparities between the industries and service sectors are relatively modest, while in high-income countries, incomes increase, particularly in industry, and even more so in the service sector.

Table 2.5 Comparison of poverty ratio between rural and urban areas[a](World Bank's World Development Indicators)

	Rural area	Urban area
Bangladesh	35.2	21.3
India	33.8	20.9
Thailand	13.9a	7.7a
Indonesia	16.6	9.9
Nigeria	69.0	51.2
Peru	48.0a	16.1a

[a] Data pertain to 2013

Finally, let us compare the poverty ratios between rural and urban areas. If the incomes of those employed in agriculture, forestry, and fisheries are significantly lower than those of workers in the industrial and service sectors, which are often located in urban areas, then the poverty ratio in rural areas should be higher than in urban areas. Here again, due to data limitations, a comparison for 2020 is not possible. Therefore, let us examine the situation in 2010, for which more comprehensive comparative data are available. Even so, data are missing for many countries. According to Table 2.5, the poverty ratio is much higher in rural areas than in urban areas. This indicates that poverty is a far more serious problem in rural areas. Moreover, it appears that many of the poor in urban and rural areas belong to the same social strata. Many people from rural areas who were poor moved to cities in search of jobs, hoping to escape poverty, but they are likely to remain poor. Others who migrated to cities and eventually returned to rural areas are still in poverty. From this perspective, it is essential for poverty reduction to enrich rural areas and create higher-income employment opportunities in urban areas for rural workers. In the next section, we will examine this point through case studies.

2.6 Who Are the Poor?

While it is clear that many of the poor reside in rural areas, what types of income strata exist within these communities? The wealthiest are absentee large landowners, but since they reside in major cities, they are not considered rural residents. Furthermore, absentee large landowners are not present in every country; in general, large-scale landlordism was established during the colonial period. Among rural residents, the relatively wealthy are the resident landlords who live in nearby towns. Next are owner-cultivators who farm their own land, followed by tenant farmers who rent land from landlords. Some households combine both owner-cultivation and tenant farming. Although the work performed by tenant farmers and owner-cultivators is essentially the same, tenant farmers are poorer because they must pay rent.

2

Based on my field surveys in rural Asia, to put it rather roughly, about one-third of the value of agricultural production is spent on inputs such as fertilizer and machinery, another third goes to land rent or returns to land, and the remaining third is labor income. The poorest are landless agricultural laborers, who engage in simple and unstable seasonal work, such as weeding, transplanting, and harvesting. Because these are unskilled jobs, wages are low, resulting in low incomes. The reason why they remain agricultural laborers is, to a considerable extent, due to "flawed land reforms." For example, land reforms in Asia aimed to confiscate land from large landlords and transfer it to cultivators (i.e., tenant farmers). However, this policy eliminated the incentive for landlords to rent out land, leading to the eviction of tenant farmers, who are forced to be landless agricultural laborers. In fact, in Asian countries where land reform has not been implemented, there are very few landless agricultural laborers. This issue will be discussed further in ► Chap. 6.[6]

So, how poor are the households of landless agricultural laborers and members of smallholder families who own only tiny plots of land? To examine this question, detailed household survey data are required. However, household surveys conducted for research purposes usually cover only specific regions rather than the entire country, raising questions about how representative they are of the national situation. Nevertheless, by comparing several surveys, general trends can be discerned. Here, I will focus on the results of rural surveys in Asia that I conducted as a project leader together with Dr. Cristina C. David during my visits to the Philippines from 1986 to 1989 (David and Otsuka 1994), as well as the results of follow-up surveys conducted in the early 2000s (Otsuka et al. 2009).

Landless agricultural laborer households account for approximately 30% of all households in the Philippines, India, and Bangladesh. According to ◘ Table 2.6, the poorest groups are landless laborers and small-scale micro farmers (here defined as households farming 1 hectare or less), followed by somewhat wealthier smallholders (1–2 hectares), and, as expected, the wealthiest are large-scale farmers (2 hectares or more). Interestingly, the income disparities among landless laborers, micro farmers, and smallholders are surprisingly small. In some cases, landless laborer households are even better off than smallholder households. Why is this the case? This is because households with less access to land tend to earn more supplementary income from non-agricultural employment. Some landless laborers are barely engaged in agricultural work at all; in fact, they can hardly be called "agricultural laborers." The importance of non-agricultural income has grown significantly in the 2000s compared to the 1980s. Our research concludes that the main reason for the reduction in rural poverty in Asia is the increase in non-agricultural income. Of course, this is underpinned by the rapid development of the non-agricultural sector.

---

6 The above discussion is based on Otsuka (2007). A major reason for the success of postwar land reform in Japan was the thorough transfer of land carried out under the command of the occupying forces, who wielded overwhelming authority.

Table 2.6 Farm household income per capita (USD) and nonfarm income share (%) by farm size in selected countries in Asia, average of two years (the late 1980s and 2002 or 2004)[ab]

	Farm size			
	Landless	Micro (0–1 ha)	Small (1–2 ha)	Large (2 ha and above)
Philippines (1985 and 2004)				
Per capita income	1,239	1,051	1,347	3,007
Nonfarm income share	65	47	38	36
Thailand (1987 and 2004)				
Per capita income	n/a[c]	1,518	1,682	2,745
Nonfarm income share	n/a	51	44	25
Bangladesh (1988 and 2004)				
Per capita income	609	712	840	1,311
Nonfarm income share	57	57	51	41
India (Tamil Nadu) (1986/87 and 2002/03)[d]				
Per capita income	n/a	446	586	1,210
Nonfarm income share	n/a	8	3	11

[a] This table is based on David and Otsuka (1994) andOtsuka, Estudillo, and Sawada (2009)
[b] Income is expressed by PPP-adjusted USD in 2000
[c] n/a indicates data is not available. No landless households were found in Thailand in 1987, whereas income data of the landless households were not collected in Tamil Nadu
[d] One-year income spanning two calendar years

In Africa, there has been, until recently, a large amount of uncultivated land, and fortunately, there are very few landless agricultural laborer households. Therefore, Table 2.7 compares per capita income among micro, small, and large farmers in four African countries. Among these, Kenya, the most developed, has the highest income and the highest proportion of non-agricultural income. There is also a slight trend in which the share of non-agricultural income decreases from micro farmers to smallholders to large-scale farmers. Similar trends are observed in the other three countries. In other words, in Africa, where the development of the non-agricultural sector is lagging, non-agricultural employment opportunities are limited, but even so, households with less access to land seem to be supplementing their insufficient agricultural income with whatever non-agricultural income they can obtain. However, high non-agricultural income does not mean that anyone can earn a high income from non-agricultural work.

The most important determinant of non-agricultural income is educational attainment, which is highest among workers who have migrated to cities, followed by non-agricultural workers remaining in rural areas, then farmers, and finally agricultural laborers. In our studies in the Philippines and Thailand, we tracked

Table 2.7 Farm household income per capita (USD) and nonfarm income share (%) in the early 2000s by farm size in selected countries in sub-Saharan Africa[a] (Otsuka et al. 2009, p. 207)

	Farm size		
	Micro (0–1 ha)	Small (1–2 ha)	Large (2 ha and above)
Kenya			
Per capita income in 2004	698	814	1,091
Nonfarm income share in 2004	32	29	25
Uganda			
Per capita income in 2004	458	557	903
Nonfarm income share in 2004	11	11	10
Ethiopia			
Per capita income in 2003	565	558	816
Nonfarm income share in 2003	7	4	1
Mozambique			
Per capita income in 2005	347	540	557
Nonfarm income share in 2005	25	24	24

[a] Income is expressed by PPP-adjusted USD in 2000

workers who migrated to cities and surveyed their annual incomes (Otsuka et al. 2009). According to the results shown in Table 2.8, the incomes of migrants to urban areas are much higher than those of non-agricultural workers remaining in rural areas. While differences in the cost of living between urban and rural areas are one factor, the higher educational attainment of urban migrants is a major reason. Yet, the difference in schooling between migrants and remainders is small in Thailand, even though the income of migrants is almost twice as much as that of remainders as in the case of the Philippines. This indicates that quality of labor which cannot be measured by schooling years is also important. Overall, the data in Table 2.8 are consistent with our earlier conclusion based on Table 2.6 that the main reason for the reduction in rural poverty is the increase in non-agricultural income.

To summarize the discussion in this section, the causes of rural poverty can be identified as: (1) lack of land ownership or ownership of only a small amount of land; (2) low levels of education; and (3) limited non-agricultural employment opportunities. Additionally, although not discussed here, even in areas where land is owned, the proportion of poor people is high in regions with low rainfall and arid conditions (especially in inland Africa). Therefore, when comparing land ownership, it is also important to consider differences in land quality and the potential productivity of the land.

Table 2.8 Comparison of annual income and schooling years between urban migrants and those who remain in the village in the Philippines and Thailand in 2004[ab]

	Philippines	Thailand
Schooling years		
Migrants	10.9	9.2
Remainders	9.0	9.0
Annual income		
Migrants	10,752	10,676
Remainders	5,082	5,860

[a] This table is based onOtsuka, Estudillo, and Sawada (2009)
[b] Income is expressed by PPP-adjusted USD in 2000

2.7 Poverty and Income Distribution

In this chapter, we have analyzed poverty thus far; however, let us now consider the relationship between poverty and income distribution. Even if the average per capita income is high, if a small minority of wealthy individuals receive the majority of income, this results in a large number of poor people.

There is no inherent value in simply increasing per capita income. Income distribution is a major concern in economics, and various indicators have been developed to measure it. In this book, we will use intuitively understandable indicators of income distribution to advance our discussion. First, we calculate what percentage of total national income is earned by the wealthiest 10% of households. The higher this ratio, the relatively wealthier the rich are, making this figure itself a measure of inequality.

This is shown for developing countries in columns (1) and (3) of Table 2.9. In East Asia and South Asia, this ratio generally ranges between 25 and 35%. However, in Africa and South America, it often exceeded 30%, and in Kenya and Brazil, around 1990, it approached 50%. One reason for this high ratio is the establishment of large plantations during the colonial era, which created a distinctly wealthy class.

Next, we calculated what percentage of total national income is earned by the poorest 10% of households. The results are shown in columns (2) and (4) of Table 2.9. If income distribution were perfectly equal, this value would be 10%, but in reality, it is often below 4%. The lowest ratios are found in Brazil, followed by Peru and Argentina. Notably, the ratio for East Asia in 2020 is strikingly low. Indonesia has experienced a slight decline since 1990, suggesting that some people in this country have been left behind by economic growth.

Finally, we examined the ratio of the income share of high-income households to that of low-income households. For simplicity, we refer to this as the *income ratio*. I once compared this simple income ratio with other income distribution indicators for postwar Japan and recall that the correlation was extremely strong. This income ratio is likely an effective indicator of income distribution.

2

Table 2.9 Comparison of income distribution among selected countries and regions around 1990 and 2020 (World Bank's World Development Indicators various years)

	Around 1990[a]				Around 2020[b]			
	Top 10 (1)	Bottom 10 (2)		(1)/(2)	Top 10 (3)	Bottom 10 (4)		(3)/(4)
East Asia								
Indonesia	24.7	4.2	(1990)	5.9	27.9	3.2	(2020)	8.7
China	25.3	3.5	(1990)	7.2	29.4	3.1	(2020)	9.5
Thailand	36.1	2.5	(1990)	14.7	27.0	3.2	(2020)	8.4
South Asia								
Bangladesh	24.6	4.2	(1989)	5.9	27.4	3.5	(2022)	7.8
Pakistan	27.1	3.5	(1991)	7.8	25.5	4.2	(2018)	6.1
India	27.0	3.9	(1988)	6.9	26.2	3.2	(2020)	8.2
Nepal	25.0	4.0	(1985)	6.2	24.2	3.7	(2022)	6.5
Sub-Saharan Africa								
Ethiopia	33.8	3.0	(1995)	11.4	28.5	2.9	(2015)	9.8
Nigeria	31.5	1.4	(1992)	22.2	26.7	2.9	(2018)	9.2
Kenya	47.9	1.2	(1992)	38.6	28.4	3.0	(2020)	9.5
South America								
Peru	35.5	2.0	(1986)	18.2	32.9	1.7	(2020)	19.4
Brazil	48.4	0.7	(1990)	74.4	39.5	1.6	(2020)	24.7
Argentina	36.8	2.0	(1991)	18.2	30.6	1.7	(2020)	18.0

[a] The numbers in parentheses are years in which data closest to 1990 are available
[b] The numbers in parentheses are years in which data closest to 2020 are available

According to Table 2.9, this income ratio is overwhelmingly high in Brazil, followed by Peru, Argentina, Ethiopia, Kenya, and Nigeria. Of particular note is the upward trend in China's income ratio. While it has not yet reached the South American level, if income inequality continues to increase, dissatisfaction among the poor could potentially put the brakes on China's remarkable economic development.

So, what is the relationship between the income ratio and the poverty ratio? If income inequality is a major factor in poverty, there should be a positive correlation between the income ratio and the poverty ratio. This is examined in ◘ Fig. 2.3. Although Brazil stands out with a high income ratio, its poverty ratio is not particularly high. For other countries as well, there is no clear relationship indicating that a higher income ratio leads to a higher poverty ratio. If income distribution becomes more equal while per capita income remains constant, the poverty ratio should decrease. The absence of such a relationship in ◘ Fig. 2.3 suggests that factors other than income distribution may also affect the poverty ratio. As discussed in ► Chap. 1, per capita income appears to be one of the most important of these factors. Therefore, analyses like the one in this figure, which do not account for the effect of per capita income, must be considered inaccurate.

As shown in ◘ Table 2.9, the fact that some countries have income ratios several to ten times higher than others suggests that there is indeed a certain relationship between the degree of income inequality and the severity of poverty. If it is possible to increase the average per capita income while also raising the labor income of the poor, then economic development and poverty reduction can be achieved simultaneously. So, how can this be accomplished? The purpose of this book is to answer precisely this question from various perspectives.

2.8 Summary

Finally, let us review the main points discussed in this chapter.

- Both in absolute numbers and in terms of ratios, poverty in developing countries has declined significantly over the past 25 years. While this is a welcome fact, most of the reduction is attributable to rapid poverty alleviation accompanying China's economic development, rather than to internationally coordinated efforts led by the United Nations. Moreover, poverty in South Asia and Africa remains severe.
- Poverty arises from a low proportion of earners in the household, low labor income, or limited income from assets.
- While developing countries tend to have a lower proportion of workers due to a larger youth population, this alone does not account for the significant income disparity between developed and developing countries.
- As the employment structure shifts from agriculture to industry and subsequently to the service sector, the proportion of people living in poverty declines. The primary reason for this is the increase in labor income that accompanies changes in the employment structure. Therefore, changes in industrial structure and the resulting shifts in employment are crucial for poverty reduction.
- Poverty is more severe in rural areas, primarily because the poor own little land, have low levels of education, and face limited non-agricultural employment opportunities.

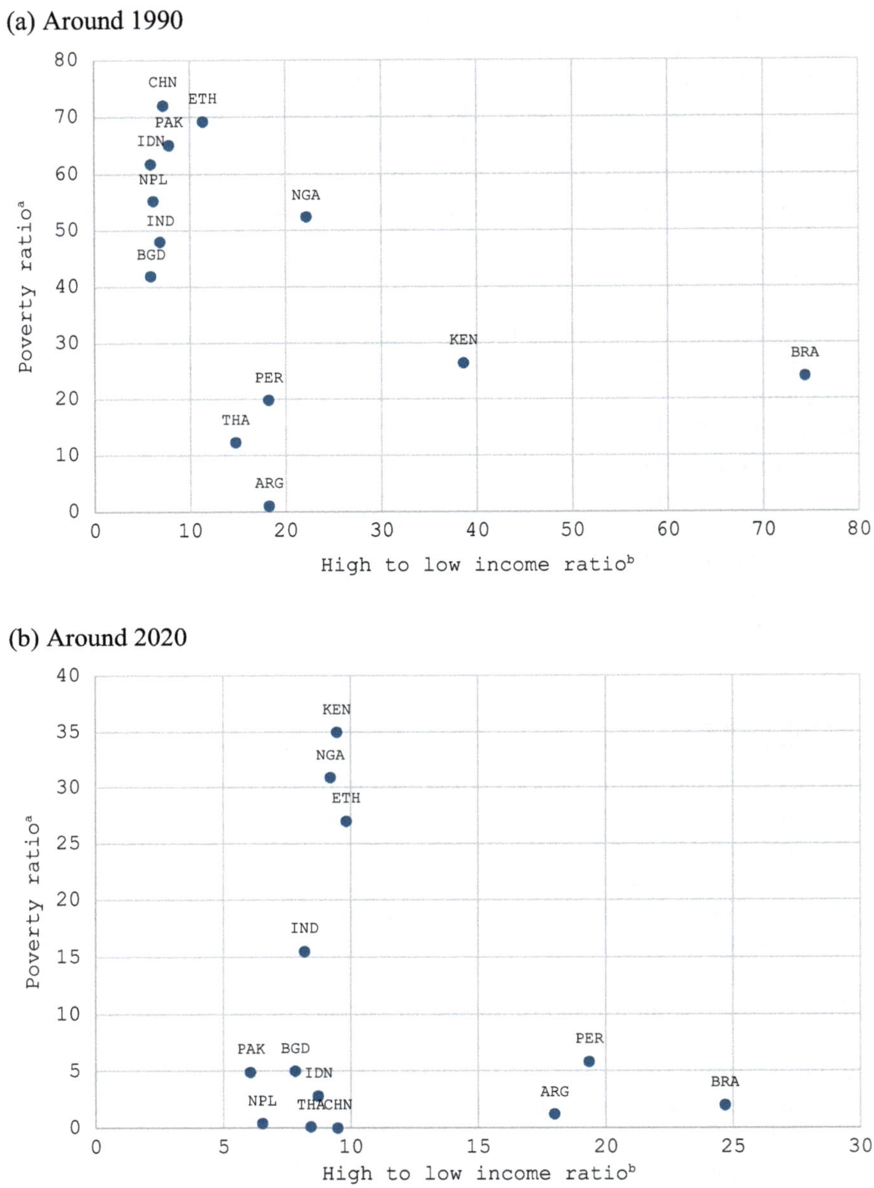

Fig. 2.3 Correlation between high to low income ratio and poverty ratio around 1990 and 2020 (World Bank's World Development Indicators various years) (Poverty line is USD 2.15 per day, Total income of top 10% households divided by total income of bottom 10% households, ETH—Ethiopia, NPL—Nepal, BGD—Bangladesh, KEN—Kenya, NGA—Nigeria, IND—India, IDN—Indonesia, CHN—China, THA—Thailand, PER—Peru, ARG—Argentine, BRA—Brazil, PAK—Pakistan)

To reduce poverty, economic development should aim to increase employment opportunities and labor income for the poor, thereby achieving both income growth and poverty reduction simultaneously.

Questions

1. Given that poverty has been declining significantly over the last few decades, should we commend the efforts made by the United Nations and aid agencies to reduce poverty?
2. Is the main reason for poverty low labor income, rather than a high dependency ratio, or the fact that the poor have little ownership of assets?
3. Is poverty likely to be severe in countries where income distribution is highly unequal?
4. Are owner farmers as poor as landless workers, because they are engaged in the same kind of farming activities?

References

Becker, G.S. (1964). *Human capital.* Columbia University Press.

Chen, S., & Ravallion, M. (2010). The developing world is poorer than we thought, but no less successful in the fight against poverty. *Quarterly Journal of Economics, 125*(4), 1577–1625.

David, C.C., & Otsuka, K. (Eds.). (1994). *Modern rice technology and income distribution in Asia.* Lynne Rienner.

Otsuka, K. (2007). Efficiency and equity effects of land markets. In R. E. Evenson & P. Pingali (Eds.), *Handbook of agricultural economics, Volume III.* Elsevier.

Otsuka, K., Estudillo, J.P., & Sawada, Y. (Eds.). (2009). *Rural poverty and income dynamics in Asia and Africa.* Routledge.

World Bank. (various years). *World development indicators.* World Bank DataBank. d Bank.

Why Can't We Eradicate Poverty?

Contents

K. Otsuka, *A Primer on Development Economics*,
Classroom Companion: Economics, https://doi.org/10.1007/978-981-95-5397-6_3

3.1 Introduction

3

In today's world, where the internet enables vital information to circulate globally in an instant and scientific advances such as induced pluripotent stem (iPS) cells allow for the artificial creation of organs, why do we still struggle to resolve the longstanding and serious issue of poverty? What makes this problem so difficult to solve in the first place? Developed countries provide foreign aid to developing countries, but is aid alone sufficient to eliminate poverty? Or have there been fundamental errors in development policy thus far? The purpose of this chapter is to discuss these fundamental questions.

► Section 3.2 points out that the driving forces behind economic development are stocks, such as human capital and infrastructure, and that increasing these stocks requires substantial time and financial resources. ► Section 3.3 then addresses the effectiveness and limitations of foreign aid. In ► Sect. 3.4, I raise the question of whether the lack of an effective development strategy is a primary reason why poverty persists. ► Section 3.5 evaluates recent debates in development economics.

3.2 Accumulating Stocks Requires Time and Money

The first point to recognize is that the productivity of workers, firms, and the overall economy is determined by human capital, physical capital, infrastructure, social capital, and intellectual capital—all of which are forms of stock. Needless to say, economic development requires increased productivity, and to achieve this, these stocks must be expanded.

As explained in ► Box 3.1,human capital essentially refers to the quality of individuals as workers. *Physical capital* here refers to machinery, equipment, and buildings owned by the private sector, typically measured in terms of value. *Infrastructure* refers to public capital provided by the government, including roads, railways, ports, airports, and so on.[1] Since private entities may sometimes operate railways and similar assets, the distinction between private physical capital and public infrastructure is not always clear-cut.

Infrastructure is sometimes referred to as social overhead capital, but this term differs from the concept of social capital discussed here. *Social capital*, in this context, refers to the degree of trust in human relationships. Social capital is closely related to institutions such as transactions, contracts, unions, and the provision of public goods. When social relations are strong, contracts can be drafted, agreed upon, and enforced more effectively, making the contractual system function efficiently. Similarly, when interpersonal trust is high, collective activities such as union activities become more active, and the provision of public goods proceeds smoothly. Collaborative work within and between firms also becomes more efficient.

---

1 Although not discussed in this book, in addition to such hard infrastructure, there is also soft infrastructure, such as legal systems that protect property rights and antitrust laws that ensure fair market transactions.

Intellectual capital refers to the stock of scientific, technical, and managerial knowledge useful for production. While both social capital and intellectual capital can be understood conceptually, they are difficult to measure in practice. When individuals acquire scientific, technical, or managerial knowledge useful for production through education or training, this increases the stock of human capital.

Sending children to school is an investment in human capital, but it does not immediately translate into higher productivity. Over time, as the stock of human capital accumulates, it eventually leads to increased productivity. Similarly, investment in research typically results in the gradual creation of new knowledge, which accumulates and ultimately enhances production efficiency.

Generally, it takes considerable effort to increase stocks that are important to the economy. While this may seem self-evident, it is a crucial point. Moreover, it is important that these stocks are complementary. When firms invest in cutting-edge equipment, they must also hire capable workers who can utilize such equipment effectively or retrain their existing workforce. As investment and employment rise and business activity becomes more vigorous across many firms, infrastructure development becomes necessary to support logistics. Companies must also build trust-based relationships (social capital) with subcontractors and retailers to facilitate smooth transactions. However, raising these stocks across the board cannot be achieved overnight. In the following sections, we will examine: (1) market transactions and social capital, (2) long-term changes in educational attainment, (3) accumulation of physical capital, (4) infrastructure development, and (5) accumulation of intellectual capital.

3.2.1 Market Transactions and Social Capital

Voluntary transactions benefit both buyers and sellers. Therefore, the fundamental principle of a liberal economy is that transactions should be as free as possible. This is the core of the market mechanism, also known as the principle of the invisible hand. Because this is such an important concept, I would like to provide a brief explanation in ▶ Box 3.1.

Box 3.1 Understanding the Principle of the "Invisible Hand"

The most fundamental concept in economics is the invisible hand proposed by Adam Smith. Many microeconomics textbooks fail to explain this point thoroughly, which I find truly regrettable, as it is the basic principle of a liberal economy.

Suppose a consumer voluntarily purchases a product at a certain price. Why? Because the consumer believes that the satisfaction gained exceeds the price paid. In other words, a certain *surplus* (satisfaction in excess of the amount paid) is generated.

Conversely, suppose a firm voluntarily sells a product at a certain price. Why? Because the selling price is higher than the cost of production, it results in a profit. Thus, a surplus (profit) is generated.

What happens if both consumers and firms are allowed to engage in voluntary transactions as much as they wish? Transactions will continue until there are no more mutually beneficial opportunities for consumers and firms. At that point, there are no "good deals" left that would make both producers and consumers better off, and no further transactions will occur (strictly speaking, this assumes that each transaction is small enough not to affect the terms of other transactions). This is a kind of ideal state.[2]

In this example, the firm is the seller and the consumer is the buyer, but the specific economic agents acting as buyers or sellers are not important. For example, when a worker sells labor services to a firm, the invisible hand principle still applies. Interestingly, the consumers and firms in these examples are self-interested individuals who care only about their own benefit. When self-interested economic agents pursue their own interests, a socially optimal state is achieved as if guided by an "invisible hand." This was Adam Smith's great insight.

For this reason, Smith advocated free market transactions, and even today, nearly all economists emphasize the role of markets. However, as will be explained in ► Box 3.3, it is also extremely important to recognize that markets can "fail."

However, it is not sufficient to leave everything to the principle of the invisible hand. There are various cases in which the invisible hand fails. Here, let us consider one such example: the problem of *asymmetric information*, where buyers cannot ascertain the quality of the product they intend to purchase. In short, this is the problem that sellers may deceive buyers by selling inferior goods at high prices. This is an issue we frequently encounter in everyday life: when something looks delicious, but it actually isn't. Everyone has probably experienced buying fruit that turned out to be completely tasteless, despite expecting it to be delicious. Similarly, excessively high prices for souvenirs at a tourist spot are a comparable situation.

So how do consumers resolve the problem of not knowing the quality of the goods they wish to purchase? The same issue applies to firms that buy raw materials, components, or services. While various solutions can be considered, in reality, *trust* and *reputation* play a major role. For example, Toyota Motor Corporation enjoys a reputation as an excellent automobile manufacturer. As a result, consumers feel confident purchasing Toyota vehicles. Other Japanese as well as European automakers have likely earned similar trust from consumers. Leading department stores and supermarkets strive to establish a reputation for selling reliable products, enabling customers to shop with confidence. Even highly reputable companies, such as department stores or supermarkets, would see their rep-

2 In economics, this is called Pareto optimality.

utation quickly decline and sales drop sharply if they were to sell inferior goods at high prices, potentially even facing bankruptcy. Such trust and reputation are the result of sustained efforts over time. While it may be possible to make short-term profits by deceiving consumers, long-term gains are built on the trust earned through honest business practices.[3]

There are other ways to eliminate dishonest practices. One is to leverage local or familial ties. Landowners, for instance, prefer to lease land to diligent and trustworthy tenant farmers—often relatives or people who have lived nearby for a long time and whose character is well known. The prevalence of family-run businesses is largely due to the desire to employ trustworthy family members.

In manufacturing, it is common to find industrial clusters where numerous firms supplying components are concentrated around final assembly companies. This is because proximity makes it easier to verify a company's reputation and to build trust-based relationships. In short, social capital plays a crucial role in ensuring the smooth functioning of market transactions.

What happens, then, when market transactions become active in an environment lacking social capital? In Japan, during the rapid economic growth of the 1960s, a real estate boom was triggered by a surge in housing demand. Many real estate agencies opened, but social capital had yet to be established. The result was a proliferation of fraudulent transactions by unscrupulous real estate agents. Over time, competition led to the establishment of reputation and trust, driving out dishonest agents and leaving only honest ones, but the process was marked by considerable turmoil.

A notable example is the collapse of socialist economies and the rapid introduction of market economies in the early 1990s. Although market transactions were liberalized, former socialist countries had few individuals or organizations familiar with free market practices, and lacked social capital (trust in distributors). The result was dysfunctional distribution systems, rampant fraud, and a sharp decline in gross domestic product (GDP), accompanied by economic chaos (see ◘ Fig. 3.1). In Russia, where marketization was particularly abrupt, GDP was halved, and it took more than 15 years to return to previous levels.

Although there is no definitive evidence, the structural adjustment policies imposed by the World Bank and the International Monetary Fund (IMF) on African governments in the 1980s—requiring them to halt direct government intervention in markets as a condition for loans and aid—also appear to fit this pattern. Generally, structural adjustment is considered to have failed. Indeed, if we look only at the short-term effects, this assessment is accurate. In places where markets did not previously exist, they do not emerge or function easily, and structural adjustment likely leads to sluggish transactions. However, as business peo-

---

3 Unfortunately, in Japan, it was revealed in the fall of 2013 that well-known restaurants and restaurants operated by top hotels and department stores had been misrepresenting the ingredients they used. This was a fraudulent act that exploited the trust they had built with consumers over the years. Such actions undermine the very raison d'être of these restaurants, and they are likely to suffer devastating consequences.

3

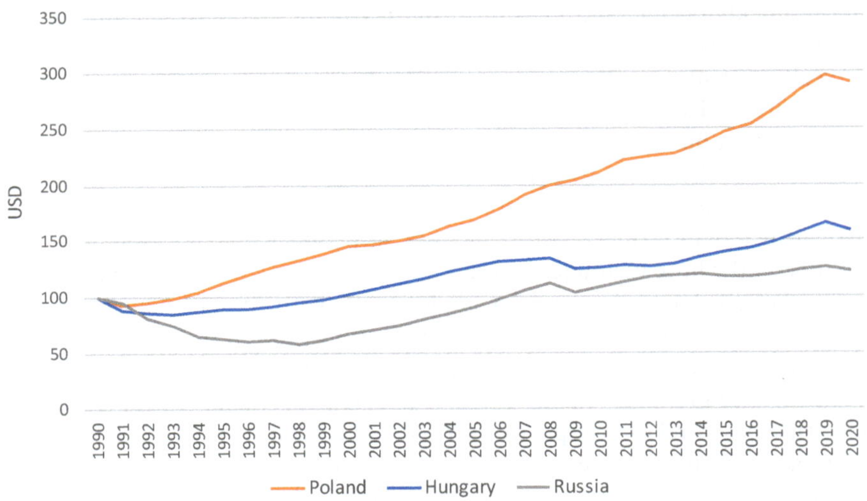

Fig. 3.1 Changes in the index of real GDP from 1990 to 2020 in countries belonging to the former Soviet Union (1990 = 100) (World Bank's World Development Indicators various years)

ple gained the necessary knowledge through experience and trust (social capital) was gradually established, it is possible that, in the long run, structural adjustment contributed to the development of efficient markets.

A good example I am familiar with is the milk trade in Kenya and Uganda. Until the 1990s, the inefficient public sector had a monopoly on milk distribution, but private businesses were eventually allowed to enter the market. As their numbers gradually increased and competition intensified, the efficiency of milk trading clearly improved. While I am not familiar with earlier times, in the rice markets of African countries I have visited, female traders are ubiquitous. This indicates that the market is functioning properly. Recently, African economies have performed much better than before, and I am quite convinced that at least part of this improvement can be attributed to structural adjustment.

3.2.2 Long-Term Changes in Educational Attainment

If asked to identify the most important stock variable for the economy among human capital, physical capital, infrastructure, social capital, and intellectual capital, most development economists would unhesitatingly choose human capital. No matter how well-developed physical capital and infrastructure may be, if human capital is lacking—that is, if the abilities of managers and workers are low—production efficiency will be low. Conversely, with sufficient human capital, it is possible to develop technology and enhance production efficiency, while gradually accumulating physical capital and infrastructure by reinvesting part of the increase in GDP. In fact, it is believed that the rapid postwar recovery of defeated nations such as Germany and Japan, which lost much of their physical capital

Table 3.1 Long-term changes in average schooling years of productive-age population in Japan, South Korea, and the United States[a] (Godo 2011)

	Japan	South Korea[b]	US
1890	1.3	n/a	6.5
1900	2.0	n/a	7.2
1910	3.0	n/a	7.7
1920	4.3	0.6	8.3
1930	5.6	0.8	9.1
1940	6.5	1.1	9.8
1950	7.6	n/a	10.5
1960	8.7	3.3	11.3
1970	9.8	4.8	12.0
1980	10.7	6.9	12.8
1990	11.5	9.0	13.5
2000	12.3	10.5	14.0

[a]Productive age refers to 15–64 years old
[b]Data before 1945 includes North Korea

and infrastructure during World War II, was due to the retention of highly skilled human capital.

Human capital is formed through formal education, parental education, workplace training, and efforts to maintain health. Among these, formal education is particularly important. Educated workers are likely to acquire workplace skills more quickly, are more likely to become parents who value education, and tend to have greater health awareness. The level of formal education appears to represent the overall level of human capital. However, the role of parental education should not be overlooked. The tendency for children to enter the same occupations as their parents is partly due to parental education. Thus, human capital has an intergenerational accumulation aspect. Even in the case of formal education, raising its overall national level requires both increasing the quantity and quality of teachers and schools, as well as investing significant time in children's education itself.

Table 3.1 shows the long-term changes in average years of schooling in Japan, South Korea, and the United States, as estimated by Professor Yoshihisa Godo (2011). According to these estimates, the average years of schooling in the United States was 6.5 years in 1890, a level Japan reached 50 years later in 1940. In 1940, the average in the United States was 9.8 years, a level Japan attained 30 years later in 1970. In contrast, South Korea's average years of schooling lagged behind Japan by 20 to 30 years. As this demonstrates, raising educational attainment is a long-term process.

3

Table 3.2 Comparison of average schooling years of adult population (over 15 years of age) in 1950, 1980, and 2010 in selected countries and regions (Barro and Lee 2013)

	1950	1980	2010
High-income countries			
Japan	6.73	9.10	11.60
US	8.40	12.03	13.18
UK	6.39	8.41	12.24
France	4.33	5.96	10.68
East Asia			
Indonesia	1.09	3.63	7.61
China	1.61	5.31	7.95
Thailand	2.04	3.64	7.99
S. Korea	4.50	8.13	12.05
South Asia			
Bangladesh	0.93	2.25	5.91
Pakistan	0.99	2.15	5.02
India	0.99	2.34	6.24
Nepal	0.11	0.99	4.23
Sub-Saharan Africa			
Ghana	0.68	4.53	7.00
Senegal	1.76	2.49	2.74
Kenya	1.16	3.41	6.14
South America			
Peru	2.83	6.10	8.88
Brazil	2.08	3.04	7.89
Argentina	4.85	7.30	9.51

Table 3.2 presents the average years of schooling for the population aged 15–64 in major countries from 1950 to 2010. Fortunately, in almost all countries, educational attainment has risen rapidly. Of course, due to differences in educational quality, direct comparisons should be made with caution. However, as long as average years of schooling have increased to a large extent, there is no doubt that educational attainment has improved in substantive terms.[4] It is also

4 One of the objectives of the Millennium Development Goals is to ensure that all children receive at least a primary education, and it is said that aid for this purpose has been particularly active in Africa. However, it has been pointed out that as enrollment rates have increased, the number of students per teacher has risen, resulting in a decline in the quality of education.

noteworthy that, in 2010, the average years of schooling in Africa was unexpectedly high, surpassing South Asia and almost comparable to East Asia. However, for Africa, data were available only for three countries with relatively high educational attainment, so generalization may not be appropriate. Nevertheless, it is quite possible that improvements in educational attainment have supported the recent growth of African economies.

3.2.3 Accumulation of Physical Capital

In low-income countries where wages are low, it is rational to employ labor-intensive production methods that utilize simple tools and machinery, relying heavily on manual labor. In such contexts, this approach is more cost-effective. However, as the economy develops and wages gradually rise, capital-intensive production methods that economize on labor and utilize machinery more effectively become increasingly advantageous. For example, while conventional lathes (machines that rotate work about a horizontal axis and shape it with a fixed tool) are commonly used in Africa, computer numerical control (the computerized operation of machining tools used in manufacturing) lathes are standard in advanced economies. Factories where robots perform most of the production work, with few human workers present, represent the epitome of capital-intensive production. As these examples illustrate, long-term economic development is closely tied to the accumulation of physical capital, accompanied by technological advancements. ◘ Figure 3.2, using data from Godo (2013), shows the long-term changes in labor productivity and the capital-labor ratio—calculated as the amount of capital per worker—for Japan and South Korea. This data includes not only private sector physical capital but also infrastructure stock, and for Japan, it spans nearly 150 years, from 1872. It should be noted that the vertical axis is logarith-

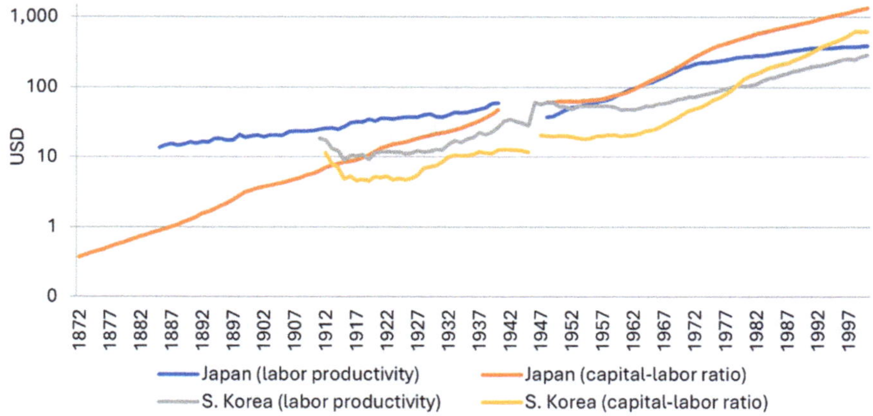

◘ Fig. 3.2 Long-term changes in labor productivity and capital-labor ratio in Japan and South Korea (Godo 2013)

mically scaled, which means that small numerical changes appear larger, while large changes appear smaller. Readers familiar with semi-logarithmic diagrams will recognize that the slope of the curve in this figure represents the growth rate. A steep upward slope indicates rapid growth, while a flat curve indicates little or no change.

3

Several interesting trends can be observed from this figure. First, labor productivity and the capital-labor ratio move in the same direction. Intuitively, if each worker operates a larger amount of capital, output per worker should be higher. Therefore, the similar direction of change in both variables is consistent with common sense. Second, the growth rate of the capital-labor ratio exceeds that of labor productivity (i.e., the slope of the capital-labor ratio curve is steeper). Since labor productivity is closely related to per capita income, this suggests that substantial capital accumulation is required to raise per capita income. Third, it becomes clear that capital accumulation is an extremely long-term process. In both Japan and South Korea, citizens have been saving for over a century; these savings have been channeled into investments, resulting in accumulated capital. This figure thus underscores that economic development is a highly protracted process. In ◘ Fig. 3.2, the capital-labor ratio is presented in price-adjusted USD; however, it is not straightforward to convert the capital-labor ratios of different countries into comparable, price-adjusted dollar terms. Therefore, international comparisons often rely on growth rates by country or region (see ◘ Table 3.3).

Comparing the data in this table with the experiences of Japan and South Korea yields some interesting insights. First, as in the cases of Japan and South Korea, international comparisons also show that labor productivity and the capital-labor ratio move in the same direction. Not only China but also other East Asian countries have experienced rapid growth in both labor productivity and the capital-labor ratio. In contrast, in Africa, except for the 1960s, growth in both labor productivity and the capital-labor ratio has been sluggish. Second, the growth rate of the capital-labor ratio generally exceeds that of labor productivity. The only exception is Africa, where labor productivity has grown faster than the capital-labor ratio. In Africa, it appears that labor productivity has been improved, at least to some extent, through effort and the use of limited capital. Nevertheless, without increasing the capital-labor ratio, it is unlikely that labor productivity will continue to rise over the long term. Enhancing the return on investment, fostering an environment conducive to active investment, and accumulating capital over the long run are critical challenges not only for Africa but for all countries.

3.2.4 Infrastructure Development

Even within the broad category of infrastructure, there are many different types, such as roads, railways, electricity, water and sewage systems, and ports. Here, I would like to consider the length of paved roads per capita as an indicator of the development of transport infrastructure in this sub-section. While the length of roads depends on a country's topography and population density, there is no

Table 3.3 Comparison of average annual growth rates of labor productivity and capital-labor ratio among selected countries and regions (Bosworth and Collins 2003)

	Labor productivity	Capital-labor ratio
Developed countries (22)		
1960–70	3.9	3.7
1970–80	1.7	2.6
1980–90	1.8	2.0
1990–2000	1.5	2.3
1960–2000	2.2	2.6
East Asia(7 countries excluding China)		
1960–70	3.7	4.9
1970–80	4.3	7.7
1980–90	4.4	6.9
1990–2000	3.4	6.6
1960–2000	3.9	6.6
China		
1960–70	0.9	0.0
1970–80	2.8	4.6
1980–90	6.8	6.0
1990–2000	8.8	9.1
1960–2000	4.8	4.9
South Asia (4)		
1960–70	2.2	3.4
1970–80	0.7	1.7
1980–90	3.7	2.9
1990–2000	2.8	3.4
1960–2000	2.3	2.9
Sub-Saharan Africa (19)		
1960–70	2.8	2.0
1970–80	1.0	3.7
1980–90	-1.1	-0.3
1990–2000	-0.2	-0.3
1960–2000	0.6	1.4
South America (22)		
1960–70	2.8	2.3
1970–80	2.7	3.4

(continued)

3

Table 3.3 (continued)

	Labor productivity	Capital-labor ratio
1980–90	-1.8	0.0
1990–2000	0.9	0.6
1960–2000	1.1	1.7

Numbers in parentheses are the number of countries included in the data. Regional averages are taken as weighted averages, with weights being the GDP

doubt that roads are a representative form of transport infrastructure. This is especially true in developing countries, where railways are often underdeveloped and the role of roads is even more significant. Nevertheless, the condition of roads in developing countries is generally poor.

I recall various scenes I have witnessed, such as the bumpy roads and traffic congestion in Dhaka, the capital of Bangladesh, and the unpaved mountain roads in northern Vietnam, where vehicles can only travel at 20–30 km per hour. When road conditions are poor, transportation costs rise, which in turn increases the prices of goods purchased and lowers the prices of goods sold. As a result, for example, the price of chemical fertilizers in landlocked African countries is reportedly two or even three times the international price. On the other hand, the prices of agricultural products remain low. It is therefore understandable that many African farmers make little use of chemical fertilizers. In addition, the prices of essential goods such as fuel are also high in inland Africa, which is one of the factors impeding poverty reduction.

Examining the data on paved road length per capita in Table 3.4, it is evident that there has been remarkable growth in East Asia. In particular, Thailand has clearly made significant investments in road infrastructure. Although data for China are incomplete, the length of paved roads increased by 60% in just five years from 2005 to 2010.[5] In contrast, South Asia has seen only modest improvements. Furthermore, in Africa, not only is the per capita length of paved roads extremely short, but there has been no significant increase in this area over the past 20 years. This situation hinders logistics and makes it difficult to realize the region's economic development potential. Overcoming this will require massive infrastructure investment sustained over a long period.

5 According to the China Statistical Yearbook, the per capita length of "graded roads" in 1990 was 0.65 m. Since graded roads are thought to correspond roughly to paved roads, this also indicates the rapid progress of road construction in China. I am grateful to Professor Liu Deqiang for pointing this out.

Table 3.4 Length of paved roads per capita among selected countries and regions (meters)[a] (World Bank's world development indicators various years)

	1990	2010	
High-income countries			
Japan	1.4	2.1	
US	25.0[b]	21.2	
UK	6.3	6.7	
France	15.2	15.8	
East Asia			
Indonesia	0.7	1.1	(2009)
China	n/a[c]	1.6	
Thailand	1.1	2.7	(2006)
S. Korea	0.9	1.7	
South Asia			
Bangladesh	0.1	n/a[c]	
Pakistan	0.8	1.1	
India	1.1	1.7	(2008)
Nepal	0.1	0.4	(2008)
Sub-Saharan Africa			
Ethiopia	0.1	0.1	(2007)
Nigeria	n/a[c]	0.8	(2004)
Kenya	0.3	0.2	
South America			
Peru	0.3	0.6	
Brazil	1.1	1.1	
Argentina	n/a[c]	1.8	(2003)

[a]Data are available only up to 2010. The numbers in parentheses are years in which data closest to 1990 are available
[b]Although no data on the length of paved roads is reported in 1990, I assumed that 100% of raods were paved
[c]No data are available

3.2.5 Accumulation of Intellectual Capital

Intellectual capital here refers to the stock of scientific, technological, and managerial knowledge. In earlier research, all these factors contributing to productivity growth were collectively referred to as *technological progress*, but in recent years, the importance of managerial knowledge in utilizing technology has come to be recognized. Broadly defined, technological progress, encompassing improvements

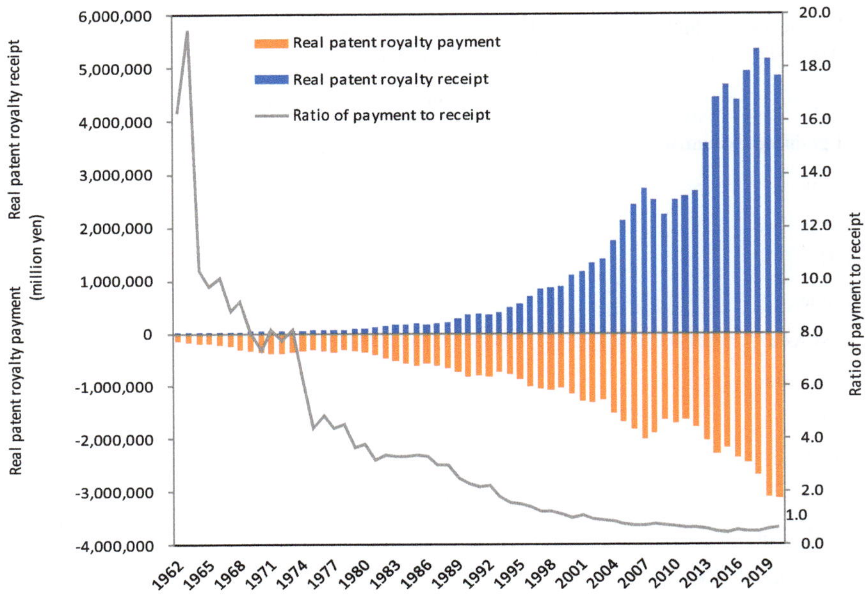

Fig. 3.3 Changes in real patent royalty payment and receipt in Japan (Deflated by GDP deflator reported by the Cabinet Office of Japan (68SNA, 93SNA, 2008SNA) (Science and Technology Agency of Japan, Kagakugijutu Yoran [indicators of science and technology] various years)

in management as well as advances in education, is recognized as a key engine of economic growth, making intellectual capital a vital component of economic development. However, objectively measuring the stock of intellectual capital is a challenging task. The number of researchers, engineers, and managers holding academic degrees is one possible indicator; however, obtaining internationally comparable data is challenging, and there are also issues with variations in the quality of degrees between countries and universities. Let us first consider the level of technological knowledge by comparing payments and receipts of patent royalties. If a country's technological level is low, it is rational to pay royalties to use foreign patents rather than develop technology independently. However, as the country's technological level rises, it will begin to collect patent royalties instead.

Figure 3.3 illustrates this for postwar Japan, for which exceptionally comprehensive data are available. During Japan's period of rapid economic growth—when the economy was expanding at an average annual rate of 10%, similar to present-day China, especially in the 1960s—Japan overwhelmingly imported technology. In 1963, payments for patent royalties were nearly 20 times greater than receipts. This was a form of legal imitation. In addition, reverse engineering, in which imported machinery was disassembled and analyzed, was also widespread, though it bordered on illegality. In fact, such imitation was a driving force behind Japan's economic development. Even after this period, real payments for patent royalties continued to increase, suggesting that technological imitation persisted. As a share of GDP, payments for patent royalties rose from 0.13% in 1980 to 0.34% in 2010. Meanwhile, patent royalty income increased even more rapidly as Japan's technological level improved. Around the year 2000, receipts from patent royalties began to catch up with payments; however, by this time, Japan had entered a period of low growth, and the pace of economic growth had slowed.

It is not possible to draw definitive conclusions based solely on Japan's experience. But it is reasonable to assume that when a country's technological level is low, rapid economic growth can be achieved by imitating the advanced technologies of more developed nations. However, as the scope for imitation diminishes and the country reaches the stage where it must develop its own technologies, the pace of economic growth appears to slow down. As shown in ◘ Fig. 3.3, this process is time-consuming. Ironically, economic growth tends to decelerate when the technological level is high, likely because the process of developing original technologies involves significant challenges and difficulties.

A similar trend to Japan's long-term experience can be observed in the international comparison of the number of patent applications and the share of applications by residents in 1990 and 2020 (◘ Table 3.5). While the quality of patents varies widely and there are qualitative differences between countries, making simple comparisons of patent numbers is inappropriate, ◘ Table 3.5 nonetheless provides a general indication of these trends.

In high-income countries, except for the United States, the number of patent applications has remained stable, and the proportion of applications by domestic residents is high. This likely reflects a consistently high level of technological knowledge and strong domestic technological development capabilities. In East Asia, the number of patent applications has generally increased significantly, and the share of applications by domestic residents has also risen sharply, indicating an improvement in technological capabilities. In South Asia, by contrast, the growth in patent applications has been slower, and the share of applications by domestic residents remains low, suggesting that technological progress has stagnated and there is a strong reliance on foreign technology. In Africa, there are very few patent applications by domestic residents, indicating an even lower capacity for technological development.

These facts strongly suggest that, as was the case for Japan in the past, successful economic development in developing countries requires reliance on foreign technology in the early stages, followed by improvements in the level of technological knowledge and, eventually, the strengthening of indigenous technological development capabilities as the economy advances.

3.3 Is Aid Insufficient?

The target of allocating 0.7% of gross national income (GNI) to official development assistance (ODA) has been repeatedly reaffirmed among Organisation for Economic Co-operation and Development (OECD) member countries (developed nations) since 1970. However, as shown in ◘ Table 3.6, the average ODA-to-GNI ratio among the core OECD members (or Development Assistance Com-

Table 3.5 Number of patent applications and proportion of applications by residents in 1990 and 2020 in selected countries (WIPO's IP Statistics various years)

	1990		**2020**	
	No. applications	**Proportion by residents (%)**	**No. applications**	**Proportion by residents (%)**
High-income countries				
Japan	360,704	92.3	288,472	78.8
US	171,163	53.0	558,305	45.6
UK	28,238	68.4	20,649	58.1
France	16,638	74.4	14,313	89.2
East Asia				
Indonesia	480	1.0	8,160	16.0
China	10,137	57.5	1,497,159	89.8
Thailand	1,940	3.8	7,525	11.5
S. Korea	25,820	35.2	226,759	79.6
South Asia				
Bangladesh	108	29.6	402	10.0
Pakistan	547	4.2	900	37.6
India	3,820	30.0	56,771	40.8
Nepal	0	n/a	0	n/a
Sub-Saharan Africa				
Ethiopia	0	n/a	0	n/a
Nigeria	258	4.7	1,008	40.7
Kenya	0	n/a	376	90.7
South America				
Peru	268	18.3	1,267	9.9
Brazil	7,537	31.7	24,338	21.7
Argentina	2,910	32.8	3,492	26.6

n/a means not applicable, as the denominator is zero

mittee [DAC]) was 0.33% in 1990–91, and remained almost unchanged at 0.32% in 2016–17. Norway's ratio is the highest among OECD countries, exceeding 1%. The United States has a relatively low ratio, but it allocates a substantial budget to military aid, making direct comparisons with other countries inappropriate. In this context, Japan's ODA-to-GNI ratio of 0.22% in 2016–17 must be considered extremely low. Moreover, in absolute terms, Japan's ODA has been declining. Unfortunately, this is an abnormal situation. ► Box 3.2 will examine this issue in greater detail.

Table 3.6 Amount of net ODA (million USD) and its ratio (%) to GNI (OECD, Development Finance Statistics various years)

	1990–1991		2016–2017	
	Total amount of ODA	Ratio to GNI	Total amount of ODA	Ratio to GNI
Japan	14,031	0.32	11,134	0.22
US	17,118	0.20	34,270	0.18
UK	4,123	0.30	18,322	0.7
France	11,056	0.61	10,324	0.41
Norway	2,512	1.15	4,162	1.06
Total of OECD DAC (Development Assistance Committee) member countries	84,700	0.33	144,814	0.32

Box 3.2 Has Japan Ever Been a Major Donor?

The straightforward answer to this question is yes. Japan's total official development assistance (ODA) increased steadily from the 1970s through the 1980s, and from 1989 to 2000, Japan was the world's top donor almost every year (see Fig. 3.4). In my view, this led to a public perception that "Japan is providing too much ODA." However, a more objective assessment should recognize that a country's commitment to aid should be measured not by the total amount of ODA, but

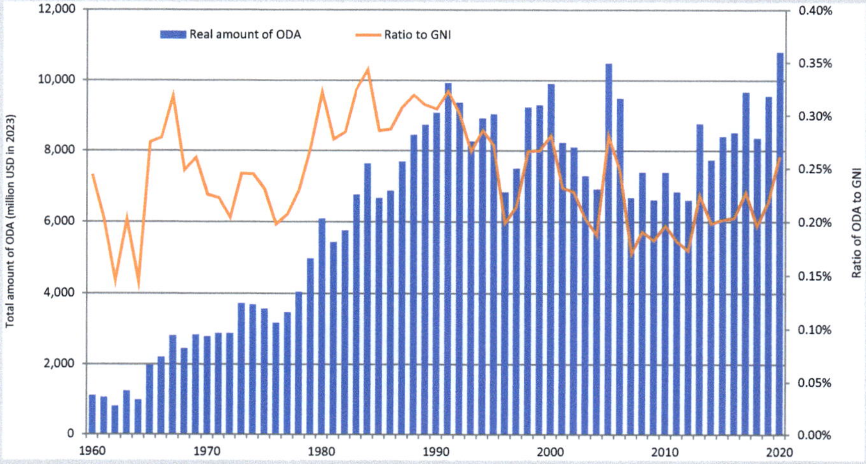

Fig. 3.4 Real amount of ODA and its ratio to GNI of Japan (OECD's Data Explorer various years)

3

by the ratio of ODA to GDP, or the per capita ODA contribution. Even if a country's total ODA is large due to its large population size, if the per capita contribution is low, it cannot be said that the country is particularly committed to ODA. This was precisely the case for Japan. The ODA-to-GNI ratio was about 0.3% around 1990, which was not particularly high by international standards, and it has continued to decline, often falling below 0.2% since 2007. In other words, while "Japan was a major ODA donor, it was not particularly enthusiastic about ODA"—this is the correct interpretation.

◘ Figure 3.5 clearly illustrates this point. In 2015, Japan's per capita ODA contribution was among the lowest of all OECD member countries (which are mostly advanced economies). South Korea, which contributes less than Japan, is a relatively new member, while Greece and Portugal are countries whose economies are at risk of collapse. Compared to Norway, which ranks at the top, Japan's per capita ODA contribution is less than one-tenth of that of Norway.

However, some argue that because Japan has a high proportion of concessional loans, the increase in principal repayments on past loans has led to an apparent decrease in net ODA disbursements. Indeed, ◘ Fig. 3.5 shows net disbursements. Moreover, the fact that repayments are high reflects the generation of positive returns to investments in the past. Nevertheless, not deducting principal repayments on concessional loans from ODA contributions equates lending with granting, which is also problematic. Ultimately, it must be said that Japan has become a "small ODA contributor not strongly interested in ODA." Understandably, Japan faces severe fiscal constraints. However, Japan is no longer a reliable advanced country from the perspective of developing nations. Given the current situation in which the Trump administration in the United States is unenthusiastic about aid, it is more important than ever to seriously consider how this will affect Japan's position in international politics.

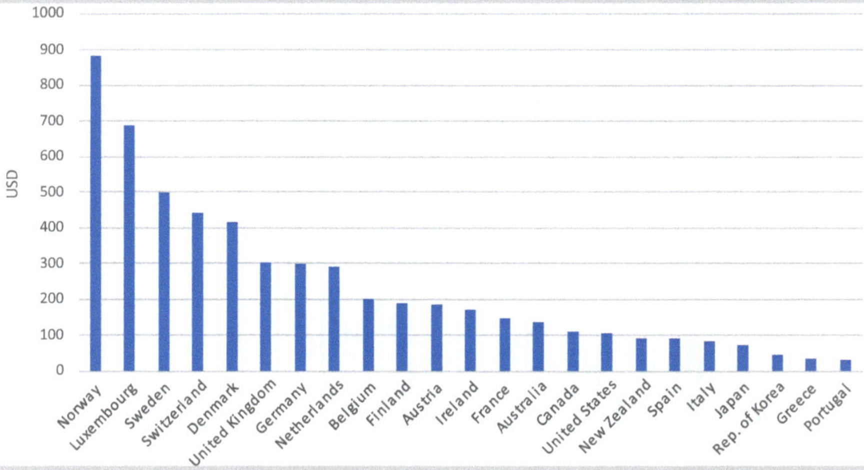

◘ **Fig. 3.5** ODA per capita in OECD development assistance committee (DAC) countries (based on 2015 USD) (OECD's data explorer various years; World Bank's World Development Indicators various years)

Table 3.7 Ratio of net ODA received to GNI and ratio of net inflows of FDI to GDP in 1990 and 2020 in selected developing countries (%) (World Bank's world development indicators various years)

	1990		2020	
	ODA/GNI	FDI/GDP	ODA/GNI	FDI/GDP
Indonesia	1.58	1.03	0.12	1.81
China	0.56	0.97	0.00	1.72
Thailand	0.94	2.86	0.04	−0.86
Bangladesh	5.55	0.01	1.38	0.41
Pakistan	2.33	0.61	0.88	0.68
India	0.44	0.07	0.07	2.41
Nepal	9.81	0.16	5.20	0.38
Ethiopia	8.13	n/a[a]	4.96	2.23
Nigeria	n/a[a]	1.09	0.79	0.55
Kenya	14.39	0.67	3.99	−0.01
Peru	1.60	0.16	0.25	0.33
Brazil	0.04	0.21	0.04	2.59
Argentina	0.13	1.30	0.03	1.27

[a] No data are available

Even if advanced countries are making reasonable efforts to provide aid, is ODA truly sufficient for developing countries to rapidly increase various forms of capital? To examine this, Table 3.7 presents the ratio of total ODA received by major developing countries to their GNI, as well as the ratio of foreign direct investment (FDI) to GDP. In 1990, the countries with high ODA-to-GNI ratios were Bangladesh, Nepal, Ethiopia, and Kenya, at levels ranging from about 5% to 14%. These countries belong to the group of least developed countries, indicating that ODA is heavily allocated to such nations. Bangladesh has experienced significant economic growth, so its ODA-to-GNI ratio dropped sharply by 2020, while Ethiopia's ratio has declined gradually. In any case, it is clear that ODA accounting for 5% or even 10% of GNI is insufficient to rapidly and substantially increase human capital, physical capital, infrastructure, and intellectual capital in developing countries.

Because ODA is quantitatively much smaller than FDI, some argue that FDI is more important than ODA. But is this really the case? Certainly, FDI brings new technologies, management know-how, and international networks to developing countries through foreign-affiliated companies, providing local firms with more opportunities to acquire valuable new knowledge. According to one expert, more than half of India's leading entrepreneurs have previously worked for foreign companies.

An interesting fact that can be gleaned from ◘ Table 3.7 is that in 1990, FDI in Bangladesh was virtually nonexistent and far below ODA. Why is this the case? FDI only flows to developing countries with a certain level of infrastructure and a workforce of sufficient quality. Countries with natural resources, such as oil or natural gas, like Nigeria, are exceptions; however, FDI generally tends to avoid the poorest countries. Therefore, to attract FDI, developing countries must achieve a certain degree of development.

By 2020, the ODA-to-GNI ratios for China and Thailand—two East Asian countries—were close to zero. Countries such as Bangladesh, Nepal, and Kenya have also seen their ratios decline. While more micro-level and detailed analysis is needed, it appears that ODA has played a role in increasing investment in infrastructure and education in the poorest countries, thereby contributing to their economic development and eventually serving as a catalyst for attracting FDI.

In conclusion, ODA alone cannot dramatically accelerate the development of developing countries. Still, if ODA is used for investments in infrastructure and education—areas that cannot be left entirely to the market—it can stimulate development in the poorest countries and eventually help realize growth that involves FDI. For this reason, ODA must serve as a catalyst to promote private investment.[6]

3.4 Lack of Knowledge on Effective Development Strategies

To promote economic development in developing countries, it is essential to invest limited resources efficiently and accumulate stocks that benefit the economy. Investment should be directed toward areas where market failures exist. If the invisible hand is functioning and transactions are occurring at a socially optimal level, then intervention by governments or international organizations is unlikely to yield significant results.

For example, suppose Company A, which is experiencing high revenue and profit, plans to build a factory with financing from a bank. Assume the bank offers loans at an annual interest rate of 10%, and Company A can borrow as much as it wishes. Company A anticipates that constructing a factory and purchasing machinery with a loan of JPY 10 billion will yield a return well above 10%. However, since production still cannot keep up with demand, the company considers borrowing an additional JPY 5 billion. Upon calculation, it is found that the marginal return on this additional investment would be approximately 10%. Consequently, Company A decides to borrow a total of JPY 15 billion from the bank.

At this point, should the government provide any support to this company? The answer depends on whether there are positive externalities and market failure. For instance, if Company A's new factory serves as a model for other firms and leads to the development of the entire industry, the social rate of return would

6 This issue was examined in Momita et al. (2019).

exceed 10%, making it desirable for the government to support the expansion of Company A's investment. ► Box 3.3 provides further explanation of market failures. For governments of developing countries, international organizations, or even governments of developed countries to effectively support the economic development of developing nations, they must be able to design what to invest in, where, and in what sequence to maximize economic development. In reality, however, this is rarely achieved. The following sections will provide evidence for this.

Box 3.3 Market Failures

If the principle of the invisible hand functions properly, economic management can be left to the market. However, there are many cases where this does not work effectively.

First, there is the problem of information asymmetry. For example, buyers may be deceived because they cannot ascertain the quality of the goods they purchase. To prevent such fraudulent activities, the enforcement of laws and the establishment of judicial systems are important, but taking every minor issue to court would be prohibitively expensive.[7]

Second, and related to the first point, is the problem of imperfections in the credit market. Lenders may not be able to assess the repayment ability of borrowers, nor can they always verify whether the borrowed funds are being used for sound, profitable purposes. Moreover, investment returns are uncertain, and if things go poorly, returns may turn negative, contrary to expectations. Especially when borrowers lack collateral, there is a risk of loan default. In such cases, lenders may become reluctant to lend, resulting in promising investments being deprived of necessary funding. This constitutes a failure of the financial market. The same applies to investment in education. It is well known that the rate of return on educational investment is generally high, but the returns are uncertain, and there is no guarantee that the loaned funds will be repaid. Furthermore, human capital cannot serve as collateral; therefore, public financial institutions, such as banks, do not provide loans for investment in human capital.

Third, market failure occurs in the presence of external economies or diseconomies. This refers to situations where third parties, other than the direct participants in a transaction, either benefit or suffer losses. For example, suppose a company emits pollutants during the production of goods it sells. This company, as well as those who purchase its products, are highly satisfied with free transactions, but residents living near the factory are suffering harm. If the damage caused by these pollutants (that is, negative externalities) is ignored, production will exceed the socially desirable level, and free transactions will not maximize total social surplus.

---

7 In cases where strong information asymmetry prevents the market from functioning at all (for example, crop insurance), the market is said to have failed. In such cases, the government should adopt policies (such as legal frameworks) to facilitate the establishment of the market.

From the perspective of economic development, external economies such as the spillover of technical knowledge and managerial know-how from innovative firms to follower firms are important. For example, suppose an innovator earns JPY 100 million in profits from a newly developed technology, and imitator firms also earn a total of JPY 100 million in profits by copying it.

In this case, the social benefit is JPY 200 million. However, since the innovator considers only the private benefit, the effort devoted to innovation will fall short of the socially optimal level. In the example discussed earlier, the innovative firm is the one that built the new factory. Even if the return on investment for this firm is, say, 15%, the social return—including the profits of imitator firms—might be as high as 30%. In such a case, the government should support Firm A and encourage increased investment. In other words, when external economies exist, the government should support such activities.

Fourth, there is the issue of providing public goods. Public goods are goods or services that many people can consume simultaneously and from which it is difficult to exclude those who do not pay. Typical examples include public roads and national defense services. For a self-interested individual, it is rational to let others bear the cost while enjoying the service for free. However, if everyone behaves this way, public goods will not be provided. Unless the government, a civic group, or a community organization bears the cost, there will be a socially insufficient supply of public goods. All facilities that provide these services are called public goods, and the government should be responsible for their provision.

When there is information asymmetry, imperfect credit markets, external economies or diseconomies, and a shortage of public goods, it is desirable for the government to intervene appropriately. However, government intervention can sometimes lead to socially undesirable outcomes. For example, corrupt political leaders may support only those firms with which they are connected. This is called government failure. Therefore, in practice, policy recommendations must weigh market failure against government failure.

3.4.1 Agricultural Development

◘ Figure 3.6 shows the average yield per hectare of major grains (rice, wheat, maize, sorghum, millet) by region. In Southeast and South Asia, the adoption of high-yielding varieties of rice and wheat, the use of chemical fertilizers, and investments in irrigation systems led to significant increases in grain yields from the late 1960s. This is known as the Green Revolution (Otsuka, 2013). Prior to this, in tropical Asia, explosive population growth had left almost no uncultivated land, and stagnating grain yields from existing farmland raised fears of mass starvation. The Green Revolution averted this crisis. As will be discussed again in ► Chap. 4, the Green Revolution was a technological transformation that transferred high-yielding technology systems developed in temperate regions, such as Japan, to the tropics. It was a major revolutionary technological change in which science was used to adapt technology to overcome differences in climate.

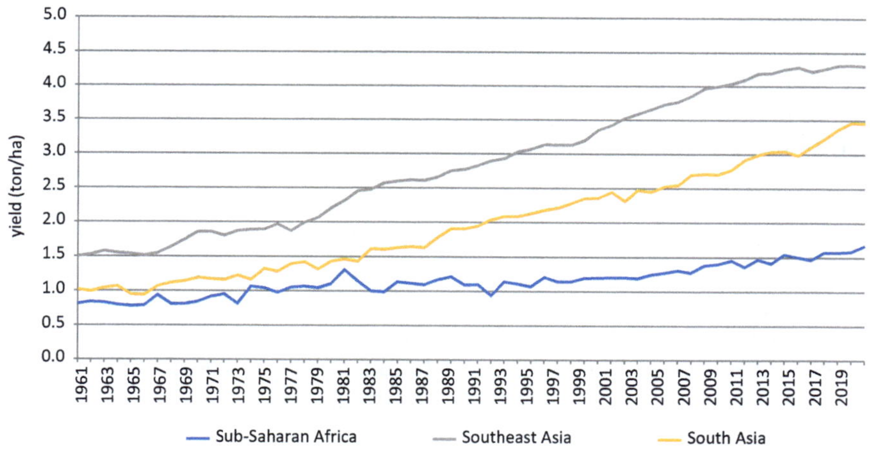

Fig. 3.6 Changes in yield per hectare of five major cereals (rice, wheat, maize, sorghum, and millet) in Sub-Saharan Africa, Southeast Asia, and South Asia (ton/ha) (FAOSTAT various years)

It is probably fair to say that the Green Revolution was the most important technological revolution in human history after the Industrial Revolution. Many Japanese made significant contributions to this achievement. This is something Japan should be proud of internationally, but unfortunately, in Japan, the negative aspects of the Green Revolution (such as heavy use of chemical fertilizers and pesticides) are often emphasized, while its importance and the contributions of Japanese people are little known.

Even within the tropics, the Green Revolution has scarcely occurred in Africa. As a result, grain yields are much lower than in Asia, and growth remains sluggish. In Africa, as in tropical Asia during the 1960s, the amount of unused, high-quality arable land is decreasing while the population continues to grow, leading to chronic food shortages (Holden and Otsuka 2014). Consequently, despite agriculture being the main industry, Africa imports large quantities of rice and wheat. This has fueled a growing desire to bring about a Green Revolution in Africa as well. The establishment of the Alliance for a Green Revolution in Africa (AGRA) in 2006 by the Gates Foundation and the Rockefeller Foundation is one manifestation of this aspiration.

It is understandable that transferring the temperate-zone technological system to tropical Asia to achieve the Green Revolution was challenging, but why has a Green Revolution not occurred in Africa, which shares a similar tropical climate to Asia? Why can't the high-yielding technologies developed in tropical Asia be transferred to Africa? Indeed, Africa's staple foods are maize and coarse grains (such as sorghum and millet), rather than rice and wheat, which are widely cultivated in Asia. Recently, however, consumption of rice and wheat has been increasing in Africa, and these grains can no longer be considered minor crops. Nevertheless, it is difficult to say that a Green Revolution has taken place for these crops in Africa.

My answer to the question of why the Green Revolution has not occurred in Africa is that an effective development strategy has not yet been identified (Otsuka et al. 2024). Despite a strong recognition of the critical importance of increasing food production, success has not been achieved, which can only be attributed to the lack of an effective strategy.

The World Bank's (2007) publication, *World Development Report 2008: Agriculture for Development*, is a highly regarded work involving many prominent agricultural economists interested in agricultural development. However, it contains little discussion on how to increase grain production in Africa. It remains unclear whether the problem lies in insufficient development of appropriate technologies, malfunctioning technology dissemination systems, inadequate farmer education, severely underdeveloped infrastructure, dysfunctional markets for chemical fertilizers and improved seeds, or significant constraints in the provision of finance to farmers.

3.4.2 Industrialization

What about industrialization? The share of the industrial sector in GDP and the proportion of workers in industry are indicators of industrialization. ◘ Table 3.8 shows the share of the manufacturing sector in GDP generation, which remains low in Africa in both 1980 and 2020. In the 1960s and 1970s, Africa adopted import-substitution industrialization policies, whereby governments supported domestic production of goods that had previously been imported. However, firms protected by government subsidies and import barriers became inefficient. These policies were gradually phased out under pressure from the World Bank and the IMF. Yet, the manufacturing share in GDP steadily declined.

In contrast, East Asia has seen a rising share of manufacturing in GDP. Somewhat unexpectedly, China's share has decreased; however, this may be because its share in 1980 was artificially inflated as a result of the forced heavy industrialization under socialism.

Another indicator of industrialization's progress is the share of manufactured goods in total exports. Even if products can be sold domestically, they cannot be sold abroad without sufficient competitiveness, making this indicator more suitable for measuring the degree of industrialization. In particular, exports to major developed countries require products to meet certain quality standards. The right half of ◘ Table 3.8 shows the share of manufactured goods in total exports. According to this data, except for Indonesia, which previously exported large amounts of energy resources, East Asia maintains a high and rising share of manufactured goods in its exports. In South Asia, although the share of manufacturing in GDP is low, the proportion of manufactured goods in exports is comparable to that of East Asia. Thus, even in South Asia, the manufacturing sector plays a crucial role in earning foreign exchange.

In contrast, while the share of manufactured goods in Africa's exports has increased, its level in 2020 remains low and is not comparable to the situation in

Table 3.8 Share of manufacturing GDP and share of manufactured products in export in 1980 and 2020 in selected countries (%) (World Bank's World Development Indicators various years)

	Share of manufacturing GDP (%)		Share of manufactured products in export (%)	
	1980	**2020**	**1980**	**2020**
High-income countries				
Japan	27.2	20.1	94.7	86.1
US	n/a	10.5	65.5	60.2
UK	25.5	9.0	71.5	68.3
France	22.8	9.2	73.3	77.2
East Asia				
Indonesia	13.0	19.9	2.3	46.6
China	40.2	26.3	47.7 (1984)	93.5
Thailand	21.5	25.6	25.2	71.6
South Korea	24.4	24.8	89.5	89.4
South Asia				
Bangladesh	13.8	20.6	67.6	95.8 (2015)
Pakistan	15.9	11.4	48.2	74.7
India	16.2	14.1	58.6	71.0
Nepal	4.3	4.5	30.5	45.4
Sub-Saharan Africa				
Ethiopia	4.9 (1981)	5.3	n/a	13.0
Nigeria	n/a	12.7	0.1 (1981)	7.9
Kenya	12.8	7.6	12.1	27.9
South America				
Peru	23.5 (1979)	12.3	16.8	9.3
Brazil	33.5	10.7	37.2	25.0
Argentine	29.5	14.6	23.2	14.4

n/a means no data are available
Numbers in parentheses are years in which data closest to 1980 and 2020 are available

Asia. In conclusion, Africa has thus far failed to industrialize, whereas Asia has been more successful. Within Asia, East Asia's manufacturing sector accounts for a much higher share of GDP than in South Asia, indicating a greater degree of industrialization success. Why is this the case? Africa's lack of industrialization is not due to a lack of interest. Anyone who speaks with people in Africa will quickly realize their strong passion for industrialization as a path to prosperity. Similarly, India, where industrialization has stagnated, has not abandoned its aspirations for industrial development. Leaders in both Africa and South Asia are deeply interested in understanding how East Asia achieved rapid industrialization. Nevertheless, if Africa and South Asia have not succeeded in industrializing, it can only be concluded that effective industrialization policies remain elusive.

Is the problem a lack of infrastructure, insufficient formal education, low technological standards, a shortage of promising entrepreneurs, or inadequate access to finance? If all of these are lacking, where should one begin? No one has definitive answers to these fundamental questions.

3.4.3 Supporting the Development of the Service Sector

As seen in ◘ Tables 1.5 and 2.3, the service sector is expanding in nearly every country. While detailed data are lacking, the growth of modern service industries that utilize computers likely plays a significant role. As exemplified by call centers, relatively simple tasks for high-income countries are being outsourced to developing countries. One characteristic of these modern service industries is that they do not require large-scale infrastructure, factories, or major equipment. Furthermore, IT-related industries are less affected by government regulation. Since firms from advanced economies provide technical guidance, technological constraints are minimal. As a result, these industries have developed spontaneously, largely independent of government support measures. However, considerable education and proficiency in English are required for employment in this sector. Consequently, the service industry tends to develop in developing countries with a large pool of highly educated, English-proficient individuals, such as India and the Philippines.

In urban India, a growing movement—even among lower castes—is emerging to invest in education in order to secure well-paying service sector jobs. The fact that the service sector is developing in almost all developing countries, despite the absence of government support policies, demonstrates that this industry can grow without a government-led development strategy. If governments wish to support the development of this sector, they should invest in higher education. However, this creates a dilemma: as the service sector expands through such policies, the income gap between the educated and uneducated widens. In other words, a trade-off arises between efficiency and equity. This does not mean that policies to foster the service sector through educational investment should be abandoned, but it is essential to simultaneously create jobs for those with lower educational attainment. To achieve this, the development of labor-intensive manufacturing industries that can generate large-scale employment is indispensable.

If modern service industries develop without a corresponding expansion of manufacturing industries, there is a risk that growing income inequality will lead to serious social discontent.

3.5 Recent Debates in Development Economics

Before concluding Part I, I would like to explain for interested readers how the discussions in this book differ from recent debates among economists regarding development. I will begin by selecting several internationally prominent and recently published works on development issues in developing countries, and then clarify where their arguments align with or diverge from the perspectives presented in this book.

From the standpoint of their influence, I have chosen three books: *The End of Poverty* (Sachs 2005), *The White Man's Burden* (Easterly 2006), and *Poor Economics* (Banerjee and Duflo 2011). In addition, it is worth noting that Banerjee, Duflo, and Kremer, who are associated with the third book, were awarded the 2019 Nobel Prize in Economics for applying experimental methods, originally developed in the natural sciences, to the field of development economics.

The End of Poverty argues that alleviating poverty requires increasing various forms of capital, such as human capital through investment in education and health, as well as enhancing the physical and intellectual capital (for example, agricultural technology), and improving infrastructure for their benefit. This perspective is not novel and is consistent with the arguments in this book. The key difference lies in Sachs's proposal to achieve these goals rapidly through a substantial increase in foreign aid. In contrast, this book advocates for prioritizing and making effective use of limited aid resources.

The White Man's Burden offers a thorough critique of the arguments in *The End of Poverty*. Easterly contends that there is little evidence to suggest that aid has contributed to economic development or poverty reduction. Countries that have achieved significant economic development—such as Japan, China, Taiwan, South Korea, Hong Kong, Singapore, Turkey, and Chile—have done so without relying on aid. *The White Man's Burden* criticizes much of foreign aid as lacking substance, being conceived by bureaucrats and politicians in developed countries who are unfamiliar with the realities of poverty, and as utopian schemes that are detached from practical realities. The first goal of the Millennium Development Goals (MDGs)—halving poverty—serves as an example of such ambitious yet unrealistic objectives. The book further points out that the accountability for aid is often unclear, resulting in much of it being wasted. Therefore, as argued in *The End of Poverty*, simply increasing aid will not be effective in reducing poverty.

While I do not have sufficient expertise to definitively judge Easterly's claims, I do not fundamentally disagree with his main points. I also recognize that aid officials often lack adequate knowledge of local conditions, and, as Sachs himself notes in *The End of Poverty*, it is highly unlikely that a mere substantial increase in aid alone could resolve the problem of poverty. Easterly points out that, in order to analyze the effectiveness of aid, social experiments such as those conducted by Banerjee and Duflo, the authors of *Poor Economics*, are effective—specifically, randomized controlled trials (RCTs). An RCT, for example, involves randomly dividing farmers into two groups, providing chemical fertilizer to only one

3

group, and then measuring the impact on productivity and income. Because the two groups are randomly selected, their average characteristics are virtually identical. Thus, by comparing the productivity and income of the two groups after the intervention, the effect of the fertilizer distribution program can be rigorously measured. In practice, most aid programs select participants based on specific criteria rather than randomly. For example, only the poorest farmers may be eligible to receive fertilizer. In such cases, there are likely to be significant pre-existing differences in characteristics and behavior between the targeted and non-targeted groups, making it impossible to rigorously determine whether any observed differences in productivity or income are truly due to the project. RCTs are used to measure such effects as accurately as possible. Influenced by Banerjee and Duflo, research employing RCTs has now become extremely popular among graduate students and young researchers specializing in development economics.[8]

The usefulness of RCTs as analytical tools is widely acknowledged. I myself have conducted research using RCTs.[9] However, there are numerous issues with the arguments of Banerjee and Duflo, who insist exclusively on RCTs. Ravallion (2012), an expert on poverty issues, raises several questions in his review of Banerjee and Duflo's book: (1) Can the results of an RCT conducted in a specific place and time be generalized to other locations and periods? (2) While RCTs resemble experiments in the natural sciences, are they truly conducted with such rigor? (3) How are important topics selected for RCTs? (4) Is there a risk that important development policies outside the scope of RCTs are being overlooked?

Issues such as (1) arise because RCT results are likely to be influenced by differences in culture, climate, policy, and other factors. An example of (2) would be farmers who receive chemical fertilizers through an RCT but resell them to friends who were not selected, rather than using them themselves. As for (4), the development support policies for agriculture and manufacturing advocated in this book are relevant. How meaningful is it to invest heavily in constructing industrial zones, invite only randomly selected firms, and compare their performance to those not selected? It would be far more economically rational first to identify promising firms and allow only those to operate in the industrial zone. Thus, while development support policies are important, they are often ill-suited to RCTs.[10]

In short, RCTs should not be regarded as a panacea, but rather as one useful research method among many. We should maintain a broad perspective on reality, identify what is crucial for economic development, and, where appropriate, apply RCTs—while remaining aware of their limitations.

A common shortcoming of these three books is the complete lack of analysis regarding the mechanisms of economic development. Consequently, there is a to-

8 For further discussion on this point, see Otsuka (2019, 2024).

9 There is also an ethical issue of whether it is acceptable to abandon those who were not selected in the RCT. Personally, I believe that if a project is found to be effective, it is the responsibility of researchers to extend the project to those who were not included in the initial RCT.

10 Public infrastructure such as roads cannot be allocated to users at random.

tal absence of analysis on strategies for promoting economic growth. According to my definition, which emphasizes development strategy, the discussions in these books do not qualify as development economics. Rosenzweig (2012), a leading scholar in development economics, offers a fundamental critique: "While Banerjee and Duflo's book considers supporting the poor through subsidies and grants, it lacks a perspective on reducing poverty through economic development." I fully agree. I believe that empirical economic analysis of the mechanisms of economic development is essential for constructing effective development strategies. Without understanding how economies develop and the factors that hinder or promote this process, it is impossible to design effective development support measures. For this reason, this book conducts empirical analysis in ► Chaps. 4 and 5 and discusses economic development strategies in ► Chap. 7 based on those findings. Here, I will summarize my views on the role of RCTs in development economics in ► Box 3.4.

Box 3.4 RCTs and Development Economics

The establishment of randomized controlled trials (RCTs) as a method of analysis in development economics is highly significant. Compared to conventional regression analysis using real-world data, RCTs, which utilize artificially generated data, enable a much more rigorous analysis. For example, consider the question of whether microcredit—providing low-interest loans without collateral to poor rural women under a group liability system—is effective in reducing poverty. Microcredit providers such as the Grameen Bank do not lend to the poorest individuals who lack repayment capacity, but rather to those who are somewhat better off. This makes it difficult to determine the true impact of microcredit on poverty alleviation. Suppose, then, that all poor individuals are randomly assigned to two groups, and only one group receives loans. If the two groups had the same standard of living initially, but the group that received loans subsequently shows a clear improvement, this provides strong evidence of the effectiveness of the intervention.

I would like to express my sincere respect for the widespread adoption of these analytical tools. Therefore, I have nothing but praise for the awarding of the Nobel Prize in Economics to Banerjee, Duflo, and Kremer, and no intention whatsoever to raise objections.

However, a significant concern is that the impact has been so great that many young researchers aspiring to work in development economics now mistakenly believe that research using RCTs is the core of the field. The question, "Is there a topic where I can use an RCT?" has become a common issue among young researchers today.

I believe that without a solid sense of reality, it is impossible to address important real-world issues. The microcredit example discussed earlier is a fairly typical case of an RCT, but what policy implications can actually be drawn from such research? If, for instance, no difference in living standards emerges between groups, should we conclude that microcredit is ineffective? I do not think so. It is necessary to investigate why such an outcome occurs. What I observed in rural Bangladesh was that most housewives used microfinance to purchase dairy cows. This is not a profitable business, and even without applying an RCT, it is unlikely to have a transformative impact on poverty reduction.

Today, the majority of research in development economics employs RCTs, whether it is distributing deworming medicine or eyeglasses to children free of charge, showing farmers videos about new technologies, or increasing tenants' share of output. However, do these studies truly contribute to poverty reduction? Why were these particular topics chosen in the first place? I cannot help but feel that many of them are selected based on researchers' ideas rather than careful observation of the field.

I believe that economic development, accompanied by the creation of better jobs, is fundamental to poverty reduction. Returning to the topic of microcredit, unless profitable jobs can be identified, no amount of lending to rural housewives will ever solve the problem of poverty. I believe that devising policies to create profitable employment for poverty reduction is at the very heart of development economics.

What is essential is to first cultivate a strong sense of reality, identify truly important analytical issues, carefully consider the applicability of all analytical methods—including RCTs—and mobilize the full extent of researchers' theoretical knowledge to conduct thorough and meticulous empirical analysis. Choosing research topics simply because RCTs can be used is clearly misguided.[11]

3.6 Summary

Finally, let me briefly summarize the key points of this chapter.

- Productivity is determined by stocks such as human capital, physical capital, infrastructure, social capital, and intellectual capital, and the accumulation of these requires both funding and time. For this reason, low-income countries cannot become wealthy overnight.
- To promote economic development, it is necessary to allocate limited resources to areas where markets fail. Investment in education, the core of human capital, is likely to be insufficient due to household financial constraints. Physical capital is also likely to be underprovided because financial markets do not function adequately. In the case of infrastructure, its public good nature almost certainly means that investment falls below the socially desired level. New technologies developed by innovators tend to be imitated by followers, but since innovators act in their own interest, investment in the development of innovative technologies is often insufficient. While it is not difficult in theory to discuss areas where markets fail, it is challenging to identify in reality where markets fail significantly.

11 For a more detailed discussion, see Otsuka (2024).

- Aid from developed to developing countries is relatively small in relation to the GDP of developing countries, and relying solely on it cannot substantially increase the critical stocks necessary for development. However, if aid is effectively allocated to areas where markets fail, it can significantly contribute to economic development.
- However, it remains unclear where investments should be directed. In other words, effective development strategies are not yet fully understood. This is precisely why Africa has struggled with economic development, and why South Asia lags significantly behind East Asia. In this sense, development economics is still a largely underdeveloped field.

Questions

1. Since it takes time and requires huge resources to increase the stock of human capital, physical capital, infrastructure, social capital, and intellectual capital to achieve economic development, it is desirable to make long-term development plans.
2. Since markets fail in a number of cases, it is not appropriate to rely on market mechanisms for development.
3. Why do you think the Green Revolution successfully took place in Asia, but not in Sub-Saharan Africa?
4. Since the service sector has developed in high-income countries, low-income countries should promote the development of the service sector, while skipping industrialization, in order to catch up with high-income countries.

References

Banerjee, A.V., & Duflo, E. (2011). *Poor economics*. Public Affairs.

Barro, R., & Lee, J. (2013). A new data set of educational attainment in the world, 1950–2010. *Journal of Development Economics*, 104, 184–198.

Bosworth, B.P., & Collins, S.M. (2003). The empirics of growth: An update. *Brookings Papers on Economic Activity, 34*(2), 113–179.

Easterly, W. (2006). *The white man's burden*. The Penguin Press.

Food and Agriculture Organization of the United Nations. (various years). FAOSTAT food and agriculture data. ► https://www.fao.org/faostat/en/#home.

Godo, Y. (2011). Estimation of average years of schooling for Japan, Korea, and the United States. *PRIMCED Discussion Paper Series*, No. 9. Hitotsubashi University.

Godo, Y. (2013). The role of education in the economic catch-up in East Asia. Paper presented at the PRIMCED International research workshop, March 8.

Holden, S.T. & Otsuka, K. (2014). The role of land tenure reforms and land markets in the context of population growth and land use intensification in Africa. *Food Policy*, 48(1), 88-97.

Momita, Y., Matsumoto, T., & Otsuka, K. (2019). Has ODA contributed to growth? An assessment of the impact of Japanese ODA. *Japan and the World Economy, 49*(C), 161–175.

Organisation for Economic Co-operation and Development (OECD). (various years). Development finance statistics: Data on flows to developing countries. ► https://www.oecd.org/en/data/datasets/development-finance-statistics-data-on-flows-to-developing-countries.html.

Otsuka, K. (2013). Food insecurity, income inequality, and the changing comparative advantage in world agriculture. *Agricultural Economics*, *44*(51), 7–18.

Otsuka, K. (2019). Technology transfer and agricultural development: A comparative study of Asia and Africa. In K. Otsuka and K. Sugihara (Eds.), *Paths to the emerging state in Asia and Africa*. Springer.

Otsuka, K. (2024). *Transforming poor economies: Effective development strategies for agriculture and industry*. Edward Elgar.

Otsuka, K., Jayne, T., Mano, Y., & Takahashi, K. (2024). Toward a sustainable Green Revolution in Sub-Saharan Africa: The case of maize and rice. *Food Policy, 129*, 102762.

Ravallion, M. (2012). Fighting poverty one experiment at a time: A review of Abhijit Banerjee and Esther Duflo's Poor Economics: A radical rethinking of the way to fight global poverty. *Journal of Economic Literature*, *50*(1), 103–114.

Rosenzweig, M. (2012). Thinking small: A review of Poor Economics: A Radical Rethinking of the Way to Fight Global Poverty by Abhijit Banerjee and Esther Duflo. *Journal of Economics Literature, 50*(1), 115–127.

Sachs, J. (2005). *The end of poverty*. Penguin Press.

Science and Technology Agency of Japan. (various years). Kagakugijutu yoran (indicators of science and technology). ► https://www.nistep.go.jp/en/?page_id=52

World Bank. (2007). *World Development Report 2008*: *Agriculture for development*. World Bank.

World Bank. (various years). *World development indicators*. World Bank DataBank.

World Intellectual Property Organization (WIPO). (various years). IP statistics. ► https://www.wipo.int/web/ip-statistics

What is Happening?

Hunger Must Be Prevented at All Costs

Contents

K. Otsuka, *A Primer on Development Economics*,
Classroom Companion: Economics, https://doi.org/10.1007/978-981-95-5397-6_4

4.1 Introduction

4

Human death is always tragic. Among all causes, dying from starvation due to lack of food is arguably one of the most harrowing. Without food, physical strength declines, leading to illness and eventually death. For this reason, it is often difficult to distinguish between those who die from disease and those who die from starvation. Consequently, it is impossible to accurately estimate the number of starvation deaths. For example, during the Great Leap Forward in China from 1959 to 1961, famine caused by policy failures resulted in the deaths of an estimated 36 million people—an approximation at best.

In this chapter, I will address Malthusian famine, which arises when food production fails to keep pace with population growth. This is because the risk of this classic tragedy remains a persistent concern. At first glance, famine may appear to be caused by natural hazards, such as severe droughts; however, in many cases, it is the underlying imbalance between food supply and population that is exacerbated by such hazards. If sufficient food is produced in normal years, it can be stockpiled, and much of the damage can be prevented.

Some argue that global food production far exceeds the amount required for the survival of the world population, and that famine occurs because distribution systems fail to function properly. However, there is a distinction between availability and accessibility. Those most vulnerable to starvation are the poor, who lack purchasing power. The idea of eliminating waste in developed countries and establishing a system to ensure equitable food distribution to all is idealistic and, in reality, nearly impossible. The fundamental solution to end hunger lies in the stable increase of food production in impoverished regions.

► Section 4.2 notes that with economic development, new agricultural problems emerge, including food shortages, widening income gaps between farmers and urban workers, and declining food self-sufficiency. ► Section 4.3 shows that the food shortages experienced by Asia in the 1960s are similar to the food problems currently facing Africa. ► Section 4.4 examines how Asia overcame these challenges, while ► Sect. 4.5 considers whether Africa has the same potential. ► Section 4.6 warns that if Asia's smallholder-based agriculture loses its vitality, as happened in Japan, the region could become a major food importer. Should this occur, already rising global food prices would escalate even further. ► Section 4.7 discusses how the world grain market is closely interconnected and how food shortages in Asia could drive up global food prices, directly impacting food-insecure regions such as Africa.

4.2 Economic Development and Agricultural Issues[1]

In societies where uncultivated land is abundant, food production can be increased simply by expanding farmland as the population grows. Thus, agricultural problems do not arise. If land is considered a natural form of capital, then

1 The discussion in this section is based on Otsuka (2013).

abundant capital supports people's livelihoods. In such societies, shifting cultivation is typically practiced. After a plot is farmed, it is left fallow for 20 to 30 years, allowing large trees to regrow and soil fertility to recover, making cultivation possible again. This cyclical system also helps maintain the forest environment to a considerable extent.

However, as the population continues to grow, the area of uncultivated land decreases, fallow periods become shorter, and soil fertility declines. If no productivity-enhancing technologies are developed under these conditions, the increase in agricultural output will be unable to keep pace with population growth, resulting in food shortages. This is the state of famine predicted by the classical economist Thomas Robert Malthus. Such famines are particularly likely to occur in densely populated regions, such as Asia and Africa. This is the first major agricultural problem.

To overcome food security challenges, it is essential to develop and disseminate improved high-yielding crop varieties, carefully till the land and control weeds, and apply chemical fertilizers to increase land productivity (yields). At this stage, the level of economic development remains low, and wages are not particularly high. In contrast, the prices of machinery such as tractors are relatively expensive, so physical labor, often coupled with draft animals, remains the primary means of cultivation. When a family of two or three works the land, the maximum cultivable area is typically around two hectares. While it is possible to expand the cultivated area by hiring laborers, this approach is rarely successful in agriculture—a defining characteristic of the sector (see ▶ Box 4.1). Given that the average size of crop cultivation farming in the United States now exceeds 100 hectares, a two-hectare operation is considered small-scale or even subsistence farming.

Box 4.1 Family Farming as the Foundation of Agriculture.[2]

Unlike factory production, agricultural production takes place over large areas, within which subtle differences in soil, slope, and the incidence of pests and diseases exist. In such an environment, it is extremely difficult to supervise hired laborers to ensure they work diligently and attentively. As a result, hired labor is generally limited to simple, easily monitored tasks such as weeding, transplanting, and harvesting. Tasks that require judgment—such as land preparation, water management, and the application of fertilizers and pesticides—are typically performed by family workers. For this reason, family farming constitutes the foundation of agriculture. Even in the United States, where farm sizes are large, family farms remain the predominant type. In developing countries where labor costs are low, the use of machinery is not economically viable, making reliance on family labor a rational management strategy. However, in many regions of Africa, the presence of sleeping sickness prevents the keeping of draft animals, leaving tractors or manual labor as the only options for tillage. In such areas, the use of tractors may be more efficient.

2 The discussion here is based on Hayami and Otsuka (1993).

Nevertheless, since hired labor is generally expensive, small-scale family farming remains the most efficient model. In fact, small-scale operations that rely on family labor tend to achieve higher land productivity than large-scale farms dependent on hired labor.

Conversely, in advanced economies where labor costs are high, it is more cost-effective to introduce large-scale machinery that saves labor. The efficient use of machinery favors larger farms, making large-scale operations the dominant approach. Does this mean that large-scale plantation management is efficient? Plantations producing bananas, pineapples, sugarcane, and similar crops are, in fact, inefficient for the same reason: It is difficult to supervise hired labor effectively. However, these plantation crops must be processed while still fresh. To keep processing plants operating at full capacity, there are advantages to integrating production and processing within a plantation system. Recently in Asia, however, a contract farming system—where smallholders produce crops and deliver them in an organized manner to processing plants under contract—has become increasingly prevalent.

Extremely large-scale farms have emerged in South America and former socialist countries. There are private agricultural enterprises managing as many as 100,000 hectares—an area equivalent to 32 square kilometers. Farm operations on this scale are conducted entirely with large machinery. I once had the opportunity to speak with the manager of such an enterprise in Brazil and asked how they supervised their workers. The answer was that, by using GPS (global positioning system), it is possible to know who is working where at any given time, so supervision is not an issue. While rigorous research is needed to provide a definitive answer, I believe this manager's response contains an important truth. In thoroughly mechanized agriculture, family farming is not necessarily the most efficient model.

However, there are moves to introduce this large-scale, machinery-dependent model in Africa, where wages are low. This is a grave mistake. In Africa, where land right systems are often not clearly established, it is not uncommon for land already being used by local residents to be officially owned by the state. As a result, foreign companies pay the government for land use rights, forcibly evict local residents, and cultivate the land—an ongoing tragedy. Countries such as China and South Korea are acquiring overseas farmland with direct government involvement. This represents a political failure and must be prevented at all costs. Furthermore, it is unrealistic to expect large foreign corporations to manage agricultural operations efficiently when employing local workers with whom they share neither a common language nor a shared cultural understanding.

In Asia, smallholder and subsistence farmers once played a central role in dramatically increasing grain production in response to food shortages (see ► Sect. 4.3). However, as pointed out in ► Chap. 1, agriculture is constrained by the availability of arable land and therefore cannot develop as rapidly as non-agricultural sectors such as manufacturing and services. As non-agricultural sectors advance first, an income gap emerges between farming and non-farming households. This income disparity constitutes the second major agricultural issue.

To resolve it, as during Japan's period of rapid economic growth in the 1960s, large numbers of rural youth must migrate to major cities. China is currently undergoing precisely this process of labor migration to address income disparities. During this period, those who remain in rural areas also increase their share of off-farm income. In Japan today, more than 80% of farm household income comes from non-agricultural sources, and it is not uncommon for the figure to reach 50% in other parts of Asia (Estudillo and Otsuka 2016). At this stage, governments also tend to actively implement price support and subsidy policies for agricultural products to boost farm incomes.

Following Japan, Asian agriculture faces significant challenges at this stage. As economies develop, wages continue to rise, driving up production costs, including the cost of family labor. To reduce production costs, it becomes necessary to introduce mechanization and reduce labor inputs. At the same time, efficient use of machinery favors larger-scale operations. In other words, farm consolidation becomes increasingly important at this stage. However, purchasing land is not easy, nor is it simple to lease contiguous plots of land. As a result, inefficient small-scale farms persist, and the country's agriculture loses international competitiveness.

In addition, as consumer incomes rise, preferences shift from grains to meat and dairy products, leading to increased overall demand for grains, including those used as animal feed. For example, producing one kilogram of beef requires nearly ten kilograms of grain, so if demand shifts toward domestically produced beef, grain imports surge. This constitutes the third major agricultural issue: the decline in food self-sufficiency. Japan, Taiwan, and South Korea have all experienced this phenomenon. China already imports 60% of the world's traded soybeans and is likely to join Japan, Taiwan, and South Korea in importing a broad range of grains in the near future. Thailand, with its vast farmland, is an exception; however, countries with limited arable land, such as Vietnam, Indonesia (especially Java), Bangladesh, India, and the Philippines, could follow the path of Northeast Asian countries if they achieve economic development. Should this occur, Asia's total food imports would become enormous, severely disrupting the global balance of food supply and demand. While this may seem like a speculative scenario, the following discussion will demonstrate that it is not unrealistic.

4.3 Food Security in Asia and Africa[3]

A comparison of Asian agriculture in the 1960s and recent African agriculture reveals a surprising number of similarities. To understand this, let us examine ◘ Fig. 4.1, which shows trends in population, grain harvests, and grain cultivation area. For Asia, the indices are based on 1961, while for Africa, they are based on 1995. The two graphs are strikingly similar by any measure.

3 The discussion in this section relies heavily on Otsuka and Larson (2013, 2016); Otsuka et al. (2023); and Otsuka (2024).

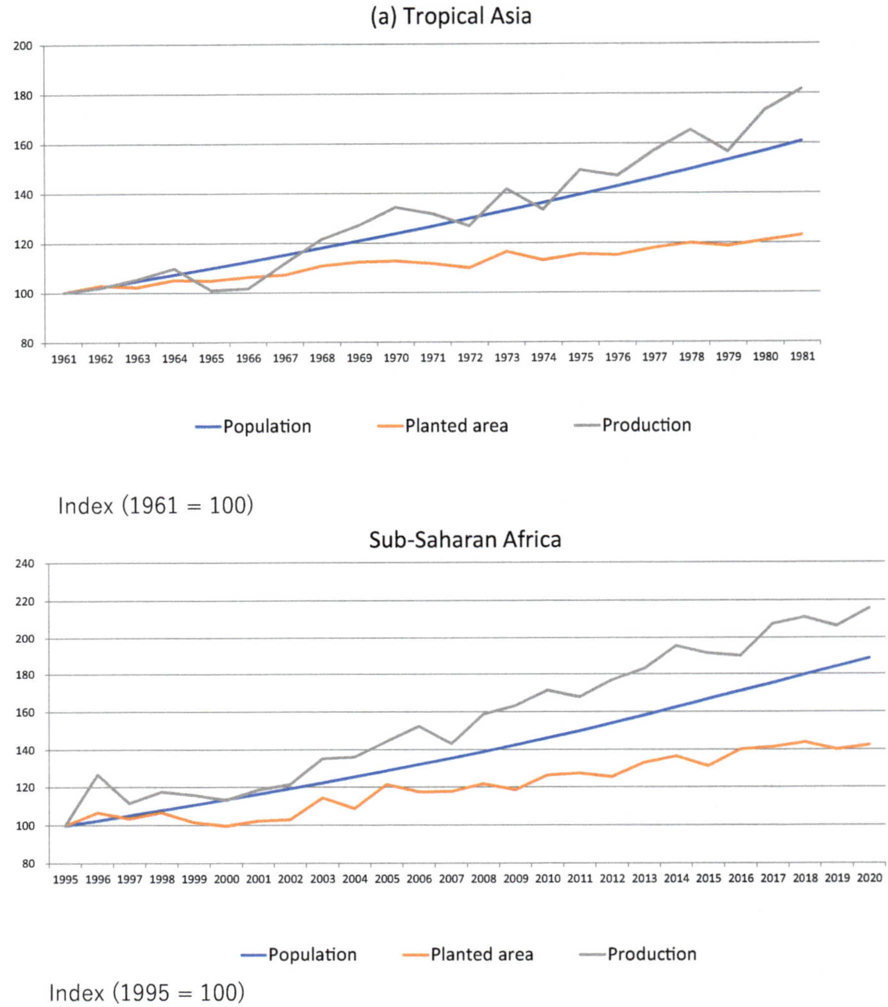

Fig. 4.1 Indexes of population, amount of cereal production, and harvested area in tropical Asia and sub-Saharan Africa (FAOSTAT various years)

Upon closer examination, it becomes clear that the mid-1960s marked a period of food shortages in Asia, as population growth far outpaced the increase in grain production. In 1965–66, drought in India exacerbated the situation; although the crisis was mitigated by wheat aid from the United States, tropical Asia faced the threat of famine. However, there was little room for expanding arable land, and the area under cultivation hardly increased. Many people became convinced that Asia would inevitably face widespread hunger. Contrary to these expectations, however, the Green Revolution began in the late 1960s, gradually enabling grain yields to surpass population growth. By the late 1970s, food shortages had become a thing of the past.

In Africa, from around 1997 to 2002, population growth once again outstripped the increase in grain production. It should be noted, however, that in some regions of Africa, root crops and bananas are staple foods, so focusing solely on grain production may not provide a complete picture. Nevertheless, during this period, food shortages became severe, prompting emergency food aid from developed countries. Despite this, as in Asia previously, the area under grain cultivation did not increase significantly. While Africa is often imagined as a vast savanna inhabited by elephants, lions, and zebras, this image applies only to a few national parks; in reality, a few countries now have large expanses of uncultivated, arable land remaining.

However, since around 2002, grain production has begun to outpace population growth. The direct causes are not entirely clear, but it is undoubtedly due in part to the efforts of African farmers to maximize the use of limited arable land and increase grain output as much as possible. If this is the case, Africa may now be facing a prime opportunity to achieve its own Green Revolution.

4.4 Tropical Asia—From Desperate Food Shortages to Increased Food Production[4]

The Green Revolution is of such critical importance that it warrants detailed examination. While the technical aspects are discussed in ► Box 4.2, this section will focus on their impact on production. ◘ Figure 4.2 presents the long-term trends in rice production, cultivated area, and yield per hectare in tropical Asia. Yield serves as an indicator of technological advancement, though it is not a strict measure, as it also depends on factors such as weather and fertilizer input. The first point to note is the dramatic increase in production: by 2020, output was more than three times higher than in the late 1960s. Second, this increase was due not to expanded cultivation area, but almost entirely to higher yields. Improved varieties, which are photoperiod-insensitive, can be grown year-round regardless of sunlight as long as water is available. As a result, double cropping became possible in irrigated areas, yet the total cultivated area did not increase significantly. These improved varieties were once referred to as high-yielding varieties, but since they perform well in well-irrigated or rainfed areas with abundant rainfall and good drainage—and not in deep-water or drought-prone regions—they are now more commonly referred to as *modern varieties*. Third, the Green Revolution, which began in the late 1960s, was a highly protracted process. While it is difficult to pinpoint its conclusion, the process likely reached a plateau around 2000, when the spread of modern varieties stabilized.

As shown in ◘ Fig. 4.3 for the cases of the Philippines and India, modern varieties gradually became more widespread. This was underpinned by the continuous development of improved modern varieties. Moreover, since modern varieties

4 The discussion in this section is based on David and Otsuka (1994).

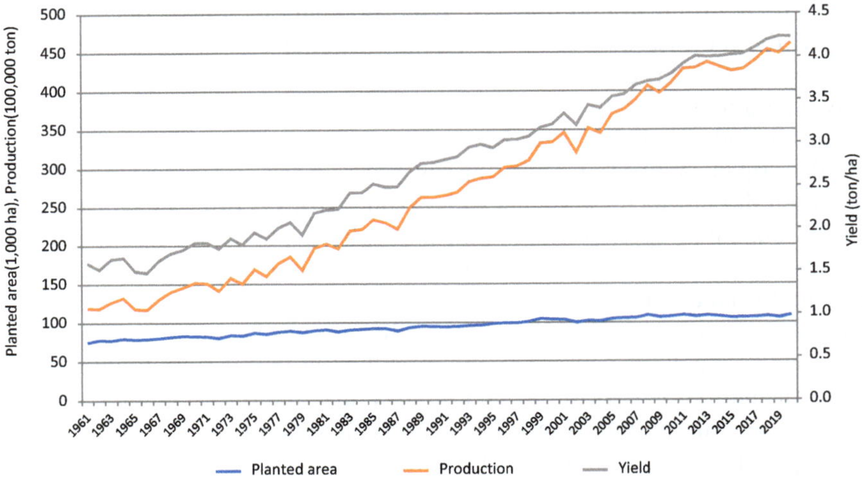

Fig. 4.2 Changes in rice yield per ha (ton/ha), rice production (million tons), and harvested rice area (1,000 ha) in tropical Asia (FAOSTAT various years)

yield even more with irrigation and allow for double cropping, the returns on irrigation investment increased. Consequently, both the Philippines and India saw expanded investment in irrigation and a higher proportion of irrigated land. Although not shown here, the use of chemical fertilizers increased even faster than yields. Chemical fertilizers are essential for realizing the high-yield potential of modern varieties, and in the early stages of the Green Revolution, there was speculation that only large, wealthy farms would benefit. In reality, however, both smallholders and large-scale farmers adopted modern varieties and increased their yields.

Box 4.2 The Green Revolution in Tropical Asia

Because modern varieties (MVs) are short and have thick stems, they do not lodge (when plants lean excessively or fall over) even when the panicles become heavy due to fertilizer application. Moreover, smaller amounts of nutrients are used for stems and leaves. The development and dissemination of such varieties for tropical regions was the essence of the Green Revolution. Japan's experience in pursuing this direction of technological development, dating back to the Meiji era, played a significant role in its realization.

The Green Revolution in rice production began at the International Rice Research Institute (IRRI) in the Philippines. Dr. Akira Tanaka (Professor Emeritus, Hokkaido University), one of the institute's first researchers, was the one who first brought the idea of developing short-statured varieties to IRRI. Although not as prominent as rice, similar developments in wheat were carried out at the International Maize and Wheat Improvement Center (CIMMYT) in Mexico. Given the similarities between the Green Revolution in rice and wheat, and my own experience as a visiting researcher at IRRI from 1986 to 1989 and as Chair of the Board of Trustees from 2004 to 2007, I would like to focus the discussion here primarily on rice.[5] IRRI was established in 1960 with support from the Rockefeller and Ford Foundations. By 1966, IR8—dubbed the "miracle rice"—had already been developed and disseminated. As is evident from the photograph in ◘ Fig. 4.4, IR8 is a short rice plant similar to those seen in Japan and the United States. However, in tropical Asia during the 1960s, only tall traditional varieties (see right side of photo) were cultivated, making IR8 truly a miracle rice. Its reputation spread worldwide, attracting visits to IRRI from dignitaries such as US President Johnson, World Bank President McNamara, Asian Development Bank President Watanabe, and the King of Thailand, all of whom praised IR8 highly.

For plants, fertilizer is equivalent to food for humans. Therefore, achieving high yields without fertilizer is impossible. IR8 was a highly fertilizer-responsive variety, with yields increasing positively responding to the amount of fertilizer applied. It is unclear who started the rumor, but in Japan, a strange claim emerged that IRRI was an agent of fertilizer companies. IR8 was also criticized for its susceptibility to pests and diseases, resulting in increased pesticide use. While such criticisms are not entirely unfounded, these debates overshadow the fact that the Green Revolution, initiated by the development of IR8, saved countless lives. Since then, IRRI has conducted research on developing varieties resistant to pests, diseases, drought, and flooding, as well as improving grain quality, water-saving cultivation methods, and reducing pesticide use. It is now estimated that varieties developed by IRRI and their descendants are cultivated in about 80% of paddy fields in tropical Asia. This achievement deserves high praise, but my current hope is that IRRI will leverage Asia's experience to help realize a Green Revolution in Africa as well.

Until the 1990s, Japan was the largest contributor to IRRI's budget, but it led the way in cutting official development assistance (ODA) and drastically reduced its contributions. The former reputation that "IRRI was nurtured by Japan" has now faded away. This represents a major failure in Japan's overseas aid policy.

There is a saying, "poverty amid plenty." Even if production increases, demand for agricultural products does not rise as quickly, causing prices to plummet and leaving farmers poorer in times of bumper harvests. Increased production is not solely due to favorable weather; technological progress also boosts output. In fact, the Green Revolution benefited consumers more than farmers, as it led to a decline in rice prices. As shown in ◘ Fig. 4.5, the real price of rice at one point fell to about one-third of its level around 1970. There is no doubt that this brought significant benefits to poor consumers, who spend about half of their income on food. According to ◘ Fig. 4.5, rice prices have been unstable, with a significant spike in 1973–74 and a somewhat smaller one around 2009. Although

5 In Japan, since 1970, rice has been in surplus, and there has been no further development of yield-increasing technologies that would lead to increased production. This has greatly diminished the potential for technology transfer from Japan to developing countries.

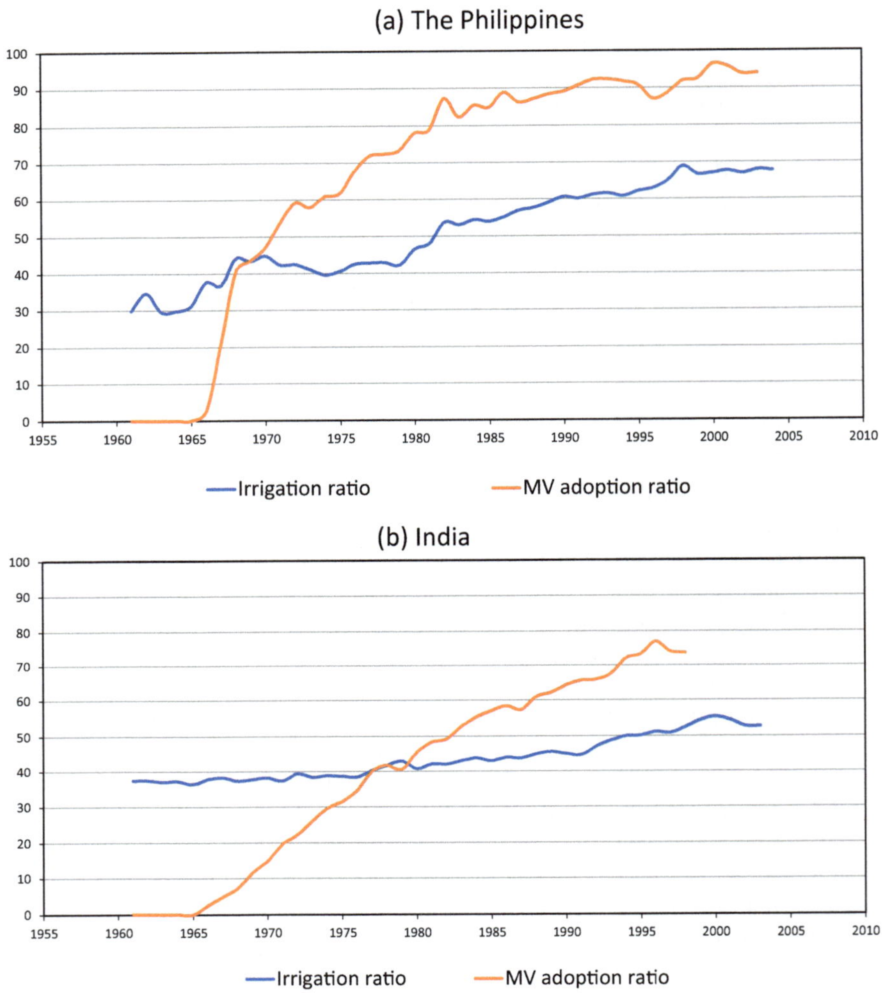

Fig. 4.3 Changes in adoption of modern rice varieties (MVs) and irrigation ratio in the Philippines and India (%) (IRRI's World Rice Statistics various years)

rice production did not decline in 1973–74, disruptions such as the US embargo on soybean exports to the Soviet Union led to market turmoil and frenzied grain speculation, resulting in a sharp price surge. Speculation also played a role during the 2009 "food price crisis." At the same time, the United States diverted large quantities of corn to ethanol production, and major grain-exporting countries imposed export restrictions. Anticipating grain shortages, speculators bought up various grains, driving prices even higher.

I personally believe that complacency has also been a significant factor contributing to the recent surge in grain prices. The long-term decline in grain prices, not only for rice but also for other grains, fostered an implicit assumption that

Fig. 4.4 Semidwarf miracle rice, IR8 (left), and tall traditional variety (right) (IRRI, World Rice Statistics)

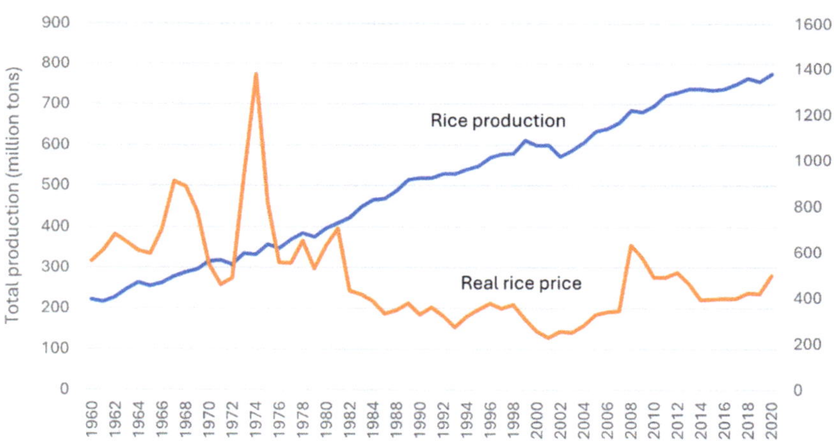

Fig. 4.5 Changes in real rice price and world rice production (FAOSTAT various years; World Bank's Pink Sheet 2025)

grain supplies were sufficient. As a result, investment in agricultural research and development was reduced, and irrigation investment was neglected. Consequently, rice production growth slowed from the late 1990s onward. This period also marked the end of the Green Revolution's initial phase. The Green Revolution drove down rice prices, creating the illusion that food would remain plentiful in the future. This illusion led to complacency in efforts to increase production, which in turn resulted in soaring grain prices—a paradoxical chain of events.

Going forward, climate change is expected to reduce grain output, and rising demand for biofuels may divert food crops for energy use. Furthermore, as demand for meat increases, grain prices are likely to continue rising unless significant efforts are made to address this trend. As will be discussed in ▶ Sect. 4.5, the stagnation of smallholder-dominated Asian agriculture is likely to exacerbate this trend.

4.5 Africa—Opportunities to Overcome Chronic Food Shortages[6]

When faced with difficulties, people strive to overcome them. For example, when crude oil prices rise, it creates problems, prompting the development of fuel-efficient vehicles such as hybrid cars. Similarly, when land is scarce and its productivity is low, making it difficult to secure adequate food, the development of modern crop varieties that increase yields per unit of land becomes essential. In economics, this is formally known as the *induced innovationhypothesis*. This is a perfectly reasonable concept, and I firmly believe it is an absolutely valid theory.

I believe that African agriculture is currently in a state of distress due to food shortages. Precisely because of this, as seen in ◘ Fig. 4.1, recent years have witnessed an increase in yields as efforts are made to overcome this situation. Africa is now presented with an opportunity to break free from chronic food shortages. ◘ Figure 4.6 shows the long-term changes in cultivated land per rural population in tropical Asia and Africa. In Africa, rapid rural population growth has led to a decrease in cultivated land per farmer, and since 2000, this figure has fallen below that of Asia around 1960. Africa receives less rainfall than Asia, and when such climatic factors are taken into account, it is clear that many African countries are

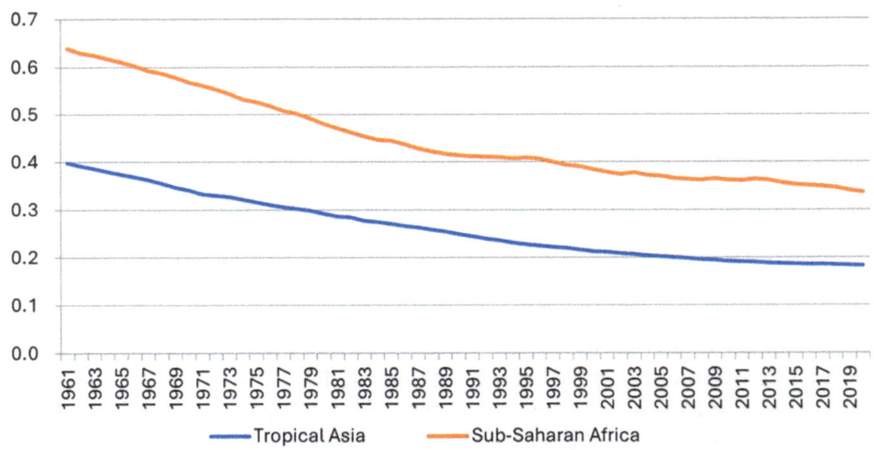

◘ **Fig. 4.6** Comparison of the ratio of arable land area to rural population between Sub-Saharan Africa and tropical Asia (ha per person) (FAOSTAT various years)

6 The discussion in this section is mainly based on Otsuka and Larson (2013, 2016), and Otsuka et al.(2023).

seriously struggling with land scarcity.[7] As suggested by ◘ Table 4.1, the scale of farm operations in Sub-Saharan Africa and Asia is becoming similar, although the farm size data for Sub-Saharan Africa are scanty. This suggests that, with the development and dissemination of yield-enhancing technologies similar to those used in Asia, sub-Saharan African agriculture has the potential for revolutionary growth.

In any industry, the quickest way to develop industries in developing countries is to introduce technologies and management practices from more advanced regions. In the case of agricultural technology, its effectiveness depends on environmental factors such as climate, so it is not always possible to transfer advanced technologies indiscriminately. However, transferring technology from Asia, which shares a tropical climate with Sub-Saharan Africa, should be relatively straightforward. In particular, Indian agricultural technologies, developed in arid regions similar to those in Africa, are highly likely to be directly transferable. Therefore, in ◘ Fig. 4.7, I have attempted a long-term yield comparison between India and Africa for rice, maize, wheat, sorghum, and millet.

From this figure, several interesting facts emerge. First, in the early 1960s, before the onset of the Green Revolution, there was almost no yield gap between the two regions. This indicates that the current yield differences are not solely attributable to disparities in production environments. Second, for rice and wheat, the Green Revolution created a significant yield gap between the two regions, but yields in Africa have also shown a gradual upward trend. This is largely due to the gradual transfer of Asian technologies to Africa. However, since wheat prefers cooler climates, its cultivation area in Africa is limited, except for regions such as South Africa and the highlands of Tanzania and Ethiopia. Third, for maize, which is the most important cereal in Africa, the yield gap between the two regions is relatively small. This suggests that achieving a Green Revolution for maize in Africa will require not only the transfer of technology from Asia but also the development of location-specific, indigenous technologies (Otsuka et al. 2024). Finally, for millet and other minor cereals, there is no yield gap between the regions. Even in India, which has advantages in almost every aspect, such as technological development capacity and infrastructure, a Green Revolution has not occurred for these crops, implying that transferring Indian technologies to Africa is unlikely to yield significant results. From these considerations, it is clear that rice holds great promise in Africa.

In irrigated areas such as the Senegal River Valley, the Mwea irrigation scheme in Kenya, and the Lower Moshi irrigation area in Tanzania, I have observed the successful cultivation of short-statured varieties developed by IRRI and improved short-statured varieties created by crossing these with local varieties. Clearly, for irrigated rice, there is strong potential for transferring Asian varieties to Africa.

---

7 For further details, see Otsuka and Place (2014) and Holden and Otsuka (2014).

Table 4.1 Comparison of farm size among selected countries (Bangladesh: 1977 Report on the Agricultural Census, 1978 Land Occupancy Survey of Bangladesh, 1996 and 2019 Census of Agriculture; India: No. 215, 26th Round 1971−72 National Sample Survey, 1980–81, 1990–1 All India Report on Agricultural Census, 2022 Agricultural Statistics at a Glance 2022; Indonesia: 1973, 1993, 2023 Census of Agriculture; Philippines: 1971, 1991, 2012 Census of Agriculture; Thailand: 1978, 1993 Agricultural Census Report, 2018 Agriculture Intercensal Survey; Ethiopia: 1989–92, 2001–02 Agricultural Census)

	Survey year	Average farm size (ha)	Proportions of farm households and farmland			
			Below 1 ha		Above 10 ha	
			Farm households	Farmland	Farm households	Farmland
Bangladesh	1976/77	1.4	49.7	28.8	n/a	n/a
	1996	0.5	86.7	42.7	0.1	n/a
	2005	0.3	n/a	n/a	n/a	n/a
	2019	0..4	91.9	67.6	n/a	n/a
India	1970/71	2.3	50.6	9	3.9	30.9
	1990/91	1.6	59.4	15	1.7	17.3
	1995/96	1.4	61.6	17.2	1.2	14.8
	2005/06	1.2	64.8	20.2	0.8	11.8
	2015/16	1.1	68.5	11.8	0.6	9.1
Indonesia	1973	1	70.4	30	5.9	10.3
	1993	0.9	70.8	29.8	0.2	3.4
	2003	0.8	74.8	n/a	n/a	n/a
	2023	1	76.7	n/a	0.3	n/a
Philippines	1971	3.6	13.6	1.9	4.9	33.9
	1991	2.1	36.6	7.3	2.4	23.3
	2002	2	40.1	8.3	2	20.5
	2012	0.9	56.9	n/a	0.1	n/a
Thailand	1978	3.7	16.4	2.5	6	23.6
	1993	3.4	21.5	3.6	4.5	23.2
	2003	3.1	13.1	n/a	2.1	n/a
	2018	3.1	23.6	n/a	n/a	n/a
Ethiopia	1989–92	0.8	72.1	36.9	0.0	0.2
	2001/02	1.0	62.9	27.1	0.1	1.4

n/a means data is not available

Fig. 4.7 Comparison of yield (ton/ha) of major cereals between India and sub-Saharan Africa (FAOSTAT various years)

As shown in Fig. 4.8, the relationship between fertilizer application and yield in Asian irrigated areas in the late 1980s, for which records are available, is almost indistinguishable from the relationship observed in recent years in African irrigated areas (David and Otsuka 1994; Otsuka, Estudillo, and Sawada 2009; Njagi 2012). In other words, in irrigated areas, the technological level is similar between Asia and Africa. However, the generally lower yields in African irrigated rice fields are due to lower fertilizer application, which in turn is caused by higher fertilizer prices. In Africa, the proportion of irrigated rice fields remains at about 15%, far lower than in Asia. While expanding irrigated areas should be a long-term goal, in the short term, it is necessary to increase yields in rainfed rice fields. According to case studies by our research group, if bunds are properly constructed, fields are carefully leveled, MVs are adopted, and fertilizers are applied,

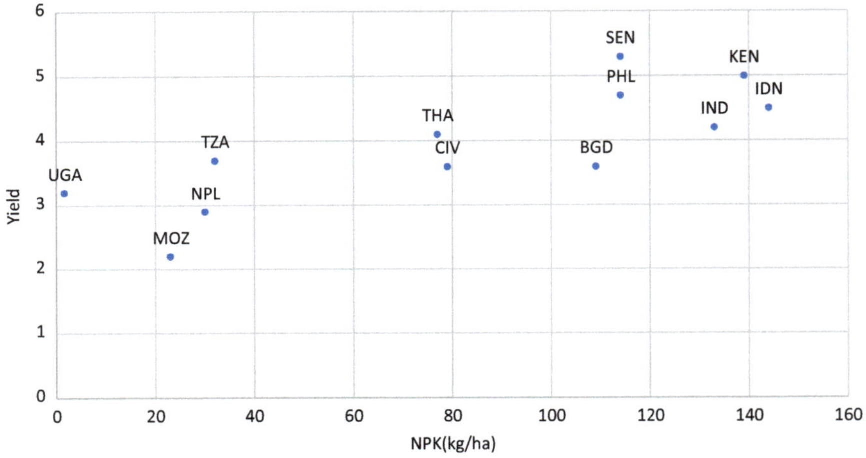

Fig. 4.8 Yield and fertilizer use per ha in selected irrigated areas in Asia and Sub-Saharan Africa (R-squared = 0.49, BGD—Bangladesh, CIV—Côte d'Ivoire, KEN—Kenya, IND—India, IDN—Indonesia, MOZ—Mozambique, NPL—Nepal, PHL—Philippines, SEN—Senegal, THA—Thailand, TZA—Tanzania, UGA—Uganda) (Njagi 2012)

yields can be increased from 1.5 tons to 2.5–3.0 tons per hectare in many rainfed areas. In short, strengthening extension activities could raise African rice yields to levels comparable to those in Asia. The main challenge, however, is the severe shortage of agricultural extension workers with expertise in rice cultivation. Nevertheless, there is no doubt that irrigated rice is the most promising crop in Africa (see ► Box 4.3).

Box 4.3 Rice is a Special Crop in Africa

About 20 years ago, I attended a conference on rice in Uganda and happened to speak with a little girl. She told me, "On Christmas, New Year's, birthdays, weddings, and funerals, I want to eat rice." At the time, I thought she was an unusual child, but that was not the case. I later learned that in many African countries, rice is considered a special crop and is traditionally eaten on ceremonial occasions such as weddings and funerals. She also said, "These days, I'm happy because I get to eat rice almost every week." Rice consumption in Africa is increasing rapidly. Currently, the average annual per capita rice consumption is about 25 kg, which is roughly double the amount from 30 years ago. In comparison, the average annual rice consumption in Japan is just under 50 kg, so the difference of 25 kg is by no means insignificant. Even in small restaurants located far from major African cities, rice is a staple on the menu. However, domestic production cannot keep pace with consumption, and one-third of the rice consumed is imported from Asia. That said, rice cultivation in Africa holds great promise. With irrigation, Africa's dry climate is even more suitable for paddy rice than Asia, due to longer daylight hours and fewer pests and diseases. Even without irrigation, the prevalence of low-lying terrain indicates that a significant amount of unused wetlands can be converted to paddy fields.

Although these are rainfed paddies, the soil is moist, making them well-suited for rice cultivation. Nevertheless, it appears that African farmers were largely unaware of the suitability of these wetlands for rice production until recently.

When I traveled through eastern Uganda in 1994, I saw many wetlands overgrown with tall papyrus. On a recent visit to the same area, however, rice paddies dominated the landscape, and papyrus had become difficult to find. Recognizing the importance of rice for Africa, Japan International Cooperation Agency (JICA) partnered with the Alliance for a Green Revolution in Africa (AGRA), an initiative strongly supported by the Gates Foundation, launched the Coalition for African Rice Development (CARD). CARD, involving the World Bank, the Food and Agriculture Organization (FAO), and research institutions such as IRRI and AfricaRice, and aimed to double rice production in Africa over ten years (2008–2018). This ambitious goal was successfully achieved, drawing significant attention from those interested in the development of African agriculture. I originally proposed the concept of CARD, and my research group has supported it through empirical studies based on farm surveys (Otsuka and Larson 2013, 2016; Otsuka et al. 2023).

In paddy fields, aquatic plants such as algae fix atmospheric nitrogen, and incoming water brings various nutrients, so soil degradation is relatively rare. In contrast, soil management is more challenging in upland fields. In densely populated regions of Africa, such as the highlands of Kenya, improved cattle breeds are raised and their manure is used as organic fertilizer to boost yields. But that is not all. Farmers widely purchase high-yielding hybrid seeds and chemical fertilizers, and practice intercropping maize with legumes that fix atmospheric nitrogen. Although research is still ongoing, it appears that a well-balanced combination of organic fertilizer, chemical inputs, and legume intercropping can dramatically increase maize productivity. Unfortunately, however, there has been little active research to date on determining the optimal combination of these practices.[8]

4.6 Unfinished Business in Asian Agriculture

Even if the food problem is resolved, addressing income disparities remains a formidable challenge. Failure to resolve this income issue can exacerbate the third agricultural problem: the decline in food self-sufficiency. The worst-case scenario of this is exemplified by Japanese agriculture.

While Japan's postwar land reform was important for the democratization of the society, it had significant long-term negative effects on agricultural development—the low level at which tenant rents were set discouraged landowners from leasing land. Although the Agricultural Land Law was amended multiple times, various restrictions continued to impede the functioning of the invisible hand, or land and land rental markets. Furthermore, the government maintained rice

8 For more details, see Takahashi et al. (2020), and Otsuka et al. (2024).

prices at extremely high levels, resulting in overproduction in the 1970s. To prevent this, policies such as acreage reduction and subsidized crop conversion away from rice were implemented. However, as the government excessively converted paddy area, soaring rice prices and shortages became a social issue in 2025. As long as policies encourage farmers to reduce rice production, there is no way for rice producers to expand their scale of operations.

4

As a result, inefficient small-scale farming was preserved, international competitiveness in agriculture was lost, and grain imports increased. While I sympathize with Japanese farmers, it is necessary to lower agricultural product prices, increase the number of people willing to relinquish their farmland, and, if needed, provide income compensation, so that farmland can be consolidated among capable and motivated farmers to achieve large-scale operations with significant scale economies.

◘ Table 4.2 compares, by scale, the average gross revenue (production value) and costs per unit of cultivated area from rice farming in 1960 and 2020, with the average of each year set at 100. In 1960, large-scale mechanization had not yet occurred, so there were no significant differences in income or costs based on the size of the farm. However, by 2020, with the advancement of large-scale mechanization, while revenues remained similar, costs differed greatly between small-scale farms of less than 0.5 hectares and medium-scale farms of 3–5 hectares. Small-scale farms are inefficient, with both labor and machinery costs per unit of land being high. Ideally, small-scale farmers would lease their land to medium-scale farmers, but this has not progressed significantly, likely due to certain regulatory constraints. The fact that farms of 5 hectares or more account for only about 5% of the total is also attributable to these restrictions.

Even so, the government has continued to protect rice production, but this has resulted in high production costs, while the production of other grains has de-

◘ **Table 4.2** Index of revenue, labor cost, and machinery cost of rice farming by farm size relative to the average in Japan in 1960 and 2020 (Ministry of Agriculture, Forestry, and Fishery of Japan 1960, 2020)

	Less than 0.5 ha	0.5–1 ha	1–3 ha	3–5 ha	Average
1960					
Revenue	98	97	103	104	100
Labor cost	111	105	96	88	100
Machinery cost	86	97	106	96	100
Total cost	105	102	99	94	100
2020					
Revenue	89	92	97	98	100
Labor cost	201	157	109	87	100
Machinery cost	141	122	111	104	100
Total cost	170	140	106	91	100

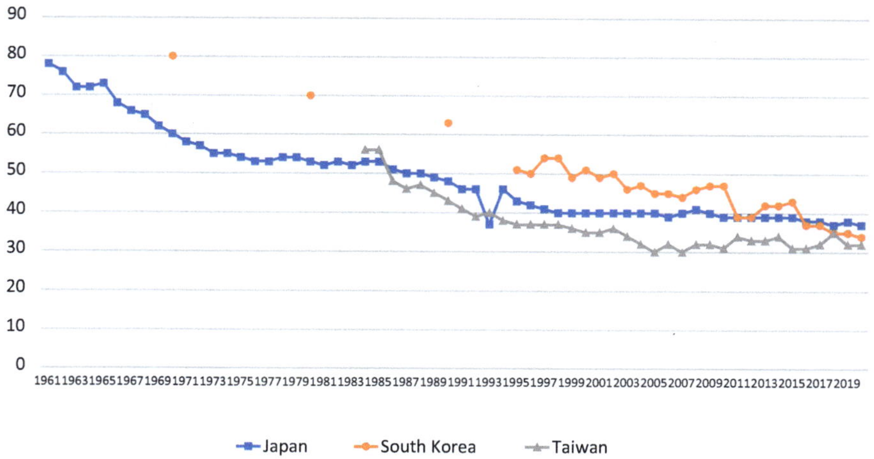

Fig. 4.9 Changes in the self-sufficiency ratio of grain in terms of calorie intake among Japan, South Korea, and Taiwan from 1961 to 2020 (%) (Ministry of Agriculture, Forestry, and Fishery of Japan, Food Supply–Demand Balance various years)

clined sharply. Consequently, the overall grain self-sufficiency ratio has rapidly decreased (see Fig. 4.9). The same issue applies to Taiwan and South Korea, which, like Japan, have maintained small-scale agriculture.

While the large-scale importation of grains by Japan, Taiwan, and South Korea is problematic, the concern is not limited to these three countries. The average farm size in China is approximately 0.6 hectares, which is only one-sixth the size of Japan's. Labor costs in China are rising rapidly, and unless farm sizes increase, production costs for agricultural products will inevitably rise. Currently, soybean imports are exceptionally high, but it is only a matter of time before imports of other crops also increase. China's purchase of farmland in Asia and Africa is undoubtedly driven by concerns about the future of its domestic agricultural production.

As shown in Table 4.1, in other Asian countries, farm sizes are decreasing due to population growth. Wages in these countries are also expected to rise, which will eventually lead to higher production costs. According to our group's research, the operational efficiency of small-scale farms in Vietnam and Java is deteriorating. If similar trends occur in highly populated countries such as India and Bangladesh, there is a significant risk that Asia as a whole will become a major grain-importing region.

Some countries in South America, such as Brazil and Argentina, with vast agricultural land, are expected to become the world's food production centers. As shown in Table 4.3, the average cultivated area per rural population in these countries is orders of magnitude larger than in Japan or China. Moreover, grain yields are increasing and are comparable to those in Japan and China. One reason for this is the implementation of scientific agriculture. In corporate farming, agricultural scientists with graduate degrees are involved in a wide range of activities, from soil management to crop breeding. In Uruguay, which ranks third in

Table 4.3 Comparison of cereal yield per ha and ratio of agricultural land to rural population in 1990 and 2020 among Argentina, Brazil, China, and Japan (FAOSTAT various years)

	Cereal yield (ton/ha)		Agricultural land (ha) per rural population	
	1990	2020	1990	2020
Argentina	2.3	5.4	6.46	33.75
Brazil	1.8	5.3	1.45	6.81
China	4.4	6.4	0.33[b]	0.62
Japan	6.1	6.5	0.56	1.96

the world for rice yields, rice milling companies employ numerous staff with master's degrees in agricultural science to provide detailed management advice. While it may be extremely difficult to achieve large-scale, scientific agriculture in East Asia, at the very least, it is time for East Asia to begin moving in that direction. Otherwise, not only will the problem of declining food self-sufficiency remain unresolved, but the situation will continue to deteriorate.

4.7 The Global Grain Market is Interconnected

Increasing production is the primary solution to food shortages in Africa; however, even if this goal is achieved, Africa is likely to remain a net importer of rice and wheat for the foreseeable future. In such a scenario, rising international grain prices would deal a severe blow to Africa. During the "food price crisis" of 2009, when food prices sharply increased globally, nationwide strikes protesting the rise in rice prices occurred in several African countries.

Figure 4.10 illustrates the long-term trends in rice export prices from Thailand and import prices in Nigeria, soybean export prices from Brazil and import prices in China, and wheat export prices from the United States and import prices in Japan. These countries are among the largest exporters or importers of each respective grain. From this, two important relationships can be identified.

First, for each grain, export and import prices have moved in nearly a parallel fashion. This indicates that the international markets for these grains are functioning properly. In the case of rice, there are instances where import and export prices cross over; this is due to the wide variety of rice types with differing qualities being traded.

Next, it can be observed that the price fluctuation patterns of the three grains are similar. This is because these grains are substitutable; when the price of one grain rises, demand shifts to others, resulting in similar price movements across all grains. In short, the global grain markets are interconnected.

This means that if Asia were to become a major grain-importing region, global grain prices would surge, and importing regions would be directly affected. The primary concern here is Africa. With climate change, global grain production

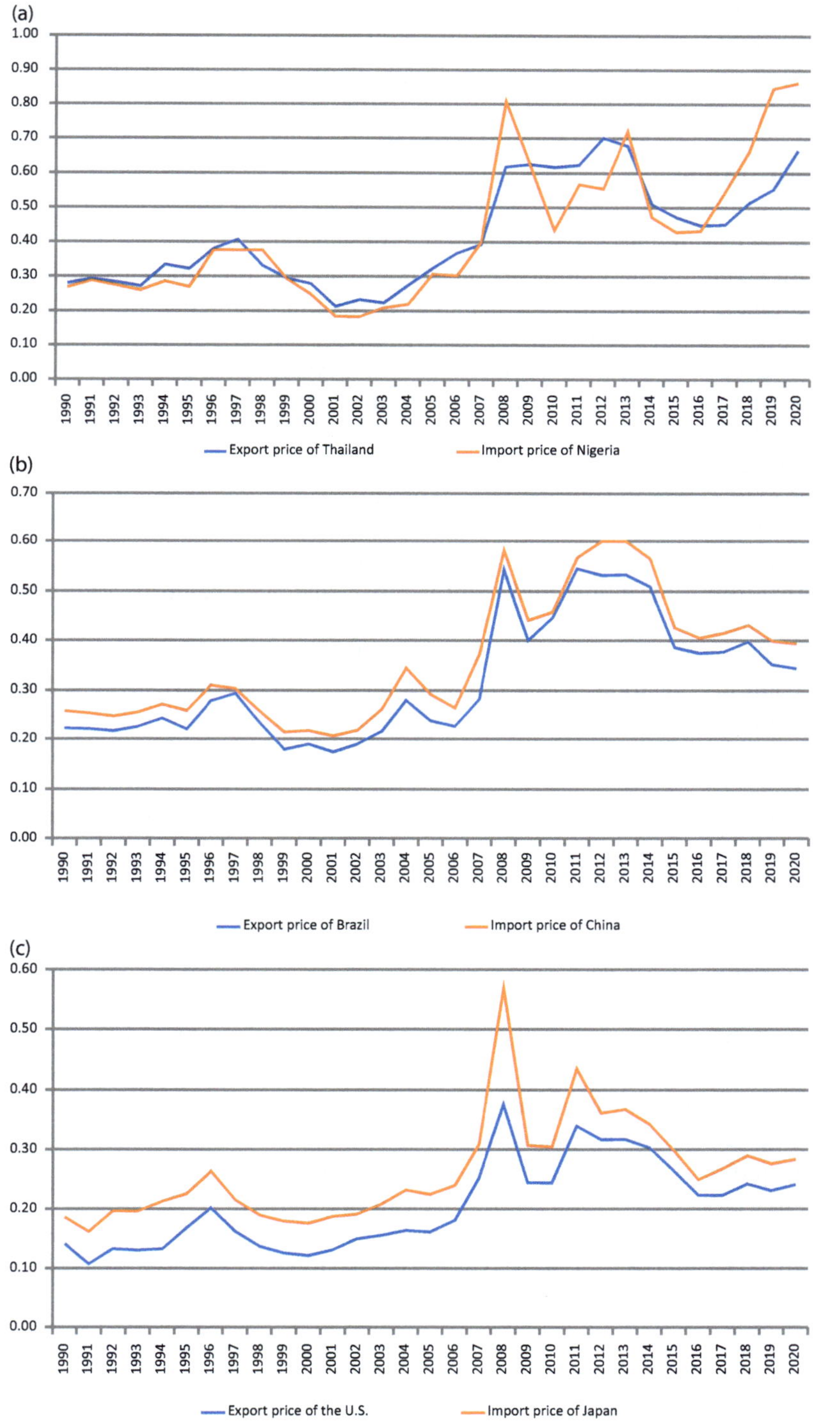

Fig. 4.10 Comparison of export and import prices of selected commodities: rice from Thailand to Nigeria (a), soybean from Brazil to China (b), and wheat from the US to Japan (c) (FAOSTAT various years)

is expected to decline, which will inevitably drive grain prices even higher. Considering these future trends in the global grain market, Africa must pursue increased grain production more aggressively than ever before.

4.8 Summary

Finally, let us summarize the discussion in this chapter.

- With economic development, there is a tendency for problems such as food shortages, widening income gaps between rural and urban areas, and subsequently, declining food self-sufficiency ratios to arise.
- The Green Revolution, centered on the development and dissemination of high-yielding varieties, made a significant contribution to solving food problems in Asia.
- In Africa, too, land is becoming increasingly scarce, and the conditions are ripe for a Green Revolution to take place.
- In many Asian countries, small-scale, labor-intensive agricultural production persists despite rising wages. As a result, the comparative advantage of agriculture is declining, and there is a risk that Asia could become a massive food-importing region.
- The global food market is interconnected. If Asia becomes a major food-importing region, food prices will soar, and the poor—who spend a high proportion of their income on food—will become increasingly impoverished. This poses a risk of widespread hunger. The situation is particularly concerning for Africa.
- In other words, humanity has not yet eliminated the possibility of hunger.

Questions

1. If the population continues to increase over extended periods in developing countries, what will happen to food security, and what must be done to maintain food security?
2. Most Asian countries are now wealthy, and their agricultural sector is shrinking compared with other sectors of the economy. What are the implications of these changes for global food security?
3. In general, nonfarm sectors grow faster than the agricultural sector. What kinds of problems will arise, and what types of polices should be adopted to prevent the increased risk of worldwide hunger and poverty?
4. If protective agricultural policies preserve small farms in Asia, what will happen to global food security or the possibility of hunger?

References

Bangladesh. *Report on the Agricultural Census*, 1977.
Bangladesh. *Land Occupancy Survey of Bangladesh*, 1978.
Bangladesh. *Census of Agriculture*, 1996 and 2019.
David, C.C., & Otsuka, K. (Eds.). (1994). *Modern rice technology and income distribution in Asia*. Lynne Rienner.
Estudillo, J.P., & Otsuka, K. (2016). *Moving out of poverty: An inquiry into inclusive growth in Asia*. Routledge.
Ethiopia Central Agricultural Census Commission. *Ethiopian Agricultural Census, 1989–92, 2001–02.*
Food and Agriculture Organization of the United Nations. (various years). FAOSTAT food and agriculture data. ► https://www.fao.org/faostat/en/#home.
Hayami, Y., & Otsuka, K. (1993). *The economics of contract choice: An agrarian perspective*. Clarendon Press.
Holden, S.T., & Otsuka, K. (2014). The role of land tenure reforms and land markets in the context of population growth and land use intensification in Africa. *Food Policy, 48*(1), 88–97.
India, National Sample Survey Organization, Department of Statistics, Government of India, No. 215, *26th Round 1971–72 National Sample Survey*.
India Ministry of Agriculture. Department of Agriculture and Co-operation. *All India Report on Agricultural Census 1980–81*.
India Ministry of Agriculture. Department of Agriculture and Co-operation. *All India Report on Agricultural Census 1990–91*.
India Ministry of Agriculture & Farmers Welfare, *Agricultural Statistics at a Glance 2022*.
Indonesia Badan Pusat Statistik (BPS-Statistics Indonesia), *Census of Agriculture 1973, 1993, 2023*.
International Rice Research Institute (IRRI). (various years). *World Rice Statistics*.
Japan Ministry of Agriculture, Forestry, and Fishery of Japan. *Survey of rice production costs,* 1960, 2020.
Japan Ministry of Agriculture, Forestry, and Fishery of Japan. *Food supply-demand balance*, various years.
Njagi, N.T. (2012). An investigation into the possibility of a rice Green Revolution in Sub-Saharan Africa: Lessons from the Mwea Irrigation Scheme in Kenya. PhD dissertation, National Graduate Institute for Policy Studies, Tokyo.
Otsuka, K. (2013). Food insecurity, income inequality, and the changing comparative advantage in world agriculture. *Agricultural Economics*, *44* (51), 7–18.
Otsuka, K. (2024). *Transforming poor economies: Effective development strategies for agriculture and industry*. Edward Elgar.
Otsuka, K., & Larson, D. (Eds). (2013). *An African Green Revolution: Finding ways to boost productivity on small farms.* Springer.
Otsuka, K., & Larson, D.F. (Eds). (2016). *In pursuit of an African Green Revolution: Views from rice and maize farmers' fields.* Springer.
Otsuka, K., & Place, F. (2014). Evolutionary changes in land tenure and agricultural intensification in Sub-Saharan Africa. In J. Lin and C. Monga (Eds.), *Handbook of Africa and Economics*. Oxford University Press.
Otsuka, K., Estudillo, J.P., & Sawada, Y. (Eds.). (2009). *Rural poverty and income dynamics in Asia and Africa*. Routledge.
Otsuka, K., Mano, Y., & Takahashi, K. (2023). *Rice Green Revolution in Sub-Saharan Africa*. Springer.
Otsuka, K., Jayne, T., Mano, Y., & Takahashi, K. (2024). Toward a sustainable Green Revolution in Sub-Saharan Africa: The case of maize and rice. *Food Policy, 129*, 102762.
Philippines. *Census of Agriculture 1971, 1991, 2012*.

Takahashi, K., Muraoka, R., & Otsuka, K. (2020). *Technology adoption, impact, and extension in developing countries' agriculture: A review of the recent literature. Agricultural Economics, 51*(1), 31–45.

Thailand National Statistical Office, *Agricultural Census Report, 1978, 1993.*

Thailand National Statistical Office, *Agriculture Intercensal Survey, 2018.*

World Bank. (various years). World Bank commodities price data (the pink sheet). ▶ https://thedocs.worldbank.org/en/doc/18675f1d1639c7a34d463f59263ba0a2-0050012025/world-bank-commodities-price-data-the-pink-sheet.

What Can We Learn from East Asia?

Contents

K. Otsuka, *A Primer on Development Economics*,
Classroom Companion: Economics, https://doi.org/10.1007/978-981-95-5397-6_5

5.1 Introduction

In order to understand cooperation and competition in the international economy, let us consider, hypothetically, a developed Country A and a developing Country B. Country A produces automobiles and electronic goods, which it exports to Country B, and imports light industrial products, such as clothing, from Country B. Suppose Country B invests in human capital, physical capital, infrastructure, social capital, and intellectual capital, and as a result, becomes able to produce light industrial goods more efficiently than before, This is beneficial for Country A, as consumers in this country can now purchase the same products at lower prices or better-quality products at affordable prices. Since there are no firms in country A producing light industrial goods, there is no domestic industry harmed by the development of Country B.

However, Country B does not stop there. Country B diligently imitates what Country A is doing, further accumulating social capital, human capital, physical capital, infrastructure, and intellectual capital, and attempts to move beyond the production of light industrial goods to manufacture and export automobiles and electronic products. In this case, what will happen to the economy of country A? If Country A is also steadily accumulating valuable stocks at a pace no slower than Country B, it may be able to produce high-tech products that Country B cannot match, and thus continue to benefit from Country B's development. However, suppose Country A does not make corresponding progress. In that case, it will find itself in direct competition with Country B. Industries in Country A will face fiercer competition than before, leading to deteriorating profitability. As a result, the standard of living in Country A may decline.

The relationship between Country A and Country B bears resemblance to the historical economic tensions between Japan and the United States. The Japan-US textile, automobile, and semiconductor disputes, among others, that arose during Japan's economic development led to a series of serious trade frictions between Japan and the United States. When Country B (i.e., Japan at the time) had a lower economic level, Country A (i.e., the United States) benefited from Country B's development. However, once Country B began exporting products in which Country A excelled, Country A began to suffer losses. In other words, competition may generate clear winners and losers.

Today, Japan is increasingly in the position of Country A in its relations with other Asian countries, much like the United States once was. South Korea and China are rapidly accumulating productive stocks and are becoming Country B, catching up with country A. If Japan were to stand still at this point, there is a real risk that it would lose in the competition and its economic situation would deteriorate.

In this chapter, ► Section 5.2 points out that international competition in manufacturing has become extremely severe and essentially zero-sum on a global scale. ► Section 5.3 examines, based on the East Asian experience, how Country B (a developing country) can leverage the advantages of being a latecomer to learn from country A (a developed country) and achieve even faster growth. ► Section 5.4 demonstrates that the core of East Asia's so-called "miraculous" development lies in learning technological and managerial knowledge from ad-

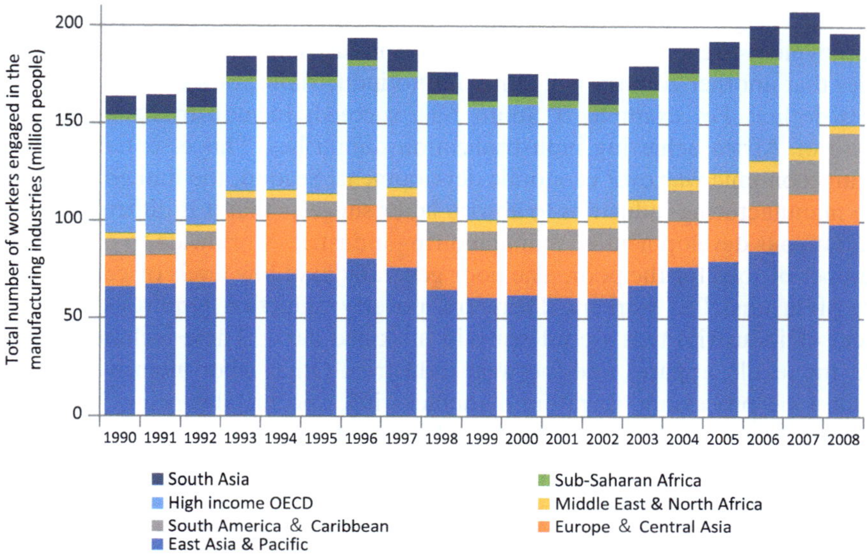

Fig. 5.1 Changes in the total number of workers engaged in the manufacturing industries in the world (World Bank 2012). Data are not available after 2009

vanced countries and rapidly accumulating intellectual and human capital. Finally, ► Section 5.5 considers whether adopting the East Asian development model could enable countries in Africa and South Asia to achieve similar progress. If these regions succeed in following the East Asian model of development, this century may shift from being the "East Asian century" to a truly global century originating from East Asia.

5.2 International Competition in Manufacturing Is Intense

It may come as a surprise, but the global employment absorption capacity of the manufacturing industries has changed very little over the long term. Figure 5.1 illustrates the trend in the number of manufacturing workers worldwide. Over the past 20 years, there has been remarkably little change (World Bank 2012).[1] During this period, global income increased, and the production of industrial goods should have grown significantly. Nevertheless, the fact that employment did not rise indicates that labor productivity in manufacturing improved rapidly, enabling a nearly unchanged workforce to produce a much larger volume of higher-quality products than before.

1 It is a basic principle that figures and tables should be reproducible. In this revision, I attempted to recalculate and update Fig. 5.1 with the most recent data, but was unable to do so. This figure was created with considerable effort together with an excellent assistant at the World Bank when I participated in writing the World Development Report. I apologize to readers that, for these reasons, Fig. 5.1 does not show data after 2009.

This is significant in two respects. First, as long as the "pie"—that is, global employment—remains fixed, the successful industrialization of one country implies that another country will either fail to industrialize or see its existing industries decline. For example, if South Asia succeeds in industrializing, the likelihood of Africa achieving industrialization diminishes. This essentially amounts to an economic war over economic development. Second, the limited capacity of the manufacturing industries to absorb labor suggests that it is difficult for the simultaneous development of manufacturing industries worldwide to create a large number of jobs for the poor. The poor generally have low levels of education and are often unskilled workers. Therefore, poverty reduction requires the development of industries that are intensive in unskilled labor. These include, for example, the textile, apparel, and footwear industries. Other labor-intensive sectors include food processing, furniture manufacturing, and metalworking. Without the development of such manufacturing industries, it is difficult to achieve poverty reduction. However, there may be inherent limits to the employment absorption capacity of these industries.

Industries that are intensive in unskilled labor are generally classified as light industries. In contrast, heavy and chemical industries are capital-intensive, while information communication technology (ICT), biotechnology, nanotechnology, and AI-related industries are knowledge-intensive. However, in the early stages of development, the production of electronic components was highly knowledge-intensive. Over time, the processes were simplified, allowing even unskilled workers to participate in production. As a result, this industry became labor-intensive, and production bases shifted from advanced economies to developing countries.

In the case of automobiles, if the goal is simply to manufacture vehicles that run, a capital-intensive production method suffices. However, producing cars with high fuel efficiency and low emissions requires a significant amount of scientific knowledge. For this reason, Japan's and Europe's automotive industry is considered high-tech, whereas China's is more capital-intensive. Thus, it is not easy to strictly categorize industries as labor-intensive, capital-intensive, and knowledge-intensive.

Despite these complexities, to observe general trends, ◘ Table 5.1 divides manufacturing into three categories—heavy and chemical industries, light industries, and others—and shows their respective shares of GDP. Since the "other" category encompasses a wide range of industries, its high share can make interpretation challenging; however, several broad trends can still be discerned from the table.

First, in high-income economies such as Japan, the United States, and South Korea, the share of heavy and chemical industries is high and shows a slight upward trend. It is likely that this category also includes knowledge-intensive industries, such as those related to new materials. Second, in middle-income countries such as China, Thailand, and India, the share of light industry is relatively high but shows a declining trend. Finally, in African countries such as Ethiopia and Kenya, as expected, the share of light industry is high, but contrary to expectations, this share has not increased significantly. This is a major concern. If light industry does not develop in labor-abundant Africa, overall economic development cannot be expected.

Table 5.1 GDP shares of heavy and chemical industries and light industries in selected countries (%)[1] (World Bank's World Development Indicators various years)

	1990			2020		
	Heavy and chemical	Light	Others	Heavy and chemical	Light	Others
Japan	34.4	13.6	52.0	54.7	15.0	30.4
US	34.4	17.3	48.4	33.6	19.1	47.3
China	28.7	29.3	42.0	35.3	21.8	42.8
Thailand	11.6	53.4	35.0	26.4[a]	22.5[1]	51.1[a]
South Korea	39.4	24.5	36.1	42.3	10.5	47.2
India	31.3	26.9	41.7	22.1	18.8	59.1
Ethiopia	3.4	82.6	14.0	16.1[b]	46.6[2]	37.3[2]
Kenya	14.0	48.0	37.9	6.2	64.3	29.5

[1]Data pertain to 2016
[2]Data pertain to 2015
[3]Heavy and chemical industries include chemical and transport industries, whereas the light industries include food processing, tobacco, textile, and apparel industries

The development of labor-intensive industries in developing countries, the focus on capital-intensive industries in middle-income countries, and the pursuit of knowledge-intensive industries in advanced economies constitute an extremely important international division of labor for the harmonious development of the world. First, this arrangement helps to some extent to avoid head-on trade wars. For example, if every country were to manufacture automobiles as a matter of national pride, trade wars would erupt everywhere. Second, and more importantly, it is an empirical fact that developing countries cannot achieve economic development without progressing through the stages of labor-intensive development, capital-intensive development, and knowledge-intensive development. In economics, this is known as the *theory of comparative advantage*. While the concept is nearly identical, in Asia, this discussion is particularly known as the *flying geese pattern*. Given its critical importance to economic development, an explanation is provided in ► Box 5.1.

Box 5.1 The "Flying Geese Pattern" Cannot Be Defied

The international economy is inherently competitive, and each country must specialize in industries where it has a comparative advantage over others to succeed. For example, prior to the economic reforms of 1978, China was a poor, agriculture-based country lacking capital. Yet, it attempted to foster capital-intensive heavy industries, such as steel and machine tools. Not only did this fail to utilize the country's abundant labor force, but it also suffered from a shortage of investment capital. It was unable to produce exportable goods, resulting in a lack of economic development.

It was Professor Akamatsu (1962) who linked the theory of comparative advantage to economic development from a dynamic perspective. Coupled with the unique term flying geese, the *flying geese pattern* continues to have many proponents among researchers even today. According to the *flying geese pattern*, in the early stages of economic development, low-income countries import even simple products such as cotton yarn. However, domestic production of these labor-intensive goods eventually becomes active, and their imports decline and exports increase. At this stage, the machinery for spinning and weaving is still imported. In the early Meiji era in Japan, domestically produced looms used hardwood instead of iron, as iron was expensive. As capital gradually accumulated and knowledge of textile machinery improved, Japan began to produce iron machines domestically and eventually exported them.

Textile machinery utilized cast-iron frames, which are technologically similar to those used in automobile body production; thus, the development of the former has led to advancements in the latter. This transition from a labor-intensive to a capital-intensive industrial structure is referred to as the flying geese pattern. This trajectory closely mirrors the history of Toyota Motor Corporation's development. This valuable theory was born out of the very history of the Japanese economy. Intuitively, the lesson of the theory of comparative advantage and the flying geese pattern is that a country should specialize in industries that make intensive use of its relatively abundant resources—whether human capital, physical capital, intellectual capital, or unskilled labor—compared to the rest of the world. There are virtually no examples of countries that have succeeded in economic development by defying this principle.

This was true for South Korea: in its rush to catch up with Japan in the late 1970s, it pursued rapid heavy and chemical industrialization but failed. Similarly, in Africa, import-substitution industrialization policies that sought to leap directly into capital-intensive modern industries, rather than steadily developing labor-intensive industries, have universally failed. "Follow the flying geese pattern" is a fundamental prerequisite for successful economic development.

In short, developing countries that lack human capital, physical capital, infrastructure, and intellectual capital have little choice but to leverage the low cost of their unskilled labor to develop industries that can compete with those of other countries through international trade. Similarly, for advanced economies with high wages to remain competitive, it is rational to specialize in knowledge-intensive industries by capitalizing on their abundant intellectual and human capital. Compared to human and intellectual capital, physical capital is relatively easy to accumulate. As a result, middle-income countries tend to specialize in capital-intensive industries. Of course, in the long run, developing and middle-income countries can achieve a comparative advantage in the production of more sophisticated goods by increasing their intellectual capital, human capital, and other valuable stocks at a faster rate than other nations.

5.3 China Thrives, Japan Lags Behind

Although signs of slowdown began to appear in the late 2010s, China's per capita GDP grew at an annual rate close to 10% for 35 years following the implementation of liberal economic reforms in 1978. In contrast, Japan's economic growth since 1990 has been a mere 1% per year. Does this mean that China's economy is exceptional, while Japan's is incompetent or lethargic? While there may be some truth to this, the fundamental answer is no. When the technological gap with leading advanced economies is large, developing countries can achieve rapid growth through imitation. China fully exploited this latecomer advantage. Similarly, during Japan's period of rapid economic growth from the late 1950s to the early 1970s, its per capita GDP also grew at an annual rate of nearly 10%.

Figure. 5.2 illustrates the growth trajectories of real per capita GDP, adjusted for purchasing power parity (PPP), from 1889 to 2020 for several countries. Since this is a semi-logarithmic graph, the slope of the curve represents the growth rate. Before World War II, Japan's economy grew at nearly the same pace as the United States. In other words, Japan did not succeed in catching up during this period, and the income gap remained. Japan's economic growth was particularly rapid after World War II. After recovering to prewar economic levels around 1955, Japan took advantage of the large per capita GDP gap with advanced economies to achieve rapid growth. A large gap meant that there were technologies and management practices in advanced countries for Japan to imitate. As shown in Fig. 3.3 in ► Chap. 3, Japan clearly achieved rapid growth by importing advanced technologies.

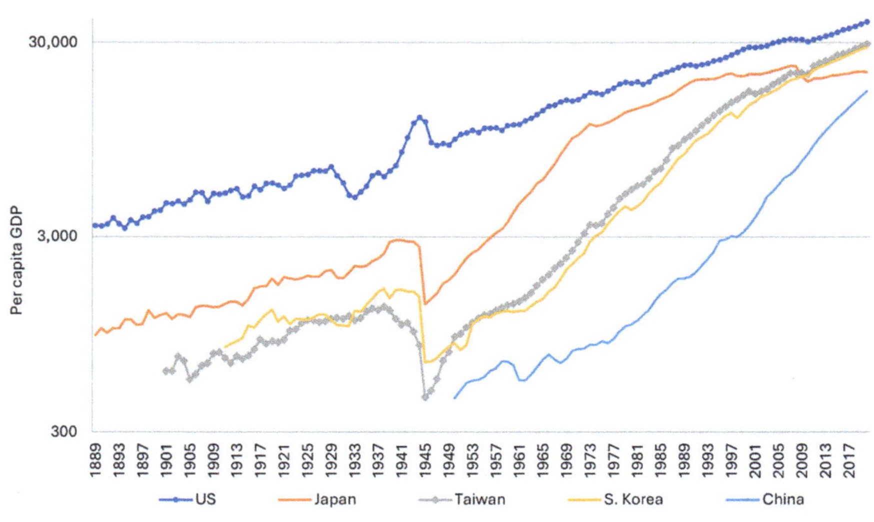

Fig. 5.2 Changes in real GDP (PPP-adjusted) per capita in the US, Japan, Taiwan, South Korea, and China (Maddison 2010 for 1890-2008; Groningen Growth and Development Centre 2025 for 2009-23)

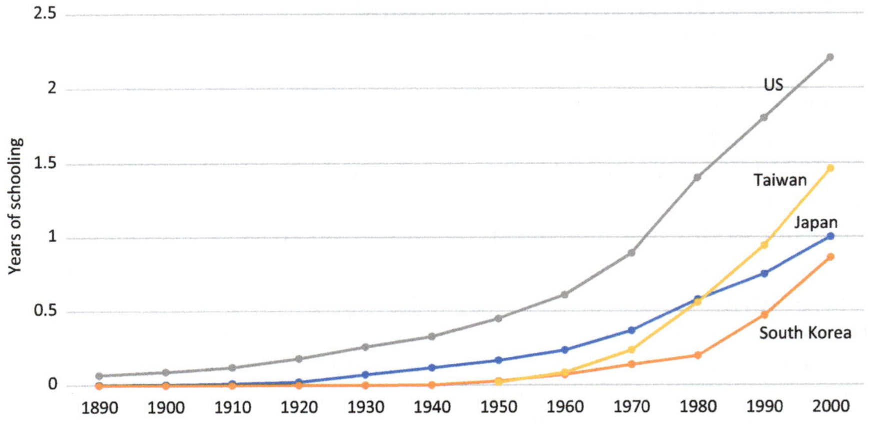

Fig. 5.3 Changes in average years of higher schooling (colleges, universities, and graduate schools) in South Korea, Taiwan, Japan, and the United States (Godo 2011)

However, as the per capita GDP gap between Japan and advanced economies narrowed, Japan's growth rate slowed. In the late 1970s, Japan entered a period of so-called stable growth, marking a shift away from its high-growth era. This shift was not because the public or politicians desired slow but stable growth. Rather, as opportunities for imitation diminished, it became necessary to develop technological knowledge independently—an extremely costly process. Thus, stable growth was not a matter of choice, but an inevitable outcome.

Interestingly, about a decade later, Taiwan and South Korea experienced similar periods of rapid and then stable growth. This supports the view that the existence and exploitation of a technological gap is key to rapid economic growth. It is also noteworthy that Japan's development served as a model, enabling other Asian countries to achieve Japanese-style or East Asian-style development in succession.[2]

China's per capita GDP remains far below that of Japan, Taiwan, and South Korea. China has achieved rapid growth by imitating not only Western technologies but also those from Japan and other neighboring countries. For example, during my research on the motorcycle industry in Chongqing, I observed Chinese manufacturers actively advertising that they could produce Honda-type or Suzuki-type motorcycles. While this is clearly a violation of intellectual property law, such aggressive imitation has propelled China's economy to become the "world's factory" in a remarkably short time. It is no exaggeration to say that the driving force behind China's dynamism is *imitation*.

2 Mahbubani (2013) states that without Japan's success, most of Asia would have ended up like Africa or the Arab world, where no country has yet joined the ranks of developed nations. Many in China also believe that without Japan's successful economic development, China's own development would not have occurred.

Even so, the Japanese economy remains sluggish. In Japan, many people seem to believe that the economy has been suffering from a downturn in the business cycle for the past 35 years, but I do not share this view. In the first place, the concept of the business cycle can explain economic stagnation lasting one or 2 years, but it cannot account for a prolonged stagnation spanning more than three decades. In my view, one major reason for Japan's economic stagnation is the lack of academic strength among the Japanese people, particularly the inadequacy of graduate-level education.

Figure. 5.3 illustrates the average years of higher education (including university and graduate school) among citizens in advanced economies. Compared to their income levels, Japanese people spend fewer years in higher education than their counterparts in the United States or Taiwan. For example, the average Taiwanese now spends about 1.5 years in university or graduate school, whereas the average Japanese spends only 1 year. It is well known that Samsung, with its large number of highly qualified employees holding graduate degrees, overwhelmingly outperformed its Japanese competitors. There is no reason to think that similar developments will not occur in other sectors of the Japanese economy in the future.

In fact, a careful examination of ◘ Fig. 5.2 reveals that South Korea and Taiwan have recently overtaken Japan in terms of real GDP per capita. If Japan is to achieve long-term economic revitalization, it must enhance graduate education, make every effort to develop internationally competitive human capital, and foster the creation of world-leading intellectual capital. Without such efforts, Japan cannot expect to advance its industrial structure, improve productivity, reduce fiscal deficits, or support its aging population. For further discussion, see ► Box 5.2.

Box 5.2 Japan Must Fundamentally Strengthen Graduate Education (3)
"What do a grain of rice stuck to the bottom of your foot and a PhD have in common?" The answer is that even if you get them, they're useless." This was the content of a front-page article in the Nihon Keizai Shimbun, a leading Japanese newspaper, two decades ago. I felt not only anger but also a sense of helplessness that left me speechless. As Japan competes as an advanced nation, its most important assets are human capital and intellectual capital. In today's world, not only in developing countries but also in advanced economies, those holding responsible positions in government and business are often individuals with doctoral degrees. This is not simply a matter of credentials. Rather, it is because those in leadership roles must have acquired advanced human capital through graduate-level training and be well-versed in cutting-edge intellectual capital. Without this, Japan cannot compete globally.

The same applies to journalists. In Europe and the United States, there are journalists with PhDs who confidently engage in debates with Nobel Prize-level economists. Turning to Japanese universities, with some exceptions, they are unfortunately not organizations that nurture internationally competitive human capital

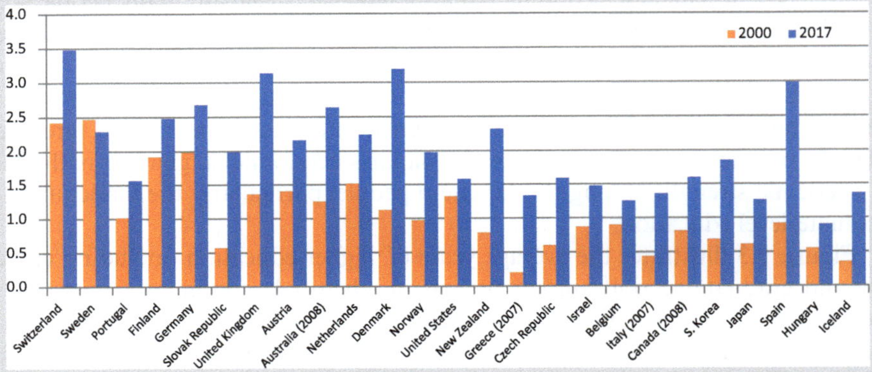

Fig. 5.4 Comparison of the percentage of PhD holders across OECD member countries in 2000 and 2017 (OECD Science, Technology and Industry Scoreboard various years). (Years in parentheses refer to the nearest years to 2000, in which data are available).

or generate frontier knowledge on a global scale. According to the 2013 OECD Survey of Adult Skills, Japanese adults ranked at the top among advanced countries in reading and mathematical literacy. However, this refers to the average, and the proportion of outstanding individuals is low. Moreover, the high average scores were found among those aged 55–65. It appears that Japan's unique corporate culture of employee training contributed to these results. In contrast, the OECD's Programme for International Student Assessment (PISA), which targets 15-year-olds, indicates that Japanese children's academic performance is not particularly high. In general, university education in Japan remains lax in many respects, and although graduate education is improving, it is still far from the global frontier. There are even doctoral programs in Japan where hardly any lectures are offered. Japanese doctoral programs are not only inferior in quality but also among the lowest in quantity among advanced countries. As shown in Fig. 5.4, the proportion of doctoral graduates in the population is lower than in South Korea, placing Japan near the bottom among advanced economies. If universities are second-rate, graduate schools are second-rate, and both public and private sector leaders possess only second-rate human capital by global standards, then the Japanese economy cannot be anything but second-rate. Unless Japan strengthens its universities and, in particular, its graduate schools, there is no bright future for the Japanese economy. This is not a problem unique to Japan. Other Asian countries, including China, should learn from Japan's mistakes.

5.4 Secrets of East Asian Economic Development

I believe there are three main reasons why East Asian countries, including Japan, have achieved successful economic development. The first is learning from abroad. This has already been made clear through the patent analysis in ► Chap. 3 and the discussions in this chapter. From the analytical framework of this book, it is important to recognize, firstly, that learning from abroad has an immediate effect on the formation of human capital and the accumulation of intellectual capital in developing countries. Secondly, it must be understood that developing industries must attempt to develop industries well-suited to the country's comparative advantage. The third factor is a strong emphasis on education and active investment in human capital. The most compelling evidence that these three factors are key to economic development can be found in the economic history of early modern Japan (see ► Box 5.3).

Box 5.3 Lessons from Japanese Economic History

As has been repeatedly pointed out, economic development takes time. This is why development economics and economic history are closely related fields. In particular, Japanese economic history is a treasure trove of research topics for development economics. Since the Japanese economy succeeded in developing over a long period from the premodern to the modern era, its history provides valuable lessons on what is important for economic development. Until recently, I believed that the introduction of modern industries, such as the cotton spinning industry represented by the Osaka Spinning Company, founded by Eiichi Shibusawa, was the driving force behind Japan's economic development since the Meiji era. However, this view is inconsistent with the theory of comparative advantage and the flying geese pattern. For a poor country like Japan in the early periods of the Meiji era (1868–1912), which had an abundance of cheap labor, it was necessary to develop labor-intensive industries. Although Japan's cotton spinning industry adopted imported modern capital-intensive technology, it transformed to labor-intensive technology, which triggered the rapid development of this industry (Otsuka et al., 1988).

Recent research in Japan's economic history suggests that, for overall economic development, the modernization of traditional industries was even more important than the introduction of modern industries. For example, in the silk weaving region of Fukui, production was carried out using handlooms until the early twentieth century, and nearly 100% of the products (namely *habutae* silk) were exported to Europe and the United States. This development pattern closely follows the basic principle of development economics that developing countries should first promote labor-intensive industries. Moreover, in some silk weaving regions, producer cooperatives have established training centers to jointly introduce foreign technologies, thereby addressing the problem of information spillovers (imitation).

As previously explained, when information spillovers exist, the private benefits to innovators are less than the social benefits, which weakens the incentive for innovation. To prevent this, the cooperatives worked together with member firms to implement activities that promoted innovation. Furthermore, these training centers were eventually reorganized into technical schools, contributing to the improvement of educational standards among those engaged in local industries (Hashino 2012). These cases vividly illustrate the importance of developing industries by leveraging technology transfer while maintaining a focus on comparative advantage.

However, this is just one example. Even without invoking the flying geese pattern, comparing Japanese economic history with the development of today's developing countries is an important research area that warrants further in-depth study, (Otsuka and Hashino 2026).

The importance of learning from abroad has been discussed previously, but the most compelling case is the development of the apparel industry in Bangladesh (Mottaleb and Sonobe 2011). There are various ways to acquire foreign technology and management know-how, including reverse engineering, borrowing foreign patents, technical and management training, and work experience in foreign-affiliated firms, making it difficult to pinpoint concrete evidence. However, the mechanism behind the development of Bangladesh's apparel industry is remarkably clear.

In 1979, South Korea's Daewoo Corporation entered into a technical partnership with Desh, a local company in Bangladesh, to launch export-oriented apparel production. At that time, however, there were no apparel companies in Bangladesh, nor were there personnel with expertise in production or management. To address this, the Daewoo-Desh alliance sent 130 newly hired university graduates to Daewoo's factories and headquarters in Korea for 9 months of intensive training, covering everything from garment manufacturing to quality control and marketing.

Remarkably, within two to 3 years of returning to Bangladesh, all 130 trainees had left the company. Some went on to establish new apparel firms, while others became presidents of apparel export trading companies, supporting the growth of other apparel businesses. As a result, the quality of Bangladeshi apparel products was high from the outset, enabling exports to developed countries. Furthermore, as shown in ◘ Fig. 5.5, the average size of apparel firms was already sub-

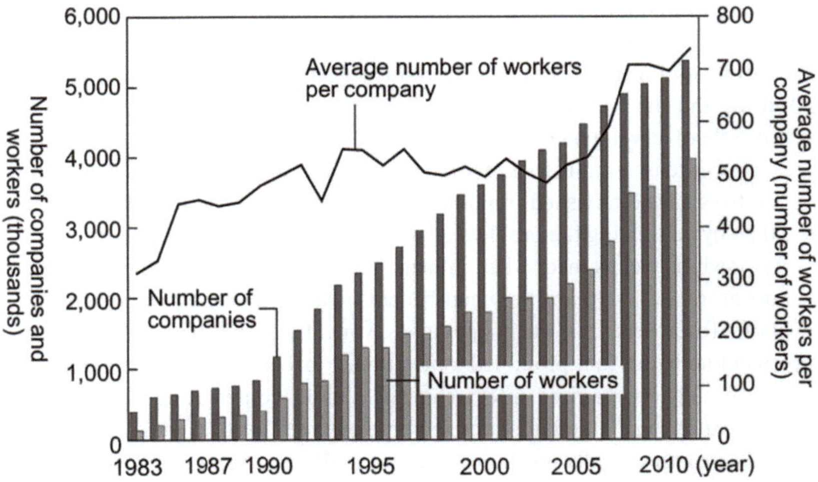

◘ **Fig. 5.5** Development of the garment industry in Bangladesh (Bangladesh Knitwear Manufacturers and Exporters Association various years)

stantial in the early 1980s, with an average workforce of 300 employees. Subsequently, Bangladeshi entrepreneurs, recognizing the importance of learning from abroad, continued to acquire technical and managerial knowledge from Japan, Singapore, Europe, and, more recently, China. As a result, apparel products now account for nearly 80% of Bangladesh's total exports, the industry employs four million people, and it has had a significant impact on improving the status of women and reducing poverty.

Bangladesh was originally one of the world's poorest countries, and foreign visitors were often shocked by the level of poverty they encountered. Many development economists believed that "Bangladesh could never develop." However, these predictions have been completely overturned. The experience of Bangladesh's apparel industry is valuable precisely because it demonstrates the importance of learning from abroad. Put differently, it is significant in that it shows that such East Asian-style development can also occur in South Asia. Subsequently, Bangladesh's pharmaceutical industry has also developed based on lessons learned from overseas.

It should be noted that while Daewoo brought enormous benefits to the Bangladeshi economy, it failed in its business venture. Consequently, no other company in Bangladesh has since provided such comprehensive training for its employees in any industry. In other words, the experience of the apparel industry in Bangladesh highlights not only the importance of learning from abroad, but also the limitations of leaving training entirely to private enterprises. In other words, because of information spillovers, it is not feasible to entrust "training" entirely to profit-oriented private firms.

It is not easy to demonstrate with data that the economies of East Asian countries have undergone structural transformation from labor-intensive to capital-intensive and then to knowledge-intensive industries. However, ◘ Table 5.1 suggests that, with economic development, there has been a shift from labor-intensive light industry to more capital-intensive heavy and chemical industries. Suppose we assume that the manufacturing sector is relatively capital-intensive and the modern service sector is relatively knowledge-intensive. In that case, it can be expected that the GDP share of the industrial sector will increase in the early stages of economic development, and eventually decline as the modern service sector expands. ◘ Figure 5.6 illustrates the changes in the manufacturing sector's share of GDP for the United States, Japan, South Korea, and China. In advanced economies such as the United States, the share of manufacturing in GDP has consistently declined, undoubtedly due to a shift toward more knowledge-intensive service industries. In Japan, the share of manufacturing peaked at around 33% in the early 1970s and has since decreased. What is particularly interesting is that in South Korea; about a decade after Japan, the share of manufacturing in GDP shifted from increasing to decreasing, and then experienced a slight uptick. Even more significant is the finding that China, too, is seeing a decline in the manufacturing sector's share of GDP. In other words, while China's manufacturing share of GDP remains exceptionally high—befitting its reputation as the "world's factory"—it is losing its comparative advantage in labor-intensive industries, and the overall relative importance of manufacturing is on a downward trend.

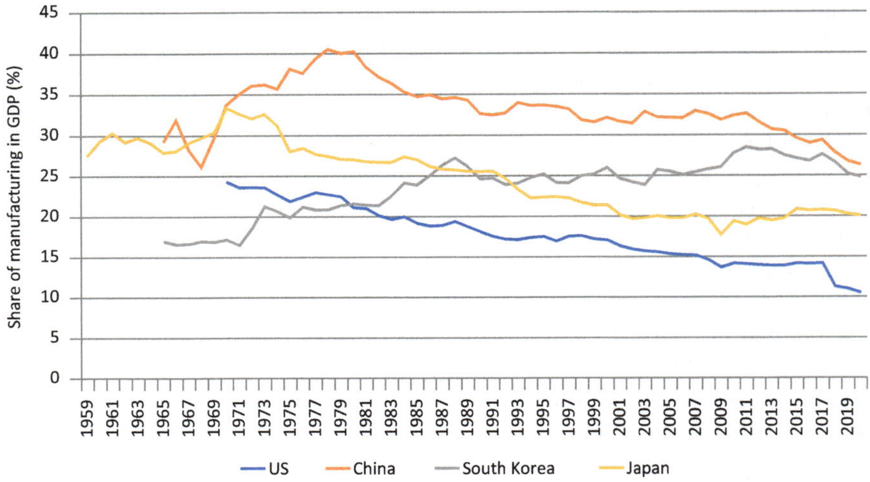

Fig. 5.6 Changes in share of manufacturing GDP in the US, Japan, South Korea, and China (%) (United Nations 1960–2017; World Bank's World Development Indicators various years)

The industrial cluster of baby clothing manufacturers in Huzhou, Zhejiang Province, which I surveyed around the year 2000, once rose to become the world's leading producer of baby clothes. However, it has since declined and is now considered a sunset industry. Today, apparel company managers in Bangladesh are confident that their international competitiveness surpasses that of China. Since the early 2000s, wages in China have risen sharply, and labor-intensive industries have already experienced significant stagnation.

Given this, which country is likely to see the development of manufacturing, particularly labor-intensive light industries, in place of China? Bangladesh, which recognizes the importance of learning from abroad, is a strong candidate. What about India? Will Pakistan or Sri Lanka experience such development? If South Asia succeeds in industrialization, the likelihood of Africa achieving the same may diminish. Does Africa have no opportunity for industrialization? While the answer remains uncertain, my view is that, as China—a major economic power—undergoes structural transformation, a fierce competition for industrialization is unfolding across all developing countries.

5.5 Can Africa Break Free from Stagnation?

The existence of a technological gap between developing and advanced countries does not automatically lead to rapid development in the former. Prewar Japan, for example, failed to catch up with advanced economies, even though it learned a great deal from them. The successful development of East Asian countries, leveraging the advantages of latecomers, mainly occurred after World War II—a phenomenon referred to as the East Asian Miracle. In contrast, Africa has largely failed to capitalize on the advantages of late industrialization.

Table 5.2 The apparel industry in Ethiopia (Sonobe and Otsuka 2011, pp. 202–205)

	Export-oriented firms	Firms managed by former tailors
No. of firms	14	7
Operation years	8	10
Schooling years of owners	16	13
Real sales value (Ethiopian birr [ETB] 1000)	2751	8342
Real value added (ETB 1000)	1376	3870
No. of workers	193	122
No. of sewing machines	248	92
% of high-speed sewing machines	74	72
Real value added per worker	6	22

For developing countries to achieve growth, it is essential to have a clear awareness of leveraging the technological gap to facilitate technology transfer, policies to promote this process, and institutional mechanisms to implement it. In my view, Africa's lack of success in industrialization stems from deficiencies in all of these areas.

Let us consider the apparel industry in Ethiopia as an example. With strong government backing, apparel factories have been constructed in industrial zones, and large enterprises have been nurtured through substantial subsidies. However, the government neither identified managers with technical or managerial expertise nor provided training in these areas. This stands in stark contrast to the success story of Bangladesh's apparel industry. As a result, as shown in Table 5.2, the 14 export-oriented firms supported by the government have large numbers of workers and sewing machines, but their sales, value added (sales minus raw material costs), and labor productivity, measured by value added per worker, remain low. Although the company presidents are highly educated, their lack of knowledge about apparel prevents them from realizing their potential. Moreover, exports—the original objective—have been sluggish, and the businesses are not profitable.

In contrast, seven large firms that rose from tailoring shops and have independently hired Korean and Indian advisors to acquire overseas expertise boast far higher productivity. Once again, companies that learn from abroad are steadily advancing. Conversely, large firms that received financial assistance and land in industrial zones from the government, much like the enterprises promoted under the import-substitution industrialization policies of the 1970s, are struggling with poor management despite using expensive sewing machines.

Although the discussion has focused primarily on Ethiopia, its case of the men's leather shoe industry is particularly noteworthy. Owing to the country's large cattle population, there is significant production of men's shoes made from cowhide. Our research group estimates that there are nearly 2000 small leather shoe factories within the capital city, Addis Ababa. However, since many of these businesses operate in small, shed-like structures to evade taxes, they are not easily visible to the public. The average number of employees per factory is about six or seven. Nevertheless, among these micro-enterprises, there are more than a dozen firms that have grown to employ several hundred workers. These firms are characterized by highly educated presidents who frequently travel to Italy, the global center of leather shoe production. Their primary objective, of course, is to "learn from Italy." Although these companies once faced a crisis due to a flood of cheap imports from China, they have since managed to drive Chinese products out of the market completely (Sonobe and Otsuka 2011).

In general, industries that are developing successfully tend to learn from abroad. While it is difficult to acquire highly advanced technologies, many firms have succeeded in their development by learning relatively simple technologies through joint ventures and other means. In Taiwan, for example, many industries have advanced by acquiring both technical and managerial expertise from joint ventures. However, unless a country can secure a certain level of human resources (or human capital) and develop basic infrastructure, it is unrealistic to expect foreign companies to invest directly in developing countries.

While there is strong support for the view that *industrialization should be pursued by attracting foreign direct investment (FDI) and learning from it*, the question of how to attract such investment must be addressed first. To create a production environment attractive to foreign firms, it is essential to first develop domestic industries to a certain extent. For instance, in countries where machinery repair is virtually impossible, foreign companies will be reluctant to enter the market.

Learning from firms established through FDI is important, but it is equally vital to acquire knowledge from abroad through technical and managerial training. In this context, Ethiopia's adoption of the Japanese-style "Kaizen" management approach (see Box 5–4) is particularly noteworthy. Such initiatives not only directly enhance the productivity of firms but may also serve as a catalyst for attracting further FDI. If this occurs, leveraging learning from abroad will further accelerate economic development, leading to even greater progress.

Kaizen has also been actively adopted in Zambia and South Africa, and the Tanzanian government has shown considerable interest in it. If African countries, starting with Kaizen, make concerted efforts to learn a wide range of technical and managerial knowledge from abroad, the manufacturing sector in Africa is likely to embark on a path of sustained growth. In doing so, they should target the imitation of technologies and management know-how that can be relatively easily learned from Asian countries with similar levels of development, particularly China and India.

Box 5.4 Ethiopia's Approach to "KAIZEN"

"Learning from abroad" is the most effective shortcut for developing countries to achieve economic growth. For Japanese, and now for those knowledgeable about the economies of Taiwan, South Korea, China, Thailand, Vietnam, and Indonesia, this is an uncontested fact. My frank impression is that African leaders lack this awareness. While there is a desire among Africans to emulate Asia's success, the motivation to actively learn from Asia remains weak. One notable exception was Ethiopian Prime Minister Meles, who passed away in August 2012.

Nearly fifteen years ago, I was invited, along with many other guests, to a party at the Ethiopian Prime Minister's residence. I brought with me a copy of T. Sonobe and K. Otsuka, Cluster–Based Industrial Development: An East Asian Model, Palgrave Macmillan (2006), which I handed directly to the Prime Minister. He was studying East Asian development and devoted considerable space in his doctoral dissertation to discussing East Asia's economic growth. At the request of the Japanese ambassador at the time, I had provided comments on his dissertation, so I was aware of his keen interest in East Asian economic development. The book I handed over contained East Since the subtitle included "Asia," I was certain that the Prime Minister would read this book. My intuition proved to be absolutely correct.

The Prime Minister read the book thoroughly, marking it with sticky notes, and requested that JICA provide large-scale instruction in Japanese management practices to Ethiopians. He established a "KAIZEN Training Center" in the country, aiming to train a large number of Ethiopian consultants capable of teaching KAIZEN. KAIZEN, already an English term in the field of management, seeks to create a more efficient workplace through the 5S principles (Sort, Set in order, Shine, Standardize, Sustain) and by encouraging QC circles. As this suggests, it is a management approach that emphasizes proposal-based participation by frontline workers (Otsuka, Jin, and Sonobe 2018). It is still too early to fully assess the results, but I am confident that significant achievements will be realized. In fact, "managerial innovation" is always crucial for the successful adoption of technology, and KAIZEN-style management is a product of the collective wisdom of many Japanese practitioners. The KAIZEN philosophy, in which both managers and workers strive together to improve operational efficiency, is already common sense among leading companies in Europe, the United States, and East Asia. I believe that KAIZEN is an indispensable tool for the development of emerging economies.

I predict that Ethiopia, which recognizes the importance of learning from abroad, will be the first country in Africa to achieve middle-income status. Should this occur, Ethiopia's experience will serve as a model for Africa's development and have a profound impact on the progress of other African nations. This would parallel the role Japan played as a model for Asia's development. Japan should make every effort to support Ethiopia's KAIZEN initiatives. Such support would benefit not only Japan and Ethiopia, but also many other African countries, and could open the door to a transition "from the Asian Century to a truly global century".

5.6 Summary

Finally, let us summarize the main points discussed in this chapter.

- Overall employment in global manufacturing has scarcely increased; growth in one region tends to be offset by declines in another, and vice versa.
- No country has succeeded in economic development without following the flying geese pattern of progressing from labor-intensive to capital-intensive to knowledge-intensive industries.
- The imitation of foreign technologies and management know-how is the driving force behind economic development in developing countries.
- The keys to East Asia's development are (1) learning from abroad, (2) promoting the growth of industries suited to local conditions, and (3) strengthening education.
- Since China is losing its comparative advantage in light manufacturing industries, intense international competition for industrialization is emerging among other developing countries, including those in Africa.

Questions

1. Why are there almost no developed countries that introduced the most modern technology from the most developed countries at their early stage of development and successfully developed thereafter?
2. What is the implication of sharp wage increases in China for the development of other developing countries?
3. Does international trade confer benefits to both importing and exporting countries?
4. While economic history examines the industrial development over a long period, development economics explores the causes of industrial development in various countries using basically cross-sectional data for a short period. What are the pros and cons of each scientific field?

References

Akamatsu, K. (1962). A historical pattern of economic growth in developing countries. *The Developing Economies*, *1*(1), 3-25.

Bangladesh Knitwear Manufacturers and Exporters Association. (various years).

Godo, Y. (2011). Estimation of average years of schooling for Japan, Korea, and the United States. *PRIMCED Discussion Paper Series*, No. 9. Hitotsubashi University.

Hashino, T. (2012). Institutionalising technical education: The case of weaving districts in Meiji Japan. *Australian Economic History Review, 52*(1), 25–42.

Hashino, T., & Otsuka, K. (Eds.). (2016). *Industrial districts in history and the developing world.* Springer.

International Monetary Fund. (IMF). (2025). *World Economic Outlook (April 2025)*.

Mahbubani, K. (2013). *The great convergence: Asia, the West, and the logic of one world.* Public Affairs.

Mottaleb, K.A., & Sonobe, T. (2011). An inquiry into the rapid growth of the garment industry in Bangladesh. *Economic Development and Cultural Change, 60*(1), 67–89.
Organisation for Economic Co-operation and Development (OECD). (various years). OECD Science, *Technology and Industry Scoreboard 2017.*
Otsuka, K., Ranis, G., & Saxonhouse, G. (1988). *Comparative technology choice in development: The Indian and Japanese cotton textile industries*. Macmillan Press.
Otsuka, K., & Hashino, T. (2026, forthcoming). Selective technology choice, adaptations, and industrial development: Lessons from successful development of the textile industries in prewar Japan. *The Developing Economies*.
Sonobe, T., & Otsuka, K. (2011). *Cluster-based industrial development: A comparative study of Asia and Africa*. Palgrave Macmillan.
World Bank. (various years) *World development indicators*. World Bank DataBank.
World Bank. (2012). *World Development Report 2013: Jobs*. World Bank.

What Must and Must not be Done?

What Developing Countries Must Not Do

Contents

K. Otsuka, *A Primer on Development Economics*,
Classroom Companion: Economics, https://doi.org/10.1007/978-981-95-5397-6_6

6.1 Introduction

Let us consider the development challenges of a hypothetical country that, although not actually existing, seems entirely plausible. This is an agricultural nation, with the majority of its population engaged in farming. However, due to its mountainous terrain and limited plains, the amount of arable land is small relative to its population. As a result, farm sizes are also small. On the positive side, like the highlands of Kenya or Sumatra, the country is situated at a high altitude near the equator, resulting in a comfortable climate year-round, with temperatures consistently between 16 °C and 25 °C. While this makes for comfortable living conditions, it has also had unintended consequences. During the colonial era, large numbers of white settlers from the colonial power immigrated to the country, displacing the local population and establishing vast estates that spanned hundreds or even thousands of hectares. In some cases, as with the *latifundia* and *haciendas* of South America and the Philippines, or the estates of East and Southern Africa, the local people were forced to work as agricultural laborers on these large farms. In other cases, as seen with the haciendas in the Philippines, the large landowners moved to the cities and became absentee landlords, employing the local people as tenant farmers. Both the agricultural laborers and the tenant farmers lived in extreme poverty, below the poverty line. Thus, escaping poverty was a dream that people desperately wished to realize.

Agricultural technology remained premodern, and farmers cultivated traditional crops using age-old methods. Naturally, yields were extremely low. Agricultural production was highly dependent on weather conditions; in good years, the country could be self-sufficient in food, but in bad years, it quickly fell into food shortages and had to rely on food aid. Therefore, improving agricultural productivity was a major challenge.

As in China, Vietnam, India, Nepal, Ethiopia, Tanzania, and many other African countries, the mountains were state-owned, but due to poor government management, the once-forested green mountains had been converted to barren hills. Valuable timber species had once grown there, but were illegally logged and sold off. As a result, farmers now struggled even to gather firewood for cooking.

Consequently, as in Ethiopia and South Asia, people resorted to drying cow and donkey dung for use as fuel. Because of the odor, kitchens were housed in separate buildings. The degraded mountains led to frequent flooding, while after several days of clear weather, the streams that should have flowed from the mountains would dry up. When this happened, women had to walk long distances to fetch water from distant rivers. As in Ethiopia, it was not uncommon for a round trip to take as long as three hours. Restoring the forests was an urgent task, both for land conservation and for improving the lives of farmers. There was also a strong desire to develop forestry by planting valuable timber species.

There were no significant industries, but the cities continued to swell with the migration of impoverished farmers. The original urban residents ran small shops, but recent arrivals from rural areas took up low-paying jobs such as street vending or collecting recyclables. Those with education sometimes found work in small companies, but wages were generally low. To break out of this situation, it was necessary to develop industries to create employment and raise wage levels.

Amid these circumstances, a charismatic new president came to power. After visiting developed countries to study their economies, the president announced the following new economic policies to enrich the nation. The policies are as follows:

1. Since the tenant farming system is exploitative and feudal, tenanted lands are to be confiscated from landlords and transferred to tenant farmers. This is expected to enhance the motivation of tenant farmers, resulting in increased productivity and reduced poverty.
2. Large-scale farms that employ agricultural workers and utilize modern, large-scale machinery will be maintained and further developed. However, white landowners will be repatriated to their home countries, and land ownership will be transferred to local residents. This will enable the creation of an efficient, modern agricultural sector under national ownership.
3. In the case of forests, *social forestry* will be promoted. Social forestry is a system in which groups of neighboring farmers in a village jointly manage the forest. In social forestry, farmers work equally and, in principle, share the income from sales of timber trees and other forest products equally among themselves. This ensures an abundant supply of firewood, allowing farmers to earn a substantial income.
4. To catch up quickly with wealthy developed countries, the development of heavy and chemical industries will be promoted, aiming for a significant increase in national income.
5. Noting that large enterprises lead the heavy and chemical industries in many developed countries, the government implements policies that prioritize large corporations. The goal is to support a large number of internationally competitive firms, thereby creating new employment opportunities for many citizens.
6. Since leaving wage determination to private enterprises does not result in sufficiently high wages, the minimum wage will be set at twice the current level. This will greatly improve the living standards of poor workers employed by companies.

While this may sound like a wonderful, rosy dream, what outcomes did these new presidential economic policies actually produce? Below, we will examine the results of each policy. It should be noted that (1) land reform has actually been implemented in countries such as India, Nepal, and the Philippines; (2) support for large-scale agriculture is currently underway in Africa; (3) social forestry has been consistently supported by aid agencies including the World Bank, Food and Agriculture Organization (FAO), and the Japan International Cooperation Agency (JICA); (4) the emphasis on heavy and chemical industries was the central strategy of import-substitution industrialization pursued by African countries after independence; and (5) support for large enterprises and (6) the establishment of minimum wages are general policies that governments have implemented in almost all developing countries.

6.2 Traditional Land Reforms

Land reform, implemented in Asia to reduce poverty and equalize income, involved the confiscation of land from landlords who owned holdings above a certain size—often with little or no compensation—and its transfer to the tenant farmers who had been cultivating it.[1] Landowners with holdings below a certain threshold, who cultivated their own land, were exempt from land reform. This policy was carried out under the slogan "land-to-the-tiller." A similar approach was taken in postwar Japan's land reform, with strong support from the occupation forces led by the Americans.

In the case of small and medium-sized landlords, rather than transferring land, the policy was to reduce land rents to a legally mandated low level. In Africa, land reform has so far focused on the establishment of property rights, differing in content from Asian land reform. For further details, see ▶ Box 6.1.

Box 6.1 Land Reform in Africa

Land reform in Africa can be broadly divided into two types. The first involves breaking up large farms, known as estates, and distributing the land to the agricultural workers employed there. In Zimbabwe, for example, a policy was implemented to return land ownership to the descendants of indigenous people who had lost their land to white settlers centuries earlier; however, in practice, it appears that politically powerful individuals acquired much of the land.[2]Unlike tenant farmers, agricultural workers generally lack experience in farm management, and without substantial training, it is difficult for them to become competent farm managers. In Asia, similar issues would arise if plantation reforms were attempted in the Philippines (sugarcane, pineapple, and banana); Malaysia and Indonesia (rubber and oil palm); or Sri Lanka (tea). Due to the difficulty of such reforms, plantation reform has been postponed in Asia.

Another form of land reform in Africa involves strengthening individual property rights to farmland. In Africa, this second type of land reform is far more important than the first. Most farmland in Africa is classified as customary land, controlled by tribal groups. Uncultivated land (such as forests) is held in common by tribe members and managed by tribal chiefs. When land is cleared with the chief's permission, the person who clears it is granted explicit use rights. Traditionally, crops are cultivated on this land for one to two years, after which it is left fallow for 20 to 30 years to restore soil fertility. During the fallow period, the land is managed by the extended family to which the original cultivator belongs. Given the long fallow period, it is not always likely that the person who cleared the land will still be alive 20 to 30 years later. As a result, the land is collectively managed and distrib-

1 The discussion in this section is based on Hayami and Otsuka (1993), Otsuka (2007), and Holden, Otsuka, and Deininger (2013).

2 The discussion in this box is based on Holden, Otsuka, and Deininger (2013) and Otsuka and Place (2014).

uted equally among family members. Because ownership is collective, the leasing and sale of land are restricted. However, in the absence of established individual property rights, there is little incentive to invest in improving land quality or value, such as building terraces, investing in irrigation, applying compost to enhance soil fertility, or planting cash crops like coffee and cocoa. This is because, without secure ownership, those who improve the land cannot be certain whether they will reap the benefits of their investment. For example, even if someone makes a great effort to cultivate coffee trees, the harvest may end up being shared among extended family members. While this may not be problematic when land is abundant, the current scarcity of farmland makes weak individual property rights a significant issue.

Furthermore, without legally recognized rights to buy and sell land, farmers cannot use their land as collateral to obtain loans from banks. Therefore, the primary objective of land reform in Africa is to establish individual property rights to farmland, for example, by issuing land ownership certificates. While this approach appears successful, land use is controlled by the extended family. So it often leads to conflicts among family members when interests cannot be reconciled, sometimes exacerbating land disputes. As population growth increases land scarcity, there is a natural tendency for individual property rights to be strengthened over extended family holdings. Issuing land ownership certificates to individuals before this process occurs organically can result in internal family discord.

How do landlords respond when they learn that a land reform aimed at transferring land to cultivators is about to be implemented? The first thing many landlords did was to change the ownership registration from their own name to those of family members, relatives, or associates, thereby reducing the size of each holding and attempting to evade the application of land reform laws. To appear as small-scale owner-cultivators, landlords expelled many tenant farmers. In many cases, they also disguised tenant farmers as hired laborers for self-cultivation. This is something I personally witnessed in the Philippines.

In India, it was reportedly common for landlords to rotate tenant farmers every season. To maintain good relations with tenants, many landlords would visit when a tenant's family member was ill or give gifts at a tenant's child's wedding, thereby building trust. As a result, landlords often employed the same tenant farmers for many years. Given these circumstances, the land-to-the-tiller policy assumed that each plot of land would have a single tenant farmer. However, to circumvent this policy, landlords began rotating tenant farmers each season. As a result, officials tasked with implementing land reform could not determine to which tenant the land should be transferred, making it impossible to carry out the land-to-the-tiller policy.

Tenant farmers, like owner-cultivators, are the principal agents responsible for farm management, including fertilizer application and water control. In contrast, agricultural laborers are engaged in simple tasks such as rice transplanting, weeding, harvesting, and threshing. Because the work of tenant farmers requires

Table 6.1 Differences in land ownership, income, and yield per ha between high- and low-caste households in Nepal (Holden, Otsuka, and Deinninger 2013, pp. 40–41)

	High caste	Low caste
No. of sample households	382	107
Average income (NPR 1000)	72.4	30.9
Average land ownership (ha)	0.64	0.17
Average cultivated area (ha)	0.63	0.35
% of tenanted area	16.8	49.5
Yield (NPR 1000 per ha)	63.8	81.8

NPR = Nepali rupees

experience and judgment, their income is higher than that of agricultural laborers. Therefore, tenant farmers who were evicted and forced to become agricultural laborers undoubtedly experienced a decline in their standard of living. On the other hand, tenant farmers who had to sign tenancy contracts with different landlords each season lost motivation, as their contracts would be terminated after the harvest regardless of whether they worked diligently or not. As a result, these tenant farmers became indifferent to activities that would benefit future production, such as maintaining soil fertility or caring for irrigation facilities.

As previously discussed, farm management that relies on hiring large numbers of agricultural laborers is inefficient. In contrast, tenant farmers are inherently as productive as owner-cultivators (Hayami and Otsuka 1993). After the eviction of tenant farmers, landlords managed their farms by hiring agricultural laborers, which led to a significant decline in agricultural productivity. Furthermore, the seasonal nature of tenancy contracts demotivated tenant farmers, causing overall agricultural productivity to fall even further.

Let us consider a concrete example. Table 6.1, taken from a study published in Holden, Otsuka, and Deninger (2013), presents the situation in Nepal. Households belonging to higher castes have more than twice the average income and nearly four times the average landholding compared to lower-caste households. Consequently, a higher proportion of lower-caste households rent land as tenant farmers. However, due to the land-to-the-tiller policy, higher-caste households are reluctant to lease land to lower-caste households. As a result, crop yields are actually higher among lower-caste households. If land could be freely rented and leased, higher-caste households would be more willing to lease land to lower-caste households, resulting in a more equitable distribution of yields. This would also narrow the income gap between the two groups. In other words, the land-to-the-tiller policy has, in fact, exacerbated poverty. Not only in Nepal, but also in India and the Philippines—countries that have adopted similar land-to-the-tiller policies—there are large numbers of landless laborers who cannot even become tenant farmers.

Fundamentally, the very objective of the land-to-the-tiller policy is deeply problematic. This is because, in Asian rural areas, the poorest are not tenant farmers but agricultural laborers. Therefore, even if the policy had succeeded, its benefits would not have reached the lowest strata of society. In short, the president of our hypothetical country failed to achieve either poverty reduction or increased agricultural productivity—both goals vanished into thin air. What, then, should have been done? While there are various debates on this issue, it is important to recognize the reality that forcibly expropriating land through the use of power will inevitably encounter resistance from politically influential landlords and is unlikely to succeed. The most effective and socially fair approach would likely be a progressive landholding tax, though this might provoke even greater resistance from landlords.

6.3 Support for Large-Scale Agriculture

The strongest evidence that there are no economies of scale in agriculture in developing countries is the fact that large-scale farms—such as latifundia, estates, haciendas, and plantations—were all established by the authority of colonial or post-independence governments, rather than through the market mechanism. If economies of scale existed, wealthy individuals would have purchased land and established large farms. However, this has not occurred. Once large-scale farms are established by force, even if they are managed inefficiently, smallholders lack the financial means to buy them out, and these large farms persist indefinitely.

Nevertheless, plantations had a certain raison d'être. Establishing a plantation required clearing the jungle and constructing infrastructure such as roads and power lines in previously inaccessible wilderness. Since crops grown on plantations must be processed while still fresh, it was necessary to manage operations so that harvesting was carried out systematically and processing facilities operated at full capacity at all times. However, the production of crops on plantations itself does not benefit from economies of scale. This is because it is difficult to monitor the largely manual work performed by laborers. In other words, as discussed in Box 4.1, *family farming remains the fundamental organization in agriculture*. In developing countries in South Asia and Africa, when comparing medium-sized farms of 3–5 hectares with small-scale farms of 1–3 hectares, the latter tend to have higher yields (production per unit of land). This is because small-scale farms primarily rely on family labor. This phenomenon, known as the *inverse relationship between farm size and productivity*, is widely observed in South Asia and Africa.

Let us compare the long-term changes in plantation-based production in the Philippines and smallholder-based production in Thailand for sugar and pineapple (see ◘ Fig. 6.1). In Thailand, where infrastructure was gradually developed, factory managers began to contract with smallholders to stagger harvest times, thereby keeping processing facilities running at full capacity. If smallholders are more efficient producers than plantations, and if transactions between the two proceed smoothly, then production efficiency in Thailand should surpass that of

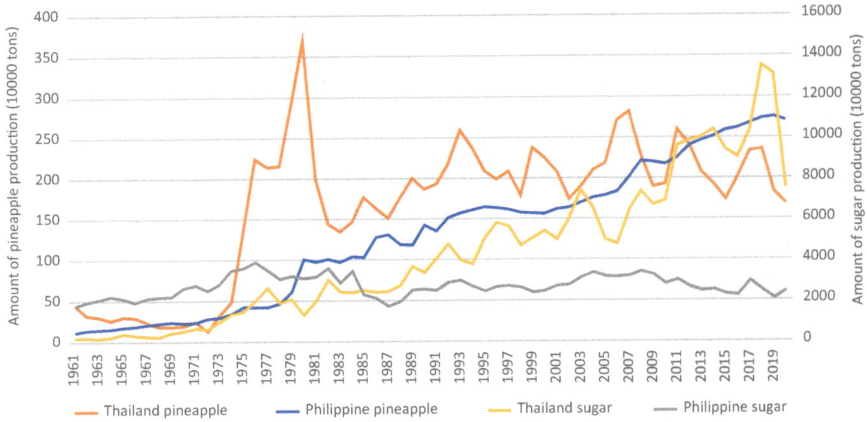

6

Fig. 6.1 Changes in production of sugar and pineapple in Thailand and the Philippines (FAOSTAT various years)

the Philippines. If this is the case, we would expect to see a greater expansion of cultivated area and increased production in Thailand. As evident from the figure, Thailand's growth in sugar production has far outpaced that of the Philippines. As Hayami (2001) pointed out, this indicates that the advantages of plantations inevitably diminish as infrastructure improves. However, in the case of pineapple, although Thailand's production greatly exceeded that of the Philippines in the late 1970s, Thai production subsequently declined, and the Philippines eventually surpassed it. One possible interpretation is that land reform dismantled pineapple plantations in the Philippines, leading to a resurgence of efficient smallholder production. Unfortunately, since some areas of Mindanao are a conflict zone, it has not been possible for me to visit and confirm this directly.[3]

Since the sharp rise in grain prices (food crisis) in 2009, there has been a surge of foreign companies seeking to purchase land and establish large-scale farms in Africa. Some of these companies are domestic. A major issue facing many African countries is that land is state-owned. In countries such as Mozambique, Tanzania, and Ethiopia, which at one time pursued socialism, farmland cultivated by smallholders is officially owned by the state. As a result, both domestic and foreign companies have acquired farmland with government approval. In some cases, it appears that local farmers have been displaced to make way for large-scale farms.[4] In Ethiopia, a major Indian corporation acquired as much as

3 In Thailand, pineapples are mainly produced for canning, which requires less stringent quality standards, whereas in the Philippines, the focus is on fresh fruit, which demands higher freshness and quality. As a result, effective coordination in production and shipment is crucial, and this may explain the advantages of plantation systems there.

4 In Tanzania, land from defunct former state-owned large farms have been sold to foreign companies.

300,000 hectares of farmland for rice production, causing significant social problems. While there is no definitive evidence and caution is warranted, it seems to me that this constitutes a policy failure at the expense of poor farmers.[5] It is also concerning that these large-scale farms have not reported their results transparently. According to experts, many foreign companies have purchased land but have not yet begun production. In some cases, rather than cultivating the land themselves, they have turned the local farmers who previously worked the land into tenant farmers. This is tantamount to the emergence of a new class of large landowners.

What, then, is the situation with large-scale farms supported by the government? Although wages are low, managing agricultural laborers is difficult, so large-scale farms are likely to use large machinery. This inevitably reduces employment opportunities for smallholders and negatively impacts their livelihoods. Moreover, since wages are already low, labor-saving measures offer little benefit to the farm operators themselves. Will large-scale machinery actually be used efficiently? For example, large machines are best suited to well-maintained, rectangular fields, but are fields in developing countries shaped in this way? Are there workers capable of maintaining and servicing large machinery? Are farm roads maintained to the extent that large tractors can pass through? Furthermore, if a large tractor breaks down, are the necessary spare parts readily available? The use of large-scale machinery is more advantageous in developed countries, where fields are typically rectangular and repair systems are well-established. Under these circumstances, it is hard to imagine that the large-scale farms envisioned by the president of our theoretical country could be operated efficiently.

Moreover, in countries like Kenya, after white landowners were expelled, it was not the indigenous people, who had lost their land to whites. The new owners were rather politically influential outsiders. Naturally, this led to friction between the two groups, resulting in political conflict.

Ultimately, the large-scale agricultural support policy of the hypothetical country's president deprived small farmers of employment opportunities, leading to stagnation in domestic agricultural production and political turmoil.

6.4 Indiscriminate Social Forestry[6]

In prewar rural Japan, there was a system known as *iriaichi* (common land). Under this system, residents of a village or settlement shared nearby woodlands, where they collected firewood, charcoal, fodder, medicinal herbs, and other forest resources. In early spring, they also conducted controlled burns to kill pests

5 However, there are cases where foreign companies provide guidance on cultivation methods and advance fertilizers and improved seeds under contract farming arrangements. This could be an effective way to overcome market failures.

6 The discussion in this section is based on Otsuka and Place (2001), Takahashi and Otsuka (2016), and Takahashi et al. (2024).

and destroy weed seeds. If residents were allowed to freely collect branches, trees, and fodder from the common land, competition would arise, and overharvesting would occur easily. This was the prevailing view in traditional economics.

Drivers who cut into a congested main road are thinking only of their own benefit, without regard for the inconvenience caused to others, which leads to severe traffic jams. Similarly, people who collect firewood often overlook the fact that their actions make it harder for others to find firewood, leading to overharvesting. This phenomenon is known as the *tragedy of the commons*.

To avoid the tragedy of the commons, rules for resource extraction were established in Japan's iriaichi, preventing overexploitation. First, an annual quota was set to ensure that resources would not be depleted, and extraction rights were, in principle, distributed equally among households. All household members participated equally in communal activities such as controlled burns and weeding. Remarkably similar practices are found today at the foot of the Himalayas in Nepal and India. Farmers who use the woodlands work together to cut vines, plant trees, hire guards, or take turns monitoring to prevent overharvesting. In many cases, resources such as firewood are distributed equally among users according to established rules.

The communal forests in Nepal and India were once degraded, but have been recovering since the introduction of joint management. There is little doubt that this joint management system is effective in preventing overexploitation. Perhaps inspired by this, aid organizations such as the Food and Agriculture Organization of the United Nations (FAO), the Asian Development Bank, the World Bank, and JICA have, since the 1970s, adopted social forestry in reforestation projects aimed at timber production. Also known as community forestry, this system, similar to Japan's iriaichi and Nepal's communal forests, requires that all farmers who use the forest participate in tree planting, jointly care for the trees, and share the proceeds from timber sales equally.

However, the results of social forestry have been disappointing. In August 2013, I was invited to an international conference organized by forestry experts in Nepal, where I had the opportunity to exchange views with them. To produce high-quality timber, activities such as pruning, thinning, and vine cutting are necessary, but according to these experts, farmers managing communal forests for timber are not actively engaging in these tasks.

If that is the case, it is not possible to produce high-quality, expensive timber. The lack of significant income from timber production means that reforestation programs hold little appeal for farmers. This is a serious issue when we wish to absorb carbon dioxide (CO_2) through reforestation and mitigate climate change, yet the reforestation programs implemented in developing countries fail to attract participants. The problem lies in the adoption of social forestry without considering the fundamental differences between coppice forests (an area of woodland in which the trees or shrubs are, or formerly were, cut back to ground level) and high-value timber forests. Like weeds, coppice trees naturally regenerate with new shoots after being cut, requiring little maintenance. In contrast, timber trees will not yield high-quality wood without careful management. In other words, to cultivate valuable timber, it is necessary to prevent overharvesting and ensure that farmers are motivated to care for the trees. Therefore, there must be incentives for farmers to care for the trees.

To understand this issue, let us consider the collapse of the Chinese people's communes. The people's commune was a large organization akin to a town, but by 1978, when the communes began to dissolve, agricultural management was carried out by production teams consisting of, on average, about 25 households. Assuming each household consisted of a couple, each production team comprised roughly 50 workers. Agricultural work was performed collectively, and the harvest was distributed equally among members. The problem was that farmers lacked motivation. Even if a farmer diligently weeded the fields, the resulting increase in production would only translate into a 2% (1/50th) increase in that farmer's income. Even when combined with their spouse's share, the increase in income would only be 4% of the additional output. Under such circumstances, there was little incentive to work hard. In 1978, when the Chinese government issued a decree allowing individual farming "as an exception in particularly poor regions," almost all people's communes were dismantled within four to five years and replaced by the household responsibility system, a form of individual management. As a result, yields per unit of land increased by 40%, and because work was completed more quickly, farmers gained more free time, which led to the rise of rural enterprises (township and village enterprises).

While social forestry is an effective system for preventing the overexploitation of forest resources, in terms of tree management, it closely resembles the people's commune. Under social forestry, Nepalese farmers lack the motivation to care for the trees. In postwar Japan, in response to soaring demand for timber, communal lands were either dissolved and converted into private forests or reforms were implemented to allocate land use rights to individuals while maintaining the communal land system. The advent of tractors drastically reduced the demand for fodder for cattle and horses, and the use of kerosene and electricity sharply decreased the need for firewood and charcoal. As a result, overharvesting of firewood and fodder ceased to be a problem. Then, a postwar housing boom drove timber prices sharply higher, prompting farmers to plant and cultivate timber species such as cedar. What is crucial here is the management of the trees, and for farmers to be motivated to care for the trees diligently, it is rational for them to own the trees themselves. Thus, the communal land system effectively collapsed.

In recent years, the privatization of public forests has also progressed in China and Vietnam. Although the details are unclear, it is presumed that developments similar to those in postwar Japan are occurring.[7] In the case of social forestry promoted by the president of the hypothetical country, the reduction in overexploitation of forest resources led to the successful restoration of coppice forests. Farmers were able to harvest firewood and fodder sustainably, and improvements in erosion and flood control meant that floods and river depletion became rare.

7 Kijima, Sakurai, and Otsuka (2000) have conducted case studies on communal lands in Japan in the postwar period.

However, the program failed to produce valuable timber and thus did not achieve the goal of increasing farmers' incomes through forestry. Therefore, while the above policy was not so disastrous as to be considered "something that should never have been done," it can be described as a policy that "should not have been preferred." If considered rationally, the president should have adopted a policy of *collective prevention of overexploitation and individual care for trees*. In other words, the land of the forest should be collectively owned and managed to prevent overexploitation of resources, while individual ownership of trees would incentivize the production of high-value timber.

If reforestation is to play any role in mitigating climate change, not only the president of this hypothetical country but also international aid organizations and national agencies that have consistently promoted social forestry should re-examine the effectiveness of social forestry initiatives.

6.5 Premature Heavy and Chemical Industrialization

Indonesia and Nigeria are often compared as examples of successful and unsuccessful industrialization, respectively (see Hayami and Godo 2005). Both countries are similar in terms of geographic size and population, and both were oil exporters. However, Indonesia succeeded in industrialization, while Nigeria failed. Why is this the case? Many studies have pointed out that, whereas Nigeria pursued rapid heavy and chemical industrialization, such as the development of its oil refining sector, Indonesia focused on labor-intensive industrialization. Another issue was that the Nigerian government subsidized investment capital for firms, lowering the cost of capital and leading to the adoption of excessively capital-intensive, inappropriate technologies. For successful industrialization, it is important not only to select industries with comparative advantage but also to adopt *appropriate technologies* (► Box 6.2).[8]

Box 6.2 Both Comparative Advantage and AppropriateTechnology Matter
While the importance of comparative advantage has often been emphasized, the concept of appropriate technology has not been discussed as extensively. Appropriate technology refers to labor-intensive technologies that should be adopted in low-wage developing countries. There are various production methods for manufacturing similar products. For example, in weaving cloth, methods range from using handlooms to high-speed looms that use air or water jets to propel the shuttle. In developing countries, capital-intensive (i.e., labor-saving) technologies similar to those adopted in advanced economies are often introduced, raising questions about

8 In addition, Nigeria has faced issues such as neglecting infrastructure investment and political instability.

whether such technologies are truly appropriate. Foreign-affiliated companies, such as joint ventures, tend to aim for high-quality and uniform products; thus, they are prone to adopting advanced, relatively labor-saving modern machinery, even in developing countries. This is because foreign firms, compared to local companies, are less adept at managing workers and therefore prefer to use more capital than labor. Similarly, state-owned enterprises and private firms receiving government subsidies for capital investment also face lower capital costs and tend to adopt modern, capital-intensive technologies.

However, when subsidies are counted, the total cost becomes high. In low-income countries, unless inexpensive labor is utilized, achieving international competitiveness is challenging. It is therefore crucial for low-income countries to select labor-intensive industries and adopt labor-intensive technologies.

Among policymakers in developing countries, there are not a few who mistakenly equate economic modernization with capital-intensive production, automation, heavy and chemical industrialization, and high-tech development. Instead, for economic development, it is essential to select industries appropriate to the country's circumstances and to achieve low-cost production by adopting appropriate labor-intensive technologies.

◘ Figure 6.2 traces the changes in the share of manufacturing in GDP and the proportion of manufactured goods in exports for Nigeria and Indonesia, going back to 1983. Until the early 1980s, both the share of manufacturing in GDP and the share of manufactured goods in exports were extremely low in both countries, with little difference between them. However, thereafter, Nigeria's share of manufacturing in GDP continued to decline, and until the mid-1990s, the share of manufactured goods in exports was virtually zero. Policies aimed at heavy and

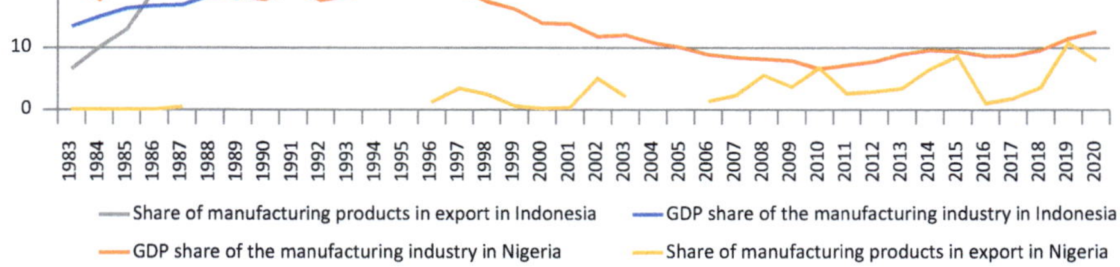

◘ **Fig. 6.2** GDP shares in the manufacturing industry and share of manufacturing products in export in Nigeria and Indonesia (World Bank's World Development Indicators various years)

chemical industrialization were unsustainable and ignored comparative advantage, resulting in almost no export activity. In contrast, in Indonesia, the share of manufacturing in GDP began to rise in the 1980s, and by the 1990s, manufactured goods accounted for around 50% of exports. The main driver was light industrial products, and Indonesia's experience strongly underscores the importance of development strategies based on comparative advantage.

While this section has focused on comparing Nigeria and Indonesia, this comparison appears to represent broader differences between the experiences of Asia and Africa. In fact, even if we consider the cases of Thailand or Bangladesh instead of Indonesia, the conclusion remains unchanged. For low-income countries, a hasty rush toward heavy and chemical industrialization does not lead to sustainable economic development.

6.6 Support for Large Enterprises

Many people tend to believe that there are economies of scale in the operation of large manufacturing factories and that large enterprises are more efficient than small and medium-sized enterprises. Certainly, when looking at giant corporations like Toyota, economies of scale seem apparent. However, Toyota outsources the production of parts and intermediate goods to thousands, even tens of thousands, of subcontractors and sub-subcontractors. If greater scale led to higher production efficiency, Toyota would conduct all production activities, including parts manufacturing, in-house. In fact, such comprehensive in-house production was characteristic of socialist enterprises, whose inefficiency is well documented. In socialist enterprises, production processes often resulted in an oversupply of some parts due to excess capacity, while other parts remained in short supply.

I do not intend to claim that there are no economies of scale in any industry. Still, East Asian examples show that cases without significant economies of scale are far more common. ◘ Table 6.2 compares the trends in the number of employees per manufacturing establishment in Japan, Taiwan, and South Korea. Here, establishment refers to a factory, and since some companies operate multiple factories, the size of an establishment does not necessarily correspond to the size of the company. However, in places like Taiwan, the overwhelming majority of cases involve one company operating a single factory. While it is important to note that these are not company-level data, it is nevertheless striking how small the average establishment size is.

As of 2000, the average number of employees per establishment in Japan and Taiwan was only about 16 to 17. In South Korea, under the Park regime in the late 1970s, policies favored large enterprises and conglomerates known as *chaebols*, resulting in a marked increase in establishment size by 1980. However, these policies ultimately failed, and after 1980, the average establishment size declined. In short, at least at the factory level, significant economies of scale are not the norm.

Table 6.2 Changes in average number of workers per factory in the manufacturing industry in Japan, Taiwan, and South Korea (Japan: various years of Industrial Statistics by Industrial Sector, Ministry of Economy and Industry; Taiwan: 1971, 1981, 1991, 2001 Industrial and Commercial Censuses of Taiwan and Fukien Area and Factory Operation Census and 2020 Economic Statistics, Ministry of Economic Affairs; South Korea: 1970, 1980, 1990, 2000 Report on Mining and Manufacturing Survey and 2020 Korean Statistical Information Service data)

Japan	**1970**	**1980**	**1990**	**2000**	**2020**
Manufacturing industry	20.9	14.9	16.2	16.4	21.3
Food and beverage	12.5	14.0	16.9	21.5	29.2
Textile	11.2	8.0	8.0	6.6	9.8
Garment	12.4	11.7	11.9	9.5	10.3
Metal products	12.3	9.3	10.3	10.4	13.0
Taiwan	**1971**	**1981**	**1991**	**2001**	**2020**
Manufacturing industry	28.2	24.0	19.0	17.2	31.8
Food and beverage	10.5	16.5	18.7	19.7	27.6
Textile	106.6	48.8	26.7	23.5	28.7
Garment	67.7	44.5	28.0	19.3	23.8
Metal products	n/a	8.6	8.5	7.8	4.6
S. Korea	**1970**	**1980**	**1990**	**2000**	**2020[a]**
Manufacturing industry	35.7	65.4	44.0	27.9	41.1
Food and beverage	22.8	39.3	46.0	28.9	n/a
Textile	70.0	81.0	46.0	23.9	n/a
Garment	17.0		36.0	17.7	n/a
Metal products	38.4	80.3	31.0	18.0	n/a

[a] Industry-wise data are unavailable in 2020 in South Korea
n/a means no data is available

Therefore, if the president of our hypothetical country implemented policies favoring large enterprises in pursuit of economies of scale, such measures would not be expected to yield effective results. In the first place, these large enterprises are not suffering from a lack of investment capital. Thus, there is no justification for supporting these companies simply to ease financial constraints. If investment subsidies were provided, there would be a risk of adopting excessively capital-intensive and inappropriate technologies.

If there is any justification for supporting large enterprises, it would be in cases where these firms are at the technological frontier, supplying skilled personnel to other companies, and providing knowledge that is widely imitated. However, if this is the rationale, the degree of support should be determined not by company size, but by the extent of their impact on other firms.

Even small companies can be outstanding. In Ōta Ward in Tokyo, for example, many small firms proudly claim, "Ours is the only company in the world capable of manufacturing this component." Such companies are at the technological frontier and are vulnerable to having their knowledge imitated by others. In fact, most of today's large Japanese corporations originated as small, family-run businesses. If the government is to provide support, it should target firms that generate knowledge spillovers or those unable to realize their growth potential due to financial constraints. Simply supporting companies because they are large is not a sound policy.

6.7 High Minimum Wages

Although this contradicts the original aim of writing an introductory book on development economics that even those unfamiliar with economics can understand, it is necessary to use the theory of supply and demand to explain the effects of minimum wages. Therefore, I will use ◘ Fig. 6.3 to illustrate the most basic supply and demand analysis. The horizontal axis represents the number of workers, and the vertical axis represents wages (either daily or monthly). As wages rise, more people are willing to work, so the supply curve (S) slopes upward. On the other hand, firms are the demanders of labor; as wages increase, they hire fewer workers, and as wages decrease, they hire more. Thus, the demand

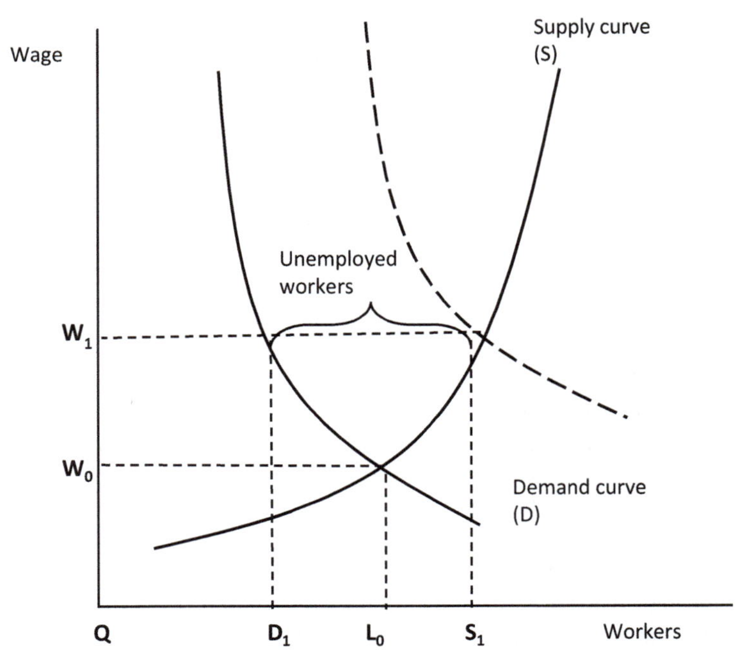

◘ **Fig. 6.3** Demand and supply curves of labor and the effect of the minimum wage law

curve (D) slopes downward. Since many workers want to work and many firms want to hire, it is assumed that neither side has the market power to set wages unilaterally.

When the wage is at the level of W_0, the number of people willing to work is OL_0, and the number of workers firms wish to hire is also OL_0. Therefore, there is neither excess supply nor excess demand for labor. While the actual labor market may not always settle exactly at the intersection of S and D, it is unlikely to deviate significantly from it. If the wage is very high, at W_1, the number of people wanting to work is OS_1, but the number of workers firms wish to hire is only OD_1. The difference between OS_1 and OD_1 represents the number of unemployed. Since the unemployed would be willing to work for lower wages, there is downward pressure on wages. Conversely, if the wage is much lower than W_0, the number of workers firms wish to hire exceeds the number of people willing to work, forcing firms to compete for labor. In this case, there is upward pressure on wages.

The minimum wage policy of the hypothetical country's president can be interpreted as raising W_0 to W_1. If the government enforces this minimum wage, the difference between S and D will result in unemployment. Those who manage to find jobs will be fortunate and better off, but those who cannot will lose their income. In other words, a minimum wage policy forces hardship on the less fortunate workers. In reality, there are differences in worker quality, and it is the poorest, lowest-skilled workers who are most affected by the minimum wage. Considering this, it is difficult to support the implementation of minimum wage laws.

Between 2010 and 2012, the Arab world experienced large-scale anti-government and pro-democracy demonstrations that led to the overthrow of several governments. One reason cited for this unrest is that government policies setting high wage levels resulted in mass unemployment. In addition, the government employed workers with university degrees—degrees that were of little practical value—in equally unproductive government positions. These jobs generated no business income to offset wage payments and consistently ran deficits year after year. As a result, the government could no longer afford to employ large numbers of workers at high wages. Consequently, unemployment continued to rise and became a major political issue. In this respect, the policies of Arab countries and minimum wage policies share a similarity: both have contributed to increased unemployment by setting high wage floors.

Returning to the issue of the minimum wage policy adopted by the president, the minimum wage imposes social costs in the form of unemployment. It, therefore, cannot be considered a desirable policy. Thus, contrary to its intentions, the new president's economic policy achieved little, except for the regrowth of underbrush in devastated forests. Moreover, it failed to promote industrial development, increased poverty and unemployment, and led to a decline in food production. What this charismatic president should have aimed for was to stimulate the development of agriculture, forestry, and industry to create employment opportunities, thereby raising wages. In terms of ◘ Fig. 6.3, this would have meant shifting the labor demand curve to the right, as indicated by the dotted line. To achieve this, it was necessary to promote industrial development and stimulate labor demand by shifting the labor demand curve in ◘ Fig. 6.3 toward the direction of the dotted line. Had this been done, both wages and employment would have increased.

6.8 Summary

There are many policies that developing country governments should avoid, but this chapter has focused on six policies that are both commonly adopted and particularly harmful. The main conclusions are summarized below.

- Land reform policies such as land-to-the-tiller programs result in the eviction of tenant farmers by landlords and a reduction in tenant landholdings, ultimately creating a class of landless agricultural laborers who are the poorest in poor rural areas.
- Support for large-scale agriculture promotes mechanization and deprives farmers of employment opportunities. Moreover, the management of large-scale farms often struggles with labor supervision and rarely succeeds as a business.
- Social forestry projects may succeed in growing trees on barren or degraded land, but due to egalitarian profit-sharing systems, there is little incentive to care for the trees, resulting in failure to produce valuable timber.
- Rapid heavy and chemical industrialization contradicts the flying geese pattern of economic development, which dictates that labor-intensive industries should develop when wages are low and capital-intensive industries should develop when wages rise. Such policies lack rationality and do not contribute to economic development.
- Support for large enterprises does not foster the growth of efficient firms in most cases, as economies of scale are generally absent.
- Minimum wage systems result in increased unemployment and ultimately undermine social stability.

Questions

1. Does the land-to-the-tiller program contribute to the equitable distribution of income and efficiency of agricultural production?
2. Are plantations and estates efficient agricultural organizations?
3. Does the subsidy for large investments in modern, capital-intensive facilities by large manufacturing firms lead to the swift development of the manufacturing industry?
4. Does the increase in the minimum wage lead to higher income for workers?

References

Food and Agriculture Organization of the United Nations. (n.d.) (various years). FAOSTAT food and agriculture data. ► https://www.fao.org/faostat/en/#home.

Hayami, Y. (2001). Ecology, history and development: A perspective from rural Southeast Asia. *World Bank Research Observer, 16*(2), 169–198.
Hayami, Y., & Godo, Y. (2005). *Development economics*. Oxford University Press.
Hayami, Y., & Otsuka, K. (1993). *The economics of contract choice: An agrarian perspective*. Clarendon Press.
Holden, S.T., Otsuka, K., & Deininger, K. (Eds.). (2013). *Land tenure reforms in Asia and Africa: Assessing impacts on poverty and natural resource management.* Palgrave Macmillan.
Japan Ministry of Economy and Industry.n.d. Industrial statistics, census of manufactures, various years.
Kijima, Y., Sakurai, T., & Otsuka, K. (2000). Iriaichi: Collective vs. individualized management of community forests in post-war Japan. *Economic Development and Cultural Change, 48*(4), 867–886.
South Korea. Statistics Korea, Report on Mining and Manufacturing Survey, 1970.
South Korea. Statistics Korea, Report on Mining and Manufacturing Survey, 1980.
South Korea. Statistics Korea, Report on Mining and Manufacturing Survey, 1990.
South Korea. Statistics Korea, Report on Mining and Manufacturing Survey, 2000.
South Korea. Statistics Korea, Korean Statistical Information Service data, 2020.
Otsuka, K. (2007). Efficiency and equity effects of land markets. In R. E. Evenson & P. Pingali (Eds.), *Handbook of agricultural economics, Volume III*. Elsevier.
Otsuka, K., & Place, F. (Eds.). (2001). *Land tenure and natural resource management: A comparative study of agrarian communities in Asia and Africa*. Johns Hopkins University Press.
Otsuka, K., & Place, F. (2014). Evolutionary changes in land tenure and agricultural intensification in Sub-Saharan Africa. In J. Lin and C. Monga (Eds.), *Handbook of Africa and Economics*. Oxford University Press.
Taiwan. Ministry of Economic Affairs, Factory Operation Census, Statistics of economics, 2020.
Taiwan. National Statistics, Report on Industrial and Commercial Censuses of Taiwan and Fukien Area, 1971.
Taiwan. National Statistics, Report on Industrial and Commercial Censuses of Taiwan and Fukien Area, 1981.
Taiwan. National Statistics, Report on Industrial and Commercial Censuses of Taiwan and Fukien Area, 1991.
Taiwan. National Statistics, Report on Industrial and Commercial Censuses of Taiwan and Fukien Area, 2001.
Takahashi, R., & Otsuka, K. (2016). Determinants of forest degradation under private and common property regimes: The case of Ethiopia. *Land Economics, 92*(3), 450–467.
Takahashi, R., Otsuka, K., Tilahun, M., Birhane, E., & Holden, S. (2024). Beyond Ostrom: Randomized experiment of the impact of individualized tree rights on forest management in Ethiopia. *World Development,* 178: 106586.
World Bank. N.D.(various years). *World development indicators*. World Bank DataBank.

What Developing Countries Must Do to Achieve Prosperity

Contents

K. Otsuka, *A Primer on Development Economics*,
Classroom Companion: Economics, https://doi.org/10.1007/978-981-95-5397-6_7

7.1 Introduction

In poor countries, 50%–80% of the population is engaged in agriculture or rural work (see ◘ Table 2.3), and poverty reduction is impossible without agricultural development. Agriculture encompasses not only grain production but also livestock, vegetables, fruit, and floriculture. For example, rose production in countries such as Kenya and Ethiopia employs hundreds of workers in large greenhouses and is essentially indistinguishable from factory production. Thus, in such cases, an industrialization strategy may be more appropriate than a smallholder-centered agricultural development strategy.

For export-oriented vegetables and tropical fruits, trading companies often provide farmers with seeds and fertilizers on credit, along with technical guidance, through contract farming arrangements. In these cases, constraints on capital and technology are minimal, and significant market failures appear to have been largely overcome.[1] Market failures are more pronounced in the production of staple grains.

For example, in the case of rice, wheat, and self-pollinating maize, anyone can reproduce improved seed varieties themselves, making it unprofitable for private firms to develop and sell such seeds. Similarly, advanced cultivation methods can be easily imitated, so it is difficult for private firms to profit from providing consulting services to farmers. Nevertheless, in Uruguay's rice sector, large rice export companies provide detailed production guidance based on soil surveys of each farm, as well as advance payment for fertilizers, storage, and milling services. It is possible that a contract farming-like production system could also be efficient for grains.[2]

However, in order to aim at achieving zero hunger, I would like to focus on how to improve the efficiency of grain production—especially rice and maize—by smallholder farmers in poor countries, particularly in Africa, through means other than contract farming.

Whether in agricultural or industrial development, the first step must be to identify promising crops or products for the country. Agricultural production is heavily influenced by climate and natural conditions, so it is crucial to select crops suited to those conditions. If high productivity has been achieved in regions with climates similar to those of developing countries, it is likely that those crops hold promise. For example, rice in Africa is a case in point. This is because rice productivity in tropical Asia, which has a similar climate, is far higher than in Africa. If adaptive research is conducted and technology is transferred from tropical Asia to Africa, there is a high potential for a dramatic increase in African rice productivity. Similarly, for staple crops such as maize, efforts should be made to improve productivity. Given that large volumes of maize are produced in Africa, the over-

1 However, contract farming may face moral hazards such as farmers using distributed fertilizers for other purposes, selling produce to non-contracted traders, or traders refusing to purchase the contracted crops (Otsuka et al. 2016).

2 In fact, in several African countries such as Côte d'Ivoire, foreign companies and smallholders have begun contract rice farming. However, at least in the case of Côte d'Ivoire, contract rice farming failed due to the companies' insufficient agricultural knowledge.

all economic impact of productivity gains in maize production is expected to be substantial.[3]

In manufacturing, it is necessary to foster industries that can be internationally competitive over the short to medium term. Ideally, the government should support industries selected by private entrepreneurs with a strong vision for the future. However, industries such as apparel, metalworking, leather, and furniture exist in every country and have achieved a certain degree of development even without government support. Industries that have developed spontaneously to some extent can be considered to possess a latent comparative advantage. If there is a nearby country with a similar cultural background, which is more industrialized, it may also be a viable strategy to promote industries that have developed in that country.

For example, Japan serves this role for South Korea and Taiwan, China for Vietnam, and India for Bangladesh. If a latecomer country selects industries appropriate to its stage of development and can imitate technologies and management practices, it may be able to establish a comparative advantage in those industries. However, the specific choice of industries should ultimately be left to the decisions of private entrepreneurs.

7.2 The Fundamental Development Strategy Is the Same for all Industries

Once the target crop sectors or industries for support have been identified, the next step is to determine where market failures exist and to promote the accumulation of intellectual capital, human capital, infrastructure, physical capital, and social capital. ◘ Table 7.1 summarizes the basic concepts. However, it is neither

◘ Table 7.1 Market failures and countermeasures

	Causes for market failure	Countermeasures
Social capital	Injustice in transactions	Rural communities, industrial clusters, and legal restrictions
Human capital	Lack of collateral for human capital investment	Support for training, extension, and education
Infrastructure	Public good	Industrial parks and general public investment
Physical capital	Imperfect information	Support for loans
Intellectual capital	Information spillovers	Support for training and research

3 In inland West Africa and similar regions, the climate is extremely arid, making it impossible to grow maize. As a result, farmers are compelled to produce drought-resistant cereals such as millet and sorghum. However, the productivity of these cereals is extremely low even in Asia, and raising their productivity is a formidable challenge (see ◘ Fig. 4.7).

easy nor necessarily desirable for the government to foster social capital directly. What the government can do is to leverage rural communities with strong mutual trust or industrial clusters where component manufacturers and final product producers are concentrated in a small area and cooperate, to promote the development of agriculture and industry. It is also important for the government to establish legal frameworks to crack down on fraudulent activities. For further discussion on industrial clusters, see ► Sect. 7.3.

Investment in human capital, particularly in education, often falls short due to difficulties in securing financing. The government should actively invest in general education, including the provision of scholarships. Training and extension activities are also important for disseminating practical knowledge to producers. It is important to note that new knowledge is transmitted from those who acquire it to others. While this diffusion is socially desirable, it creates a problem when individuals seek to obtain knowledge for free from those who have participated in training and invested in creating new ideas, without bearing the cost themselves. This is the issue of information spillover, or the "free rider" problem. If everyone is motivated to free ride, training programs that charge tuition cannot be sustained. Therefore, government support for training is necessary.

Human capital and intellectual capital are sometimes difficult to distinguish. Knowledge related to new inventions or innovations is clearly a form of intellectual capital. However, when someone acquires useful new knowledge at school or gains new management or technical skills through training, this can be seen as an increase in human capital, but it can also be regarded as an enhancement of the firm's intellectual capital. If intellectual capital can also be imitated, then the private benefits of acquiring intellectual capital may fall short of the social benefits. Ideally, government support is also desirable in this area.

Infrastructure has the characteristics of a public good, meaning that once it is in place, everyone can use it regardless of whether they contributed to its cost. This creates an incentive to free ride, which often leads to underinvestment. To prevent this, public investment is necessary. Alternatively, policies such as constructing industrial parks or special economic zones and concentrating infrastructure development in those areas can be considered. By attracting firms producing similar products to industrial parks, the development of industrial clusters can also be promoted. This is something that local governments in China have actively pursued. Regarding investment in physical capital, lenders tend to be reluctant to provide financing because they lack sufficient information about the borrower's ability or behavior. Therefore, government support is also needed for such investments.

Up to this point, the discussion has merely enumerated key issues and does not yet constitute a development strategy. Simply stating that investment in all forms of capital is important is not a strategy. A strategy must make effective use of limited resources. For example, a small unit launches a preemptive attack on the enemy at point A, anticipating that the enemy will retreat toward point B. Then the main force assembles there to launch a surprise attack—this is what constitutes a strategy.

The development strategy I envision involves determining the optimal sequence and types of capital investments. Solving this problem would provide significant intellectual support (see 7.1). In the following sections of this chapter, I will consider more concrete development strategies for both agriculture and manufacturing. However, given the many uncertainties that remain, this chapter aims to outline the contours of a desirable strategy and to draft a preliminary *blueprint.*

Box 7.1 Intellectual Support as the Most Crucial Form of Foreign Assistance

As repeatedly discussed in this book, there is no consensus among development economists or practitioners regarding effective development strategies, whether for agricultural or industrial development. In such circumstances, providing evidence that can inform the construction of effective development strategies should be considered an essential component of foreign aid activities. Unfortunately, few experts recognize this need.

Let me illustrate with an example. It is well known that Japanese aid is characterized by a higher proportion of infrastructure investment compared to other countries. Some countries are critical of this approach, while others view it favorably. However, these are merely subjective judgments. If Japan had objectively estimated the returns on its past infrastructure investments, the situation would have been markedly different. If the returns were found to be very high, Japanese aid would not only have been highly regarded but could also have contributed to improving the overall efficiency of foreign aid by influencing the policies of other advanced countries and international organizations. Alternatively, if Japan had estimated the conditions under which certain investments yield higher returns, this would have provided valuable information for the formulation of development strategies.

There is no space here for a detailed discussion, but in reality, estimating returns is not a simple task. Accurate evaluation requires both on-the-ground knowledge and methodologies grounded in economic theory. In other words, there are numerous areas in which practitioners and researchers must collaborate to deliver effective support. While it is regrettable that this was not done earlier, it is encouraging that the Japan International Cooperation Agency (JICA) has recently begun to engage development economists. This is a highly welcome development. I hope that, as a result, Japan will assume international leadership in the area of intellectual support. I myself am committed to contributing as much as possible to this effort.

7.3 Agricultural Development Strategies in Africa[4]

To resolve Africa's food shortages with a view to achieving zero hunger, realizing a Green Revolution is an essential prerequisite. This requires the development of promising crop varieties, the establishment of appropriate cultivation techniques, and the dissemination of these innovations. The modern rice variety, IR8, first de-

4 The discussion in this section draws heavily on Otsuka and Larson (2013, 2016), Otsuka et al. (2023, 2024).

veloped by the International Rice Research Institute (IRRI), was short-statured and high-yielding, inheriting these traits from Taiwanese varieties, while its adaptation to tropical environments was derived from Indonesian varieties. Generally, when transferring Asian varieties to Africa, it is desirable to conduct adaptive research to improve the varieties suited to African conditions. Interestingly, however, in the case of rice production, including the varieties themselves, a considerable degree of direct technology transfer is possible. In the Lower Moshi irrigation project in Tanzania, developed with significant support from JICA, modern varieties developed by IRRI demonstrated high yields. While some adaptive research is desirable, in the case of rice, the potential for technology transfer from tropical Asia to Africa is high. This is especially true in irrigated areas, where production environments become more similar, thereby increasing the feasibility of directly transferring improved rice varieties.

If improved technologies are developed, or if directly transferable technologies are identified, what should be the next step? It is neither investing in irrigation, nor providing subsidies to make seeds and chemical fertilizers easily accessible, nor even investing in transportation and communication infrastructure to streamline logistics. This is because farmers are still unaware of the new technologies and have not adopted them. When traditional, unimproved varieties are used, the application of chemical fertilizers yields little increase in production. Therefore, farmers show little interest in purchasing chemical fertilizers. Similarly, if improved varieties are not adopted, the presence or absence of irrigation makes little difference in yields. As a result, farmers are not particularly interested in irrigation either. Undoubtedly, the next step after technology transfer and development is the dissemination of these technologies to farmers. However, in the case of rice, there are very few agricultural extension officers in Africa who are well-versed in rice cultivation techniques. The weakness of the technology dissemination system thus constitutes the greatest constraint to the Green Revolution for lowland rice in Africa.

Conversely, strengthening this system is the most direct route to achieving a successful Green Revolution for rice. In Asia, a paddy field is defined as farmland with bunds. However, in Africa, there are surprisingly many paddy fields without bunds. Without bunds, even a brief dry spell can cause the paddy field to dry out completely. When water is lacking, weeds proliferate. Furthermore, without bunds, fertilizers applied to the field flow into neighboring fields, reducing incentives to apply fertilizers. Equally important to constructing bunds is land leveling, which involves making the paddy field flat. Land leveling is a crucial cultivation technique for ensuring uniform and healthy rice growth. In unlevelled paddy fields, some areas suffer from water shortages while others are flooded. Nevertheless, there are many unlevelled paddy fields in Africa. Estimates suggest that constructing bunds and leveling the fields can increase rice yields per hectare by at least 50%, and potentially even double them. In Asia, these basic cultivation techniques have been almost perfectly disseminated. Thus, improving rice productivity requires not only the introduction of improved varieties but also the widespread adoption of appropriate cultivation techniques. I believe that, with a

Table 7.2 Paddy yield (ton/ha) ad adoption of improved cultivation practices in Eastern Uganda[a]

	Training villages	Non-training villages
Adopters of all improved practices[b]	3.68	1.22
Adopters of 3 practices	3.02	n/a[c]
Adopters of 2 practices	2.54	1.95
Adopters of 1 practice	2.11	1.89
Non-adopters	0.79	1.47
% of users of inorganic fertilizer	3.8	0.0
% of adopters of modern varieties	41.9	5.0
No. of sample farms	150	75

[a] This table is based on Kijima (2014) and Kijima et al. (2012)
[b] Improved practices include bund construction, levelling, straight-row transplanting, and proper timing of transplanting
[c] Not available

strong technology dissemination system, realizing a Green Revolution for rice in Africa is not a mere dream.[5]

Let me present evidence. Tables 7.2 and 7.3 show the relationship between paddy yields and technology adoption in Uganda and Ghana, respectively. JICA provided training on production techniques, as well as the installation of simple irrigation facilities partially, in the two villages in Eastern Uganda. Table 7.2 shows paddy yield separately according to the number of improved cultivation practices adopted, i.e., bunding, levelling, proper timing and transplanting, and transplanting in rows, in the two training villages and one non-training village, which are located in the same areas with similar climate. It is clear that the average yield rises as more of cultivation practices adopted in the training villages. The yield of 3.68 tons per hectare, when all four improved cultivation practices are adopted, is very high even by international standard and more than a half of farmers belong to this group. The yield is only 2.11 tons per hectare when only one improved practice is adopted and only 0.79 tons per hectare when none of them is adopted. This significant difference in rice yield suggests that there is complementarity among improved cultivation practices. In contrast, the yield in non-training village is low and there is no clear relationship between the number of cultivation practices applied and the yield. I suspect that farmers do not understand meaning of improved cultivation practices in non-training village, which

5 In Africa, about 12% of paddy fields are located in flood-prone areas known as floodplains. In such regions, modern short-statured varieties are at a disadvantage, and bunds are less important. There is still no clear strategy for developing these areas, but it is necessary to examine whether submergence-tolerant rice varieties recently developed by IRRI are effective, or whether constructing dams or reservoirs upstream would be economically viable.

Table 7.3 Paddy yield (ton/ha) and adoption of improved cultivation practices in Northern Ghana (deGraft-Johnson et al. 2014)

	Non-adopters	Partial adopters				Perfect adopters
		Only modern inputs[a]	At least one modern inputs[b]	Modern inputs, bunding, and leveling	At least modern inputs, bunding, and leveling	
Yield (ton/ha)	1.46	1.7	1.95	1.98	2.33	2.59
Labor inputs (days/ha)	102	152	187	204	238	264
Factor share of labor (%)	61.5	62.6	54.6	52.8	49.5	47.6
No. of sample farms	63	78	349	37	84	47

[a] MVs and inorganic fertilizer
[b] In addition to MVs and inorganic fertilizer, at least one of the three improved cultivation practices (i.e., bunding, leveling, and dibbling) is adopted

led to the absence of the relationship between yield and the number of cultivation practices adopted.

These analytical results highlight the importance of proper technical training and demonstrate that the dissemination of new technologies can significantly enhance rice productivity. In the case of northern Ghana, as shown in Table 7.3, an Asian-style rice production technology dissemination project was implemented around the year 2000. Here, too, it is clear that yields have increased substantially through the use of modern varieties (MVs), chemical fertilizers, bund construction, and land leveling. This is a purely rainfed rice area, with no irrigation facilities whatsoever. Such production environments span a vast region, extending from northern Côte d'Ivoire to northern Nigeria, and the discovery of significant potential for yield increases in these areas is of great significance.

In rice production, the contribution of improved technologies to productivity is greater when irrigation facilities are available. This implies that the dissemination of new, improved varieties increases the rate of return on irrigation investments, thereby stimulating further investment in irrigation. In Asia, large-scale investments in irrigation infrastructure accelerated during the early stages of the Green Revolution. Whether on a large or small-scale, the effective use of irrigation facilities requires the efficient allocation of irrigation water to paddy

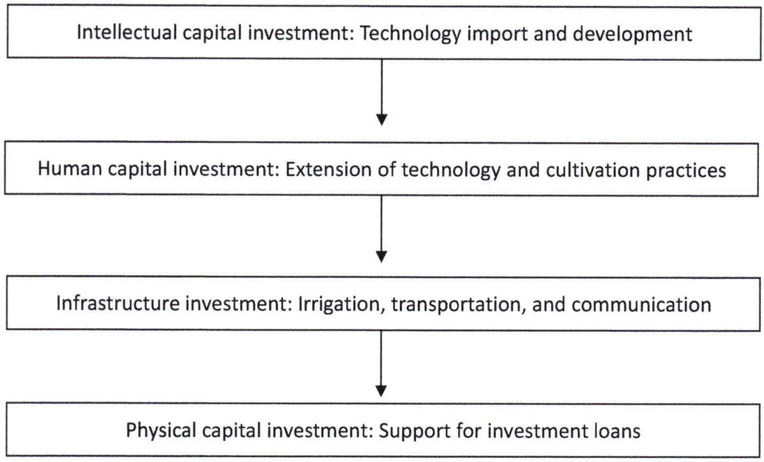

Fig. 7.1 Strategies for agricultural development

fields and the maintenance of these facilities by farmers, both of which are critically important. Therefore, social capital plays a crucial role in this context. Furthermore, the adoption of new technologies leads to increased cash expenditures, such as for fertilizers, which in turn raises the demand for credit. In Asia, a practice emerged in which rice millers who also dealt in fertilizers would advance the cost of fertilizers to farmers, to be repaid with interest after the harvest. However, this practice is observed only in some irrigated areas in Africa. The reason why such advances are made is that the young rice plants growing in the paddy fields effectively serve as collateral. There are cases in Africa where foreign companies are beginning to offer similar business models, advancing the cost of fertilizers and seeds to farmers, to be repaid with interest after the harvest. Here again, the establishment of trust between farmers and suppliers—a form of social capital—is crucial to the success of these new transactions.

Figure 7.1 summarizes the above discussion and presents a concise strategy for agricultural development. First, investment in technology transfer and development, aimed at enhancing intellectual capital (or establishing promising technologies), is a prerequisite. Once promising technologies are established, the second step is their dissemination. The third step involves investment in irrigation and the development of transport and communication infrastructure in regions where new technologies are being adopted. Finally, in areas where the demand for credit has increased, it is necessary to enhance the physical capital investment by offering credit systems.

In grain-producing agriculture, human capital—particularly education—is not especially important. Even in Asia, except for the 1970s when the spread of MVs began, there is little evidence that education had a significant impact on technology adoption or productivity improvement. As previously noted, rice is the most promising crop in Africa. In the case of rice, the water flowing into paddy fields

Table 7.4 Development of intensive maize cultivation in Kenya[a]

	2004	2012
No. of sample farms	699	692
Chemical fertilizer input (N· P· K kg/ha)	57.14	47.11
Organic fertilizer input (kg/ha)	2312	2786
Adoption rate of improved maze varieties (%)	58.30	82.20
Intercropping ratio with beans (%)	86.10	79.30
Ratio of cultivated area of Napier grass (%)	13.30	11.60
Number of non-improved cattle (per household)	1.85	1.17
Number of improved cattle (per household)	2.95	1.93
Maize yield (kg/ha)	1907	2125
Value of maize yield (KES/ha)[b]	34,829	38,082
Total value of maize and bean yield (KES/ha)[b]	45,544	46,598
Total value of yield including other crops (KES/ha)[b]	58,346	67,295

a Value is expressed by the 2009 real price
[b] KES stands for Kenyan shilling

brings various nutrients, and algae in the water and soil fix atmospheric nitrogen, resulting in minimal soil degradation. Therefore, rice can be considered the most sustainable crop.

In contrast, the management of soil fertility is more challenging for upland crops. When cultivated without fertilizers, soil fertility declines rapidly and yields decrease accordingly. To prevent this, it is necessary to replenish the nutrients that crops extract from the soil. How, then, do African farmers achieve sustainable production of upland crops? In regions with high population density, there is little opportunity to restore soil fertility through fallow periods, so farmers must maintain the fertility of their cultivated land year after year. Here, we introduce the case of maize cultivation in the highlands of Kenya, which appears to be a good example of such sustainable practice (see Table 7.4). Here, the National Graduate Institute for Policy Studies (GRIPS) has conducted periodic surveys of the same group of farmers since 2004. The first point to note is that, to maintain soil fertility, farmers apply not only chemical fertilizers but also compost (organic fertilizer) and practice intercropping with legumes. The compost is produced from the manure of crossbred cattle (hybrids of indigenous zebu and European breeds). These improved cattle are at least a few times more productive than indigenous breeds, both in terms of milk and manure production. Improved cattle are kept in barns for milking and manure collection. Consequently, farmers cultivate fodder crops—particularly Napier grass, which originates from Africa—on part of their land. Since legumes fix atmospheric nitrogen, intercropping with legumes is functionally equivalent to applying nitrogen fertilizer. As a result, intercropping is practiced on approximately 80% of maize fields. While maize yields alone are not particularly high, averaging around 2 tons per hectare, the total value of production per hectare, including legumes, is quite high and shows an upward trend.

Although this may not amount to a Green Revolution, productivity has improved significantly. Interestingly, the practices of barn-based cattle rearing, fodder crop cultivation, and compost utilization mirror the essence of the Agricultural Revolution that preceded the Industrial Revolution in England. However, there has been little research on this new technological system that combines crop cultivation and improved cattle, such as the optimal degree and method of intercropping maize and legumes, the best combination of compost and chemical fertilizers, or the ideal frequency of rotating fodder crops with maize. In other words, it is no exaggeration to say that an optimal technological system for maize cultivation has yet to be established. Moreover, the optimal system varies by location, which is a distinctive feature of maize. This is a fundamental difference from rice, for which promising technological systems have already been established and can be widely applied across regions (Otsuka et al. 2024). If a Green Revolution in maize is to be achieved, the establishment of a technological system is an urgent priority. Once this is accomplished, strengthening the system for technology dissemination will become a key issue. If the resulting increase in maize production is supported by improvements in transport infrastructure and other measures, further productivity gains can be expected. In summary, the path to a Green Revolution should proceed through the following steps: selection of promising crops → international transfer of technology and improvement of technology through adaptive research → dissemination of new technology and training→ investment in infrastructure and provision of credit.

7.4 Development Strategies for Manufacturing[6]

While the Green Revolution is critically important for achieving zero hunger, its contribution to poverty reduction is limited because its effect on employment generation is limited, according to the Asian experience (David and Otsuka 1994). To achieve the goal of eradicating poverty, it is essential to develop labor-intensive manufacturing industries that provide ample employment opportunities.

Manufacturing industries often tend to cluster geographically. During the Industrial Revolution, firms producing cotton yarn concentrated in Manchester, while steel producers clustered in Birmingham. In Japan, there have been many examples of industrial clusters: the silk-reeling industries in Okaya and Maebashi before World War II, the ongoing silk weaving industries in Nishijin and Kiryu, postwar motorcycle manufacturing in Hamamatsu, and, more recently, metalworking in Ōta Ward in Tokyo and Higashi-Osaka, as well as automobile manufacturing in Toyota City. Industrial clusters refer to regions where firms produc-

6 The discussion in this section relies on Sonobe and Otsuka (2006, 2011, 2014) and Otsuka et al. (2018).

ing similar or related products (such as final goods and components) are densely concentrated. However, pyramid-shaped clusters, such as in Toyota City—where Toyota Motor Corporation sits at the top, followed by first-, second-, and third-tier subcontractors—are rare in developing countries. Interestingly, industrial clusters are found in large numbers in Taiwan, China, Vietnam, Bangladesh, India, Pakistan, and even in Latin America and Africa. In Taiwan, clusters are so prevalent that it is difficult to find industries that are not clustered. In China, the development of manufacturing is said to have relied heavily on the growth of industrial clusters. At least in the early stages of cluster development, numerous micro and small enterprises emerge, creating employment opportunities for many unskilled workers. This job creation is critically important for poverty reduction. Some development economists mistakenly assume that Africa lacks industrial clusters, but this is a serious misconception.

Why, then, do manufacturing industries tend to cluster together? The first reason is that such clustering facilitates the formation of social capital. Industrial clusters, where firms are located in close proximity, share characteristics similar to those of rural communities, where farming households live side by side. Many entrepreneurs know each other, and any antisocial behavior quickly becomes the subject of rumors. Therefore, in order to continue operating within the cluster, entrepreneurs are expected to act with integrity. As a result, transactions of parts and intermediate goods between firms proceed smoothly. The second advantage is the ease with which new knowledge can be imitated. In several apparel industry clusters, it is reported that when a new, popular design emerges, almost all firms begin producing similar products within two to 3 days. While this is a benefit, there is also a drawback. If too many entrepreneurs focus on easy imitation, there will be little incentive for other firms to develop new products or technologies. The third advantage is that skilled workers, engineers, designers, and merchants are drawn to industrial clusters, making it easier to secure the necessary labor and services.

Industrial clusters can be classified as either stagnant or growing. Unfortunately, most clusters in Africa are of the stagnant type, while those in East Asia are predominantly growth-oriented—the key distinction between the two lies in the presence or absence of *innovation*. While innovation often brings to mind breakthroughs in technological advances, in many cases, *numerous incremental improvements* are even more important in practice. In fact, even minor innovations can have a significant impact on business performance. The typical development pattern of industrial clusters is explained in ▶ ▶ Box 7.2, which summarizes our observations in more than 25 case studies of industrial clusters in Asia and Africa. What should be emphasized here is that without *multifaceted innovation*—in product quality, marketing, labor management, and the management of procured parts—firms will not thrive.

Box 7.2 Development Patterns of Industrial Clusters

Together with my colleague Professor Tetsushi Sonobe and others, I have conducted case studies using questionnaires on more than 25 industrial clusters in Japan, Taiwan, China, Vietnam, Bangladesh, Pakistan, Ghana, Tanzania, Kenya, Ethiopia, Senegal, and South Africa (Sonobe and Otsuka 2006, 2011, 2014). Among these clusters, some have developed while others have stagnated, so there is no doubt that heterogeneity has been observed. Nevertheless, despite differences in industries and social institutions, it is also true that there are striking similarities in the development patterns of these clusters.

For products such as apparel and leather shoes, which are easy to manufacture but difficult to sell, it is often former merchants who start new businesses. On the other hand, for products such as machinery and machine parts, which are difficult to manufacture but relatively easy to sell—since many customers are knowledgeable about machinery and will accept products of a certain quality—engineers and skilled workers are more likely to become entrepreneurs. These entrepreneurs may not necessarily have high levels of formal education. Still, they are people of innate talent and ingenuity who begin producing imitations of popular imported products from advanced countries through trial and error. In developing countries, there are often many raw materials and components that are not readily available, even if they are accessible in advanced countries, making entrepreneurship a considerable challenge for adaptation.

Naturally, the quality of the products is poor. Since the prospects of these new businesses are uncertain to outsiders, lack of funding is also a major issue. In fact, initial investments are overwhelmingly financed through personal funds or loans from relatives and friends. We refer to this stage of development as the *initiation phase*. Establishing production methods and developing sales channels involves considerable challenges. Still, as long as the products are cheaper than imports, many consumers are willing to purchase even low-quality goods, resulting in substantial profits. This profit can be described as entrepreneurial profit. While starting something new is always difficult, imitation is relatively easy. To share these profits, followers begin to enter the industry. This is particularly common among employees of the pioneering firms who start their own businesses. These new firms use the same raw materials and components, adopt the same production methods, and sell similar products in the domestic market, just as the original entrepreneurs did. As the number of firms increases in this way, industrial clusters are formed (see ◘ Fig. 7.2).

During this period, imitation prevails, resulting in little improvement in product quality and productivity. If the imitators lack the necessary capabilities, the overall productivity of the cluster may even decline. We refer to this period as the *quantity expansion phase*. During the quantity expansion phase, large volumes of low-quality products flood the domestic market, leading to price erosion. As a result, as indicated by the dotted line in ◘ Fig. 7.2, the number of firms tends to increase, but profitability deteriorates. When this low level of profitability persists, the result is a stagnant industrial cluster.

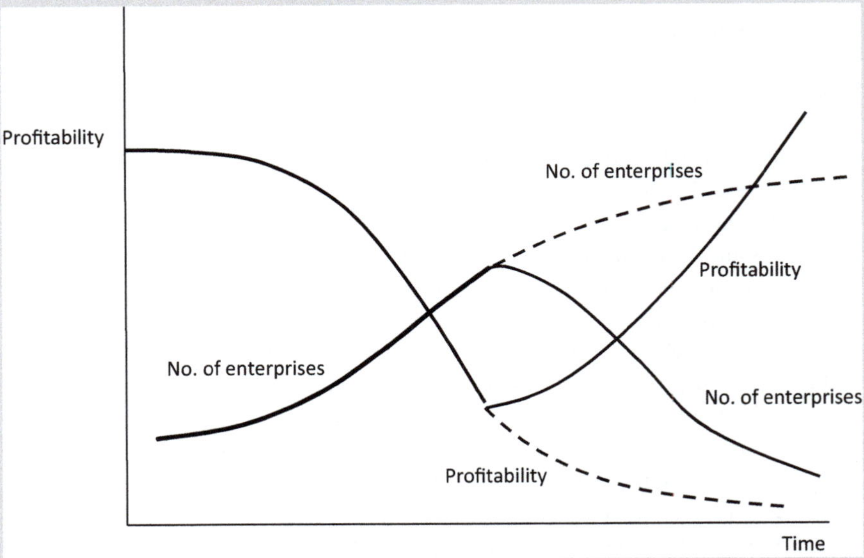

Fig. 7.2 Process of cluster-based industrial development (Sonobe and Otsuka 2011, p. 6)

The reason for poor profitability in industrial clusters is clear: it is due to low product quality. In response, innovative entrepreneurs strive to improve quality by utilizing higher-grade raw materials and components, installing more efficient machines, hiring competent designers and skilled technicians, and prioritizing quality enhancement. Although improving quality is not too difficult, it is even more difficult to convince consumers of the value of higher-quality products. For example, products from Wenzhou, China—a region known for the rapid growth of private enterprises—were once synonymous with poor quality. Although innovative entrepreneurs began working to improve product quality in the late 1980s, consumers were slow to recognize these improvements, and it was difficult to sell higher-quality products at commensurately higher prices. Because these firms used better materials and paid higher wages, their profitability initially worsened. To address this, innovative firms sought to establish brands, increase the number of sales staff to persuade consumers, and operate franchise or company-owned stores to enhance their reputation. If successful, sales would grow, profitability would recover, employment would increase, and, with luck, exports to advanced economies would become possible.

At this stage, management becomes more complex, involving labor management, quality control, and other sophisticated practices. Firms that master all these aspects achieve great success. We refer to this period as the *quality improvement phase*. Whether quality improvement occurs depends on the emergence of such *multifaceted innovation*. In other words, whether innovation occurs at the end of the quantity expansion phase determines whether the cluster evolves into a growth-oriented one or remains a stagnant industrial cluster.

It is worth recalling that "Made in Japan" was once synonymous with poor quality until the 1950s. However, through improvements in product quality, the development of quality control circles, the establishment of Japanese-style management, and advances in marketing, Japan succeeded in completely transforming this image.

Many firms unable to keep up with multifaceted innovation go bankrupt or are absorbed by more innovative companies, so the number of firms decreases during the quality improvement phase (see ◘ Fig. 7.2). Of course, the overall scale of production in the industry increases. Successful entrepreneurs tend to be highly educated, often have work experience with foreign firms, and are well-versed in overseas technology and management practices. In some cases, producer associations take the lead in establishing training centers to learn foreign technologies and raise the overall level of the industrial cluster. Such efforts were observed in Japan's prewar silk weaving clusters and in recent clusters of medical instrument manufacturers in Pakistan. Because of information spillovers, when firms are reluctant to generate and adopt innovative ideas, these actions by producer associations can be highly effective.

Here, let us consider how to revitalize stagnant industrial clusters where innovation has not emerged. The very existence of such clusters, even without government support, suggests that the industry possesses a latent comparative advantage. The government's role should be: (1) providing credit to facilitate investment in physical capital, such as factory building and machinery; (2) investing in infrastructure; and (3) promoting investment in human and intellectual capital. The key issue is where to begin.

Suppose we start by extending credit to small enterprises within these stagnant clusters. Would this pose any problems? In fact, there are serious issues. The primary challenge is identifying which entrepreneurs are promising. Among them are individuals who run family businesses as a side activity and lack both the motivation and capability to pursue multifaceted innovation. Extending credit to such individuals will not lead to high-return investments or overall industrial development. Therefore, a strategy that begins with credit provision is misguided. Nevertheless, many experts continue to believe that a lack of credit is the primary reason for the failure of the growth of small enterprises.

What about starting with infrastructure investment? The challenge here is deciding where to build roads, water and sewage systems, power lines, and ports. In the long run, it is desirable to develop such infrastructure in many regions to raise the standard of living. However, given budget constraints, priority areas must be selected. Should the focus be on urban areas, rural areas, or stagnant industrial clusters? This is a difficult decision. If the industrial cluster in question has promising prospects, it may be appropriate to concentrate infrastructure investment there, or, as seen in China and Ethiopia, to establish industrial zones with well-developed infrastructure to foster cluster formation. However, how can we determine whether a given cluster is indeed promising? Without relevant information, a development strategy that begins with infrastructure investment is unlikely to succeed.

What if we begin by providing training to managers of micro, small, and medium-sized enterprises, imparting advanced overseas technologies and management knowledge? One issue is that managers often fail to recognize the value of the knowledge gained through training. This is similar to how graduate students may not appreciate the value of graduate education until they complete their studies. However, recent empirical research (Otsuka 2024) has begun to show that management training can indeed improve managerial efficiency. If this is the case, more managers will eventually come to appreciate the value of such training. For example, when Japanese-style Kaizen management training was provided—teaching the so-called 5S principles (sort, set in order, shine, standardize, and sustain) and so on—many African managers highly value these practices. Entrepreneurs who have the capacity to understand and the willingness to implement such new knowledge have improved their business performance through training. Production costs tend to decrease, sales increase, and sensitivity to quality control improves. As a result of higher profitability, these firms seek to expand their factories through further investment.

It is important to emphasize here that training not only contributes to the accumulation of human and intellectual capital but also serves a crucial function in identifying promising firms. Just as in university lectures, the abilities of participants become apparent during training. Therefore, the first step in revitalizing stagnant industrial clusters should be investment in human and intellectual capital through training. This will lead to increased profitability and the discovery of innovative firms seeking to scale up. These are the firms that should be prioritized for access to industrial zones and infrastructure. As the performance of such firms improves, they will accumulate some internal funds, and banks will become more willing to lend. Nevertheless, the costs of constructing new large factories and purchasing new high-quality machinery can be substantial. If the future of the industry remains uncertain, the profitability of such investments is also uncertain. In such cases, the government should support the provision of credit.

To sum up, in order to develop manufacturing industries, the first task is to find out promising industries, followed by learning advanced technology and management methods from abroad through training. Further policy support for the construction of industrial zones and the provision of credit should be implemented. These are summarized as *strategies for development of the manufacturing industry* in ◘ Fig. 7.3.

The fundamental sequence—enhancement of intellectual/human capital, development of infrastructure, and accumulation of physical capital—is essentially the same in both agricultural and industrial development cases. However, in manufacturing, there are the additional challenges of selecting promising industries and products, increasing formal education, and, under government budget constraints, focusing on promoting specific regions such as industrial zones, which distinguishes it from agriculture. Transformation of capital-intensive technology learned from developed countries to labor-intensive technology adapted to labor-abundant poor economies plays a critical role (Otsuka and Hashino 2026). Regarding the selection of promising industries, it is advisable to target existing industrial clusters, at least initially. In addition, by examining the experiences of

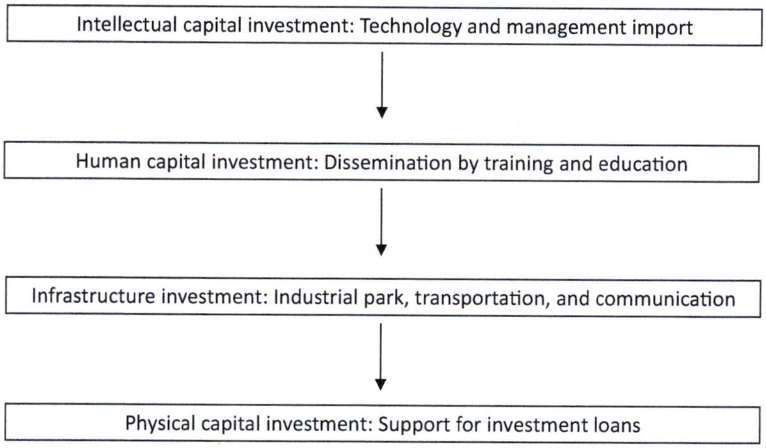

Fig. 7.3 Strategies for development of the manufacturing industry

other countries and the domestic context, consulting with experts, and engaging in discussions with international organizations such as the World Bank and aid agencies from advanced economies, it is desirable to identify industries that could establish a comparative advantage in the future. Furthermore, developing infrastructure and attracting foreign companies to industrial zones is also a desirable development strategy. Foreign firms possess advanced technologies and management know-how, providing local companies with excellent opportunities to learn from abroad. To attract FDI, however, it is crucial to eliminate unnecessary regulations and create a liberal environment that fosters production and investment. Otherwise, foreign companies may shy away from direct investment.

7.5 Development of Modern Service Industries

I have no research experience regarding modern service industries utilizing IT, nor are there many field-based empirical studies by other researchers, so I do not have a strong sense of practical realities concerning the development of the service sector. Therefore, I cannot claim absolute confidence in the discussions in this section. Accordingly, I will begin with a theoretical (i.e., commonsense-based) consideration.

In the case of IT, the costs of capital equipment and buildings are not particularly high, and if necessary, it may be possible to obtain loans from advanced-country firms that outsource work. Thus, a lack of physical capital is unlikely to be a major obstacle to business. However, in terms of infrastructure, it is necessary to construct base stations for mobile phones and install lines capable of transmitting large volumes of data. As for technology and know-how (intellectual capital) in high-income countries, firms can certainly provide guidance. The remaining issue is human capital, but many developing countries have excellent universities, and there are also a considerable number of individuals with degrees from Europe and North America. In particular, in English-speaking countries, widespread fluency in English is advantageous for the development of the IT industry.

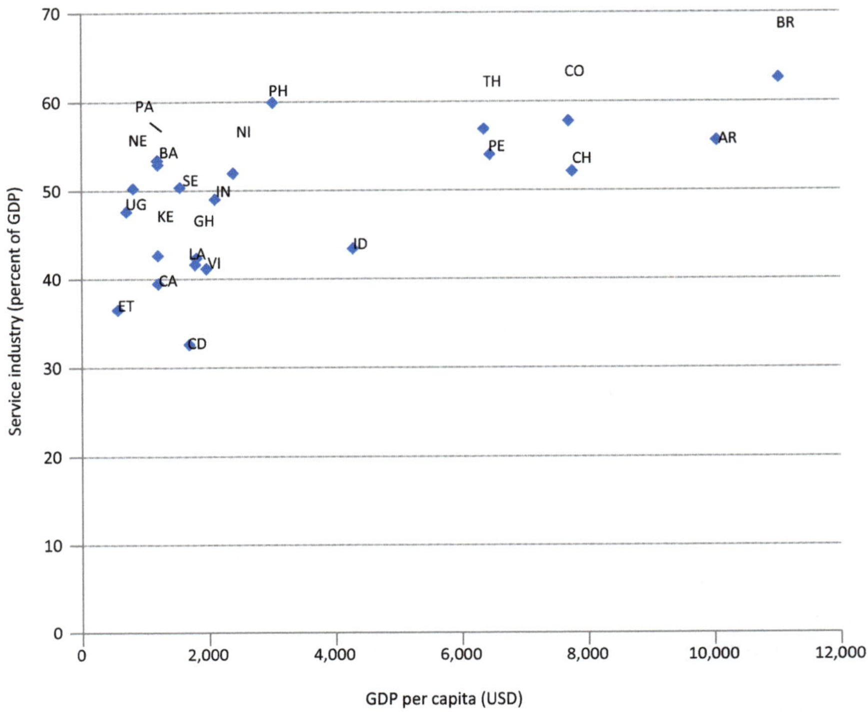

Fig. 7.4 Relationship between GDP share of the service industry and GDP per capita in 2018 (World Bank's World Development Indicators various years) (ET—Ethiopia, NE—Nepal, UG—Uganda, BA - Bangladesh, KE—Kenya, CA—Cambodia, LA—Laos, PA—Pakistan, SE—Senegal, NI—Nigeria, VI—Vietnam, CD—Côte d'Ivoire, IN—India, PH—Philippines, ID—Indonesia, GH—Ghana, CH—China, TH—Thailand, PE—Peru, CO—Columbia, AR—Argentine, BR—Brazil)

In other words, compared to the development of agriculture and manufacturing, market failures that hinder the accumulation or utilization of various forms of capital appear to be relatively minor in the service sector. Therefore, while government policy support is important for the development of agriculture and manufacturing, the government's role is less critical for the development of the service sector. Most likely, what is important is English language education and university education. This is precisely what is suggested by Fig. 7.4.

As expected, the share of the service sector increases with per capita GDP; however, several developing countries stand out above the overall trend. Among these are many countries, such as India and the Philippines, where English is an official language. This suggests that English proficiency supports the development of the service sector. Senegal, a French-speaking country, also has a high service sector share despite its low income, which can be attributed to proactive government support for the IT industry. As for university education, since it is strongly correlated with per capita GDP, it is difficult to isolate its effect from the data.

In sum, the fundamental policy likely to support the development of modern service industries is higher education, including English language instruction. The returns to English education and university degrees should be increasing for those engaged in modern service sectors. To remain competitive internationally, policies that support education are essential, and given the expected continued growth of the modern service sector, there is little room for objection to such policies. However, the modern service sector primarily creates employment opportunities for the educated and affluent. If the goal is equitable development that does not generate disparities, it is imperative not to neglect job creation in agriculture and manufacturing. Otherwise, income gaps between social strata will widen, leading to social instability and threatening the sustainability of economic development itself.

In this regard, India is a particular concern due to the impact of the modern service sector on poverty reduction. While the IT industry has developed rapidly in Bangalore and Hyderabad, it does not appear to be making a significant contribution to poverty reduction, as employed workers are predominantly highly educated and affluent individuals. Therefore, it is difficult to envision sustainable economic growth being led solely by the IT sector. As agriculture gradually becomes more mechanized, a vast number of farmers and landless laborers who lose their jobs in agriculture are expected to migrate to cities in search of non-agricultural employment. If sufficient employment opportunities cannot be provided for them, the risk of social unrest will increase.

A major reason for the development of the IT industry in India is that Indians who had worked in Silicon Valley brought advanced knowledge back to India. In other words, learning from abroad is critically important not only for the development of manufacturing but also for the advancement of service industries.

7.6 Remaining Research Issues

Empirical research in developing countries continually reveals new and intriguing topics, making it challenging to identify a definitive endpoint. Nevertheless, constructing a *development strategy for poor countries* is an urgent task that must be addressed as soon as possible. The author currently considers the two main remaining research issues: (1) pyramid-type industrial clusters and (2) development strategies for rural industries.

The industrial clusters discussed in this book are, in fact, what might be called *horizontal clusters* consisting of many similar firms, but there also exist *pyramid-type* clusters. For example, in the case of leather shoe clusters, similar factories are lined up side by side, forming a horizontal cluster. While raw materials such as tanned leather and shoelaces are necessary, the companies producing these materials are not always located within the cluster. Even when they are, there are not necessarily fixed, hierarchical business relationships. Most of the firms within the cluster are similar companies engaged in leather shoe production. As a result, the cluster resembles a landscape of single- or two-story buildings densely packed side by side. Apparel industry clusters are similar in this respect.

In contrast, the pyramid-type cluster is characterized by an assembly company at the apex, followed by first-tier, second-tier, and third-tier subcontractors. The quintessential example is the automobile industry, where thousands of companies are located around Toyota, forming what is known as a company town.

In this type of industrial cluster, assembly companies build close relationships with first-tier subcontractors to ensure a stable supply of high-quality components, often providing guidance and training to these suppliers. First-tier subcontractors, in turn, train second-tier suppliers to secure quality parts, and second-tier suppliers do the same with third-tier suppliers.

Although such hierarchical relationships exist, perfect hierarchies are rare; for example, first-tier suppliers affiliated with Toyota often supply parts to other automobile manufacturers as well. Generally, first-tier suppliers produce components using capital- and knowledge-intensive methods, while second-tier suppliers tend to produce simpler, more labor-intensive parts; this trend becomes even more pronounced at the third tier.

In the case of the automotive industry in developing countries, if there are no capable local subcontractors, foreign assembly companies often import parts from their home country's primary subcontractors or invite parts manufacturers from their home country to begin local production. In the latter case, it is also common to procure parts produced by secondary and tertiary subcontractors from abroad.

The automotive industry encompasses a vast number of related firms and, correspondingly, an enormous variety of parts, resulting in the production of a wide range of vehicles and components. While it is indisputable that innovation determines the success or failure of such a complex industry, strategies for fostering innovation are far more intricate than those for horizontal industrial clusters. Developing the pyramidal type cluster remains one of the author's future research topics.

Another major research issue is rural industrialization. Rural areas are typically poor with limited employment opportunities, while cities offer jobs but suffer from severe congestion and poor living conditions. Therefore, fostering industries in rural areas to increase employment is highly desirable. The most promising sector is food processing, with various factories and enterprises such as sugar mills, tapioca starch plants, fruit canneries, rice mills, and other businesses involved in sorting, processing, and shipping fruits, vegetables, and flowers being established in rural regions.

Many agricultural products must be processed or handled while still fresh, which gives rural industrialization a distinct advantage. Moreover, high-value fruits and vegetables are washed, fumigated, graded, and packaged at factories while still fresh, then shipped to urban supermarkets. Such simple processing activities are also considered part of the rural industry. The shift from grain-centered agriculture to fruit, vegetable, livestock, and cash crop production leads to agricultural diversification and transformation, making rural industrialization a transformative change for rural areas (Otsuka and Fan 2021).

The problem, as far as the author is aware, is that there have been very few policy efforts to foster such industries in rural areas. This is likely due to a lack of understanding of development strategies.

Interestingly, many of these industries exhibit characteristics of both pyramid-type and horizontal-type industrial clusters. From the perspective of agricultural processors, the farmers who produce the raw materials are similar to subcontractors in a pyramid-type cluster. Thus, processors have an incentive to train farmers, but there is a risk that farmers may sell their products to other companies rather than those who provided the training. Nevertheless, contract farming between farmers and processors appears to be on the rise (Otsuka and Larson 2016; Otsuka and Zhang 2021). Processors may be geographically concentrated or somewhat dispersed across production areas. However, the presence of numerous similar firms is reminiscent of horizontal-type industrial clusters.

In many developing countries, rising incomes are driving increased demand for non-cereals such as premium fruits, vegetables, and dairy products. As a result, the potential for rural industrialization is growing. Additionally, differences in climate and natural conditions are enabling increased exports of agricultural products from developing to developed countries. Therefore, the latent potential for rural industrialization is increasing. How to realize this potential is one of the key issues in industrial development strategy. The author has begun to address this research question, but has not yet reached a conclusion.

7.7 From Agricultural to Industrial Economies

Up to this point, the discussion has proceeded as if the development of agriculture and industry were independent processes. However, this is not accurate. Among agricultural researchers, many apply Albert Hirschman's (1958) concepts of *forward linkages* and *backward linkages* to argue that agricultural development leads to the development of non-agricultural sectors.

For example, when a new, highly profitable, high-yielding technology is adopted in agriculture, it generates backward linkages by increasing demand for fertilizers, pesticides, and agricultural machinery, thereby stimulating the development of industries that produce these inputs. At the same time, forward linkages may arise, leading to the growth of industries such as rice milling, transportation, and retail. Furthermore, as farmers' consumption increases, it stimulates the production of companies supplying consumer goods. Conversely, if the manufacturing industries related to agriculture develop and fertilizers or agricultural machinery become more affordable, this will, in turn, promote agricultural development. According to Hirschman, this is referred to as a forward linkage effect. However, this does not necessarily mean that producing all fertilizers and agricultural machinery domestically is desirable for agricultural development. The fertilizer and agricultural machinery industries are not labor-intensive sectors. If high-quality fertilizers and machinery can be imported at low cost, that would undoubtedly be preferable.

There are, however, advantages to the simultaneous growth of agriculture and manufacturing. In fact, a major reason for the reduction of rural poverty in Asia has been the increase in off-farm income among farming and landless households, as well as the employment of their children in non-agricultural sectors (Otsuka et al. 2009). Therefore, the development of non-agricultural sectors is essential for poverty reduction. Moreover, agricultural development increases farmers' incomes, which in turn stimulates investment in their children's education, potentially leading to employment in non-agricultural sectors and contributing to the sector's growth.

However, no research has accurately estimated the *chain of development*. Since a variety of factors trigger the development of any industry, it is not easy to estimate how each factor contributes to the growth of different industries. If the magnitude of backward and forward linkage effects could be estimated, it would be possible to target industries with large effects for development. However, in the absence of such information, it is difficult to incorporate the chain of inter-industry development into development strategies. In our research on industrial clusters, we place particular emphasis on metalworking. This is because metalworking is crucial for machinery repair and parts production, and is expected to support the future development of the machinery industry as well as other mechanized industries. Furthermore, if the metalworking industry is well-developed in a given country, it is more likely to attract direct investment from foreign companies. If this occurs, it will further promote the development of both the metalworking and machinery industries. In conclusion, while the importance of complementary relationships and linkages between industries is empirically recognized, there is currently insufficient quantitative evidence to place them at the core of economic development strategies.

7.8 Who Should Do What?

The main points discussed in this chapter are summarized in the development strategies presented in ◘ Figs. 7.1 and 7.3; therefore, a separate summary does not seem necessary, unlike other chapters. Instead, I would like to shift the perspective here and offer some thoughts on the actors responsible for implementing these strategies and the roles they should play.

- The most important actors in formulating and implementing development strategies are, without question, the governments of developing countries. However, when these governments lack the capacity to execute appropriate strategies or are unfamiliar with the successful experiences of other developing countries, international aid organizations and agencies from developed countries should provide advice.
- Non-profit and non-governmental organizations, which excel at grassroots support, are expected to make significant contributions by disseminating technical and managerial know-how and by providing credit assistance.

- In supporting the development of manufacturing industries, it is desirable for the government to identify existing industrial clusters, assess their potential, and then concentrate resources on human resource development and the construction of industrial parks. Similarly, in agriculture, policies should prioritize the development of promising crops and regions. The experiences gained in these areas will provide valuable information for development strategies in other regions.
- Researchers in development economics should collaborate with practitioners and aid organizations to: (1) empirically investigate the long-term development processes of agriculture and industry; (2) work toward theoretical formulation of these processes; and (3) make efforts to quantitatively assess the true significance of critical issues.

Questions

1. What are the proper sequences of policy supports for technology transfer from developed countries: development or adaptations of advanced technology, investment in infrastructure, and the provision of credit?
2. Since innovation is an engine of growth in any industry, should the first priority be placed on training major decision-makers (e.g., farmers and entrepreneurs) in advanced technologies and management from abroad?
3. What are the major differences in development strategies between agriculture and the manufacturing industry?
4. Why do I recommend that developing countries learn technologies and management methods from developed countries rather than generate them independently by their own efforts?

References

David, C.C., & Otsuka, K. (Eds.). (1994). *Modern rice technology and income distribution in Asia.* Lynne Rienner.

deGraft-Johnson, M., Suzuki, A., Sakurai, T., & Otsuka, K. (2014). On the transferability of the Asian rice green revolution to rainfed areas in Sub-Saharan Africa: An assessment of technology intervention in Northern Ghana. *Agricultural Economics, 45*(5): 555–570.

Hirschman, A.O. (1958). *The strategy of economic development.* Yale University Press.

Kijima, Y. (2014). On the possibility of rice Green Revolution in rainfed areas in Uganda: Impact evaluation of a management training and guidebook distribution. In: K. Otsuka and D.F. Larson (Eds.). *In pursuit of an African Green Revolution: Views from rice and maize farmers' fields.* Springer.

Kijima, Y., Ito, N., & Otsuka, K. (2012). Assessing the impact of training on lowland rice productivity in an African setting: Evidence from Uganda. *World Development, 40*(8): 1619–1633.

Otsuka, K. (2018). Kaizen as a key ingredient of industrial development policy. In: K. Otsuka, K., Jin, and S. Sonobe (Eds.). *Applying the Kaizen in Africa: A new avenue for industrial development.* Palgrave Macmillan.

Otsuka, K., & Hashino, T. (2026, forthcoming). Selective technology choice, adaptations, and industrial development: Lessons from successful development of the textile industries in prewar Japan. *The Developing Economies.*

Otsuka, K. (2024). *Transforming poor economies: Effective development strategies for agriculture and industry*. Edward Elgar.

Otsuka, K., & Fan, S. (Eds.). (2021). *Agricultural development: New perspectives in a changing world.* International Food Policy Research Institute.

Otsuka, K., & Larson, D. (Eds.). (2013). *An African Green Revolution: Finding ways to boost productivity on small farms.* Springer.

Otsuka, K., & Larson, D.F. (Eds.). (2016). *In pursuit of an African Green Revolution: Views from rice and maize farmers' fields.* Springer.

Otsuka, K., & Zhang, X. (2021). Transformation of the rural economy. In K. Otsuka and S. Fan (Eds.), *Agricultural development: New perspectives in a changing world.* International Food Policy Research Institute, mimeo.

Otsuka, K., Estudillo, J.P., & Sawada, Y. (Eds.). (2009). *Rural poverty and income dynamics in Asia and Africa.* Routledge.

Otsuka, K., Jayne, T., Mano, Y., & Takahashi, K. (2024). Toward a sustainable Green Revolution in Sub-Saharan Africa: The case of maize and rice. *Food Policy, 129*, 102762.

Otsuka, K., Jin, K., & Sonobe, T. (Eds.). (2018). *Applying the kaizen in Africa: A new avenue for industrial development.* Palgrave Macmillan.

Otsuka, K., Mano, Y., & Takahashi, K. (2023). *Rice Green Revolution in Sub-Saharan Africa.* Springer.

Otsuka, K., Nakano, Y., & Takahashi, K. (2016). Contract farming in developed and developing countries. *Annual Review of Resource Economics*, 8: 353–376.

Sonobe, T., & Otsuka, K. (2006). *Cluster-based industrial development: An East Asian model.* Palgrave.

Sonobe, T., & Otsuka, K. (2011). *Cluster-based industrial development: A comparative study of Asia and Africa*. Palgrave.

Sonobe, T., & Otsuka, K. (2014). *Cluster-based industrial developments: Kaizen management for MSE Growth in developing countries.* Palgrave.

World Bank. (various years). *World development indicators*. World Bank DataBank.

How Can the "Middle-Income Trap" Be Avoided?

Contents

K. Otsuka, *A Primer on Development Economics*,
Classroom Companion: Economics, https://doi.org/10.1007/978-981-95-5397-6_8

8.1 Introduction

The purpose of this book is to examine what should be done to achieve economic prosperity in poor countries. However, there is not necessarily a fundamental difference between raising low-income countries to middle-income status and advancing middle-income countries to high-income, developed status. Therefore, this book has also mentioned the development of advanced economies throughout. In this chapter, I aim to systematically discuss the similarities and differences between the development of poor countries and that of middle-income countries.

It is important to note that even if a country successfully attains middle-income status, this is no cause for complacency. According to the World Bank (2024), middle-income countries are defined as those with per capita incomes between USD 1,136 and USD 13,845, and 108 countries fall into this category. The problem is that many middle-income countries are unable to join the ranks of advanced economies and remain stuck at the middle-income level. This phenomenon is known as the *middle-income trap*. In this chapter, I will focus on why so many countries fall into the middle-income trap and how they can escape from it.

8.2 The Source of Development is Innovation

As discussed in ► Chap. 3, for an economy to develop, it is necessary to increase the stock of intellectual capital, human capital, physical capital, infrastructure, and social capital.[1] However, it is financially difficult and strategically unwise to expand all of these simultaneously and comprehensively. Therefore, as explained using ◘ Fig. 7.1 and ◘ Fig. 7.3 in ► Chap. 7, the correct development strategy is, first, to increase intellectual capital (that is, knowledge of science and management); foster human resources capable of utilizing new knowledge (i.e., enhancement of human capital); and thereby drive innovation. If this is achieved, the returns on infrastructure and physical capital investment will rise, stimulating further investment in these areas and supporting innovation, which in turn accelerates economic development.

To reiterate, the source of development is innovation (Otsuka 2024). Here, innovation refers to improvements in production methods and management efficiency, as well as the development of new products. For example, in Kaizen—also known as the Toyota Production System—the 5S principles (sort, set in order, shine, standardize, and sustain) are the most fundamental operational guidelines, and whether or not these are implemented makes a significant difference in product quality and production efficiency. I personally wonder whether much of the difference in production efficiency between Asian and African firms can be explained by the extent to which Kaizen is thoroughly implemented.

Earlier economic research included such innovation under technological progress, but it has become clear that not only advances in technology but also in

1 Frankly speaking, I do not have a concrete idea of how to invest in social capital or to increase trust among people, except for facilitating the development of industrial clusters, which mimic the community.

management are crucial. Peter Drucker (1985), a leading figure in management science, pointed out that 80% of innovation consists of advances in management.

Indeed, the global success of Starbucks Coffee can be attributed more to advances in management than to technological progress. Similarly, the development of logistics and courier delivery companies appears to be underpinned by management strategies that leverage IT. Therefore, in this context, I will use the term innovation to encompass both technological and managerial advances, rather than technological innovation alone. Incidentally, economics as a discipline has long underestimated the role of management.

Labor productivity increases as the amount of physical capital per worker rises. Using a more powerful computer improves labor productivity. At the same time, technological progress—such as the use of multifunctional, large-scale computers—further enhances labor productivity. In addition, if an appropriate division of labor among workers within a firm is achieved through improved management, labor productivity increases even further. In advanced economies, only about 20%–30% of improvements in labor productivity can be explained by quantitative increases in physical capital, while more than 70% is attributable to innovation.

In developing countries, perhaps because much of their growth is driven by imitation, the measured rate of productivity increase is not particularly high. In other words, the importance of innovation does not appear to be as great as it is in advanced economies. As shown in ◘ Fig. 7.2, during periods of quantitative expansion driven by imitation, productivity does not rise significantly. However, imitation occurs precisely because innovation has taken place, so the significance of innovation should not be underestimated. Moreover, even during periods of quantitative expansion, investment can occur, gradually making industries more capital-intensive and potentially leading to increases in labor productivity.

Kim and Lau (1994), through the estimation of production functions, found that the development of the Four East Asian Tigers (Singapore, Hong Kong, Taiwan, and South Korea) was explained primarily by capital accumulation (an increase in the capital-labor ratio) rather than by productivity growth or innovation. Building on this, Krugman (1994) predicted that capital accumulation without productivity improvement would lower the return on capital, eventually bringing the growth of the Four Tigers to an end. However, his prediction did not come to pass.

Hayami and Godo (2005) argued that systematic scientific research and development are gradually established as incomes rise, and thus, productivity growth will become increasingly important with income growth. This view aligns with Sonobe and Otsuka's (2006, 2011, 2014) concept of a transition to a phase of qualitative improvement. In other words, productivity does not increase during the quantity expansion phase, when the driving force for development is imitation, whereas productivity increases during the quality improvement phase due to innovation.

The World Bank (2024) has also pointed out that innovation is crucial for escaping the middle-income trap. However, it emphasizes the role of direct technology transfer from developed to developing countries or mere imitation. Since it ignores the adaptation of technology and management, it takes a different position from this book.

8.3 What Differentiates Middle-Income from Low-Income Countries?

In terms of the source of industrial development or the importance of innovation, there is no fundamental difference between the development of low-income and middle-income countries. The key distinction is that while low-income countries can learn scientific, technological, and managerial know-how from middle- and high-income countries, middle-income countries have fewer technologies and management practices left to imitate from advanced economies and must transition to systems that foster their own innovation.

As seen in ◘ Fig. 5.2, Japan, Taiwan, and South Korea experienced rapid growth rates of 10% per year during periods when their income gaps with the United States were large. This was due to their rapid acquisition of scientific, technological, and managerial know-how from the United States and other Western countries. The same applies to Singapore and Taiwan, and China's continued growth at an annual rate of 10% has also been largely due to the benefits of learning from advanced economies. Ethiopia, which is unusual in Africa for recognizing the importance of learning from abroad, has also achieved growth rates exceeding 10% per year.

It is extremely important to note that mere imitation—simple copying—often fails. This is because materials and components available in advanced economies are often not accessible in developing countries. Furthermore, in low-wage developing countries, even if the basic technological and managerial ideas are the same, it is essential to adapt them by employing more labor-intensive methods than those used in high-income countries. In other words, learning ideas of advanced technologies and management practices from advanced economies and adapting them to low-income economies is an effective means of achieving economic development. The World Bank (2024) also argues that innovation is effective in avoiding the middle-income trap.

As countries reach middle-income status and aspire to join the ranks of advanced economies, there is less to learn from advanced countries, and it becomes necessary to foster more knowledge-intensive industries than before, making it increasingly difficult to learn from abroad. Therefore, the improved intellectual capacity to learn and absorb technological and managerial knowledge from advanced economies becomes crucial. If the absorptive capacity for knowledge remains low, GDP growth rates tend to stagnate. Ultimately, for middle-income countries to continue growing and become advanced economies, it is critically important to invest in human capital to enhance their absorptive capacity of advanced knowledge. For this purpose, not only schooling but also workplace training will have to play a role. In addition, investing in science to build up intellectual capital is also essential. Since scientific knowledge generates information spillovers, the government must invest in scientific research. In these ways, a large pool of talent must be developed to skillfully incorporate and utilize new technologies and management from abroad, as well as develop new ideas of their own.

The best evidence supporting my argument is none other than the United States itself. I do not believe the average American is exceptionally intelligent. This is a country where even high-ranking government officials cannot name the member states of the Association of Southeast Asian Nations (ASEAN). Yet, why is it that the United States boasts an exceptionally high per capita income? My answer is that the US is home to numerous world-class universities and research institutions, resulting in a vast accumulation of intellectual and human capital. In the United States, extraordinarily talented researchers are paid high salaries and receive substantial research funding, enabling them to lead global scientific advancements. These outstanding individuals, in turn, mentor bright young minds in graduate schools. As a result, while there is a significant income disparity between the highly intelligent and others within the country, the average per capita income in the United States remains among the highest in the world.

The Trump administration, however, has failed to value these world-class universities and research institutions, which are a national asset, leading to a situation where many scientists are considering emigrating abroad. Should this truly occur, the United States would likely fall from being a wealthy nation to an ordinary one. Returning to the context of middle-income countries, achieving sustainable development will increasingly require broad improvements in the population's educational attainment, the enhancement of universities and graduate schools, and expanded investment in scientific research.

8.4 Asian Countries that Escaped the "Middle-Income Trap"

As shown in the first graph of ◘ Fig. 8.1, after World War II, Japan was the first in Asia to become a high-income country without falling into the middle-income trap. Japan was followed by Hong Kong, then Singapore, Taiwan, and South Korea. All of them avoided the middle-income trap and instead advanced to developed country status. Notably, during the period when their per capita GDP was around USD 5,000 and they were considered middle-income countries, the slope of their growth curves steepened, and each country experienced growth rates approaching 10% per year. However, as the per capita GDP of these five countries approached that of the United States, their growth rates slowed. This is likely because, having caught up with the advanced economies such as the US, there was less to learn from them, making it more challenging to generate innovation independently.

The reason these Asian countries were able to escape the middle-income trap was not only their relentless efforts to learn technology and management know-how from abroad, but also their enhanced absorptive capacity for knowledge. Furthermore, by improving the quality of education and increasing investment in scientific research, they cultivated a workforce of intellectuals capable of driving innovation, which contributed to their escape from the middle-income trap.

While it is difficult to measure "absorptive capacity" or "innovative capability," one indicator is the average years of schooling among workers. As shown on

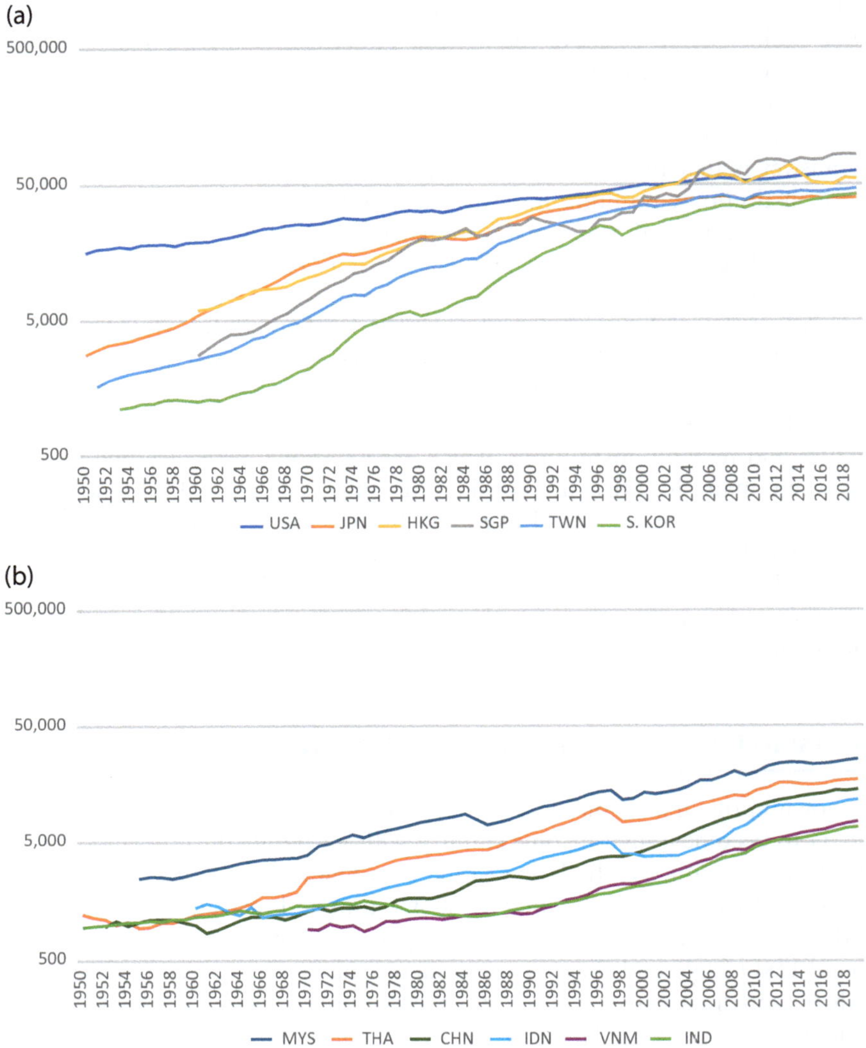

Fig. 8.1 Change in real GDP per capita in high-performing East Asian countries in comparison with the US and other middle-income Asian countries (PPP-adjusted, semi-log scale) (Groningen Growth and Development Centre 2023)
Source: World Bank's World Development Indicators various years

the upper part of Fig. 8.2 (or Fig. 8.2a), Japan, Singapore, Hong Kong, Taiwan, and South Korea rapidly increased their average years of schooling, and by around 2010 had nearly caught up with the United States. The rise in average years of schooling likely also improved the quality of education, contributed to rapid economic growth, and facilitated the structural shift from "imitation-based growth" to "innovation-driven growth."

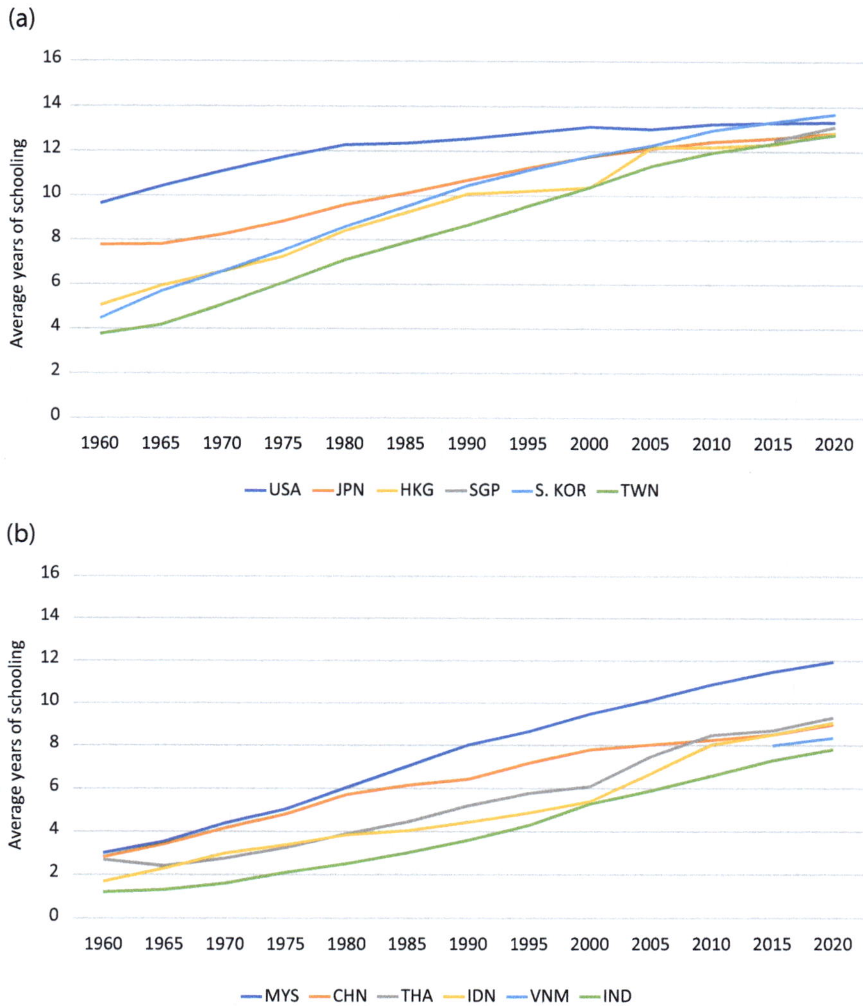

◘ Fig. 8.2 Changes in average years of schooling in high-performing East Asia countries in comparison with the US and other middle-income Asian countries (Barro and Lee 2021, 1960 to 2015; Global Change Data Lab 2023, data until 2020).

8.5 Asian Countries at Risk of Falling into the "Middle-Income Trap"

Focusing on Asia, countries such as Malaysia, Thailand, and Indonesia appear to be at risk of falling into the middle-income trap. As shown on the lower graph of ◘ Fig. 8.1 (or ◘ Fig. 8.1b), these countries have not experienced the rapid economic growth seen in Japan and the so-called East Asian Tigers, and their per capita GDP growth rates remain sluggish. Particularly noteworthy is that, in contrast to Japan and the East Asian Tigers, which accelerated their economic growth at the USD 5,000 per capita GDP level, these three Southeast Asian countries have shown a tendency for growth rates to decelerate at this stage. China, too, experienced rapid economic growth over a long period following the 1978 reforms, but its growth has clearly slowed since around 2010. These countries thus appear to be on the verge of falling into the middle-income trap.

Vietnam and India, which originally had low levels of per capita GDP, have both achieved steady growth since around 1990, almost in tandem. However, whether these two countries can continue to achieve sustained and accelerated growth and escape the middle-income trap remains uncertain.

Because the vertical axis in ◘ Fig. 8.1 is logarithmic, the income gap between the high-income East Asian countries (8.1a) and the middle-income countries (8.1b) may appear small at first glance. In reality, however, there is a substantial disparity in income. When considering the future prospects of Asia's middle-income countries, the trend in years of schooling is particularly important. As shown in Fig. 8.2b, Malaysia's increase in years of schooling is remarkable, approaching the levels seen in high-income East Asian countries. In terms of income as well, Malaysia surpasses other Asian countries and appears to be in an excellent position to escape the middle-income trap. In contrast, China, Thailand, Indonesia, and Vietnam have seen their growth in years of schooling stagnate at low levels, and do not seem to be on a trajectory of innovation-driven growth.[2] The years of schooling in these countries remain too low, raising doubts about whether they can sustain income growth as middle-income economies.[3]

8

Except for Malaysia, the years of schooling in the middle-income countries shown in ◘ Fig. 8.2b, while increasing, are still significantly lower in both growth rate and absolute level compared to Japan and the East Asian Tigers (◘ Fig. 8.2a). Considering also the disparities in the quality of education, it appears that the middle-income countries of Asia are not yet prepared, in terms of either intellectual or human capital, to break free from the middle-income trap.

8.6 Long-Term Development Strategy

For poorer countries, a sound development strategy is to invest in the human capital of farmers and small business owners, enabling them to learn advanced technologies and management practices from abroad. Given the abundance of labor in such countries, they should have a comparative advantage in labor-intensive industries and should focus on developing these industries. It is also critically important to adapt new technology and management to the economic conditions of poor economies.

However, if they succeed in this and gradually accumulate capital, fostering more capital-intensive industries, the country will eventually reach the middle-income stage. At this point, the middle-income trap awaits. To escape this trap, it

2 For Vietnam, data on years of schooling were only available for 2015 and 2020.

3 In the case of China, the years of schooling reported by the government have steadily increased, which is inconsistent with the data in ◘ Fig. 8.2.

is necessary to transition from the stage of *learning the basics of technology and management from abroad* to an economic structure that *learns advanced foreign technologies and management while also generating indigenous innovation.* Achieving this requires progress toward a new type of innovation, including enhancing school education and training opportunities, investing in scientific research, and utilizing university-generated knowledge in the private sector. If a country fails in this endeavor, it will remain stuck as a middle-income country for an extended period.

Questions

1. Discuss the role of the imitation of advanced technologies and management from developed countries in poor countries.
2. What is the main cause for a middle-income country to fall into the middle-income trap?
3. What is a major problem of the mere imitation or copying of advanced technology and management for poor countries?
4. What are the prerequisites for escaping the middle-income trap?

References

Barro, R.J., & Lee, J.W. (2021). *Barro-Lee Educational Attainment Dataset, version 3.0.*

Drucker, P.F. (1985). Innovation and entrepreneurship. Harper & Row.

Global Change Data Lab. (2023). *Our World in Data.* ► https://global-change-data-lab.org/

Groningen Growth and Development Centre. (2023). *Penn World Table version 10.01.*

Hayami, Y., & Godo, Y. (2005). *Development economics.* Oxford University Press.

Kim, Il-Gon, & Lau, L.J. (1994). The sources of economic growth of East Asian newly industrializing countries. *Journal of the Japanese and International Economies, 8*(3), 235–271.

Krugman, P. (1994). The myth of Asia's miracle. *Foreign Affairs, 73,* 62–78.

Otsuka, K. (2024). *Transforming poor economies: Effective development strategies for agriculture and industry.* Edward Elgar.

Sonobe, T., & Otsuka, K. (2006). *Cluster-based industrial development: An East Asian model.* Palgrave Macmillan.

Sonobe, T., & Otsuka, K. (2011). *Cluster-based industrial development: A comparative study of Asia and Africa.* Palgrave Macmillan.

Sonobe, T., & Otsuka, K. (2014). *Cluster-based industrial developments: Kaizen management for MSE Growth in developing countries.* Palgrave Macmillan.

World Bank. (2024). *World Development Report 2024: The middle-income trap.* World Bank.

What the World Must Address More Seriously

Contents

K. Otsuka, *A Primer on Development Economics*,
Classroom Companion: Economics, https://doi.org/10.1007/978-981-95-5397-6_9

9.1 Introduction

Climate change is as important as, if not more important and difficult to resolve than, poverty reduction. If the global environment deteriorates, it will inevitably have adverse effects on people's lives and exacerbate poverty. Conversely, even if light industry develops and poverty is reduced, if that development results in significant greenhouse gas (GHG) emissions through increased energy use, it will negatively impact climate change. In short, development economics must devise strategies that achieve the seemingly conflicting goals of poverty reduction and environmental protection simultaneously.

However, as will be examined in this chapter, there are qualitative differences between the two. Environmental issues are largely a matter of will and the formation of international consensus, whereas achieving poverty reduction requires both the will and strategies for economic development.

In ► Sect. 9.1, we will consider the shift in global development goals from the Millennium Development Goals (MDGs) to the Sustainable Development Goals (SDGs). ► Section 9.2 will explain the extent to which climate change is deteriorating the global environment and the scale of the resulting damage. ► Section 9.3 will examine the *environmental Kuznets curve* hypothesis, which posits that while environmental degradation increases with rising per capita income, it improves once a certain income threshold is surpassed. If this hypothesis holds, economic development could ultimately lead to solutions for global environmental problems. ► Section 9.4 will analyze how and to what extent developing and developed countries emit greenhouse gases, and ► Sect. 9.5 will highlight that, in order to halt climate change, it is essential for both developing and developed countries to actively participate in international efforts to reduce greenhouse gas emissions. Finally, as a conclusion to this book, I would like to outline strategies for achieving both climate change mitigation and poverty reduction.

9.2 From MDGs to SDGs

First, let us review what the United Nations' MDGs were (see ◘ Table 9.1). The MDGs consisted of eight goals, under which 21 more specific targets and 60 indicators were established. Most of these used 1990 as the baseline year and set 2015 as the target year for achievement. What impressions do readers have upon seeing these eight goals? The MDGs deserve high praise for drawing global attention to the issue of poverty. Furthermore, the concrete setting of targets, such as halving the number of the poor, is commendable in that it enabled the evaluation of progress and outcomes.

However, there are two points that must be given a "failing grade." The first is that, although the declaration aims to halve poverty, there is no discussion whatsoever on how this is to be achieved. Even if we concede that there was no clear poverty reduction strategy in place at the time the MDGs were established, it would have been imperative to develop such a strategy thereafter. Yet, there is no evidence of such efforts. The United Nations' lack of accountability is a signifi-

Table 9.1 List of the Millennium Development Goals (MDGs) (United Nations 2025)

Goal 1	Eradicate extreme poverty and hunger
Goal 2	Achieve universal primary education
Goal 3	Promote gender equality and empower women
Goal 4	Reduce child mortality
Goal 5	Improve maternal health
Goal 6	Combat HIV/AIDS, malaria, and other diseases
Goal 7	Ensure environmental sustainability
Goal 8	Global partnership for development

cant problem.[1] Under these circumstances, the goal of poverty reduction remains merely a projection rather than a target to strive for. As pointed out in ► Chapter 2, even if this goal is achieved, it may not be the result of international efforts, but rather due to the development of developing countries, particularly China. In contrast, goals such as the expansion of primary education,[2] the reduction of under-five child mortality, and the increase in measles immunization coverage appear to have been achieved to a considerable extent through international support.

The second issue is that climate change is given little attention, and its relationship with other goals, such as poverty reduction, is unclear. The seventh goal, "Ensure environmental sustainability," is exceedingly abstract, and being the seventh out of eight goals does not convey its importance. Yet, climate change is the greatest challenge facing humanity in the twenty-first century. Therefore, it is only natural that the post-2015 goals, following the conclusion of the MDGs, have been replaced by the SDGs, which place a much stronger emphasis on environmental protection.

The term *sustainable* has two meanings. The first is to achieve sustained economic development without degrading the environment. The second is to build an equitable, poverty-free economic society that ensures social stability. Even if average income increases, if income inequality worsens and poverty becomes more severe as a result, social unrest may ensue, making sustainable development unattainable. Thus, the SDGs can be interpreted as inheriting the basic stance of the MDGs while advocating for greater environmental consideration. However, as shown in Table 9.2, the SDGs encompass an extremely wide range of goals and are expressed in much vaguer terms than the MDGs. Moreover, the United Nations remains silent on the crucial issues of how to achieve poverty reduction and how to maintain and improve the global environment.

1 Since the agreement on the MDGs was also supported by the World Bank and donor countries, it may not be appropriate to place the blame solely on the United Nations.

2 However, as more children have begun attending primary school, concerns have arisen regarding a decline in educational quality, with an increasing number of primary school students unable to read or write.

Table 9.2 List of the Sustainable Development Goals (SDGs) (United Nations 2025)

Goal 1	*No Poverty* End poverty in all its forms everywhere
Goal 2	*Zero Hunger* End hunger, achieve food security and improved nutrition, and promote sustainable agriculture
Goal 3	*Good Health and Well-being* Ensure healthy lives and promote well-being for all at all ages
Goal 4	*Quality Education* Ensure inclusive and equitable quality education and promote lifelong learning opportunities for all
Goal 5	*Gender Equality* Achieve gender equality and empower all women and girls
Goal 6	*Clean Water and Sanitation* Ensure availability and sustainable management of water and sanitation for all
Goal 7	*Affordable and Clean Energy* Ensure access to affordable, reliable, sustainable, and modern energy for all
Goal 8	*Decent Work and Economic Growth* Promote sustained, inclusive, and sustainable economic growth, full and productive employment and decent work for all
Goal 9	*Industry, Innovation, and Infrastructure* Build resilient infrastructure, promote inclusive and sustainable industrialization, and foster innovation
Goal 10	*Reduced Inequality* Reduce inequality within and among countries
Goal 11	*Sustainable Cities and Communities* Make cities and human settlements inclusive, safe, resilient, and sustainable
Goal 12	*Responsible Consumption and Production* Ensure sustainable consumption and production patterns
Goal 13	*Climate Action* Take urgent action to combat climate change and its impacts
Goal 14	*Life Below Water* Conserve and sustainably use the oceans, seas, and marine resources for sustainable development
Goal 15	*Life on Land* Protect, restore, and promote sustainable use of terrestrial ecosystems, sustainably manage forests, combat desertification, and halt and reverse land degradation and halt biodiversity loss
Goal 16	*Peace, Justice and Strong Institutions* Promote peaceful and inclusive societies for sustainable development, provide access to justice for all, and build effective, accountable, and inclusive institutions at all levels
Goal 17	*Partnerships for the Goals* Strengthen the means of implementation and revitalize the Global Partnership for Sustainable Development

9.3 Climate Change and Damage Projections

We have experienced unusually hot summers, concerns over water shortages due to low rainfall, frequent strong typhoons, and an increase in sudden torrential downpours, all of which suggest that something is amiss with our climate. Photographs showing the shrinking Himalayan snowfields are particularly alarming. While these phenomena may simply reflect cyclical changes in the global environment rather than long-term climate change, there is a scientific consensus among experts that climate change is indeed occurring.

■ Figure 9.1 illustrates the deviation of annual global temperatures from the 30-year average for the period 1991–2020. Although there are short-term fluctuations from year-to-year, it is clear that global average temperatures have been steadily rising since around the late 1970s. Roughly speaking, over the past 70 years, temperatures have increased by about 0.7 °C–0.8 °C. The Intergovernmental Panel on Climate Change (IPCC), composed of researchers in meteorology and environmental science worldwide, has concluded with considerable confidence that human activities are causing global climate change.

Among human activities, carbon dioxide (CO_2) emissions are particularly significant. Burning fossil fuels such as coal, oil, and natural gas releases CO_2 into the atmosphere. Deforestation also leads to increased CO_2 emissions. The accumulation of these gases creates a greenhouse effect, enveloping the Earth much like a greenhouse. As a result, climate change, including global warming, occurs. CO_2 accounts for more than 75% of greenhouse gas emissions, but methane and substitute chloro-fluorocarbons are also greenhouse gases that contribute to global warming.[3]Methane gas is primarily emitted from rice paddies that use nitrogen fertilizers.

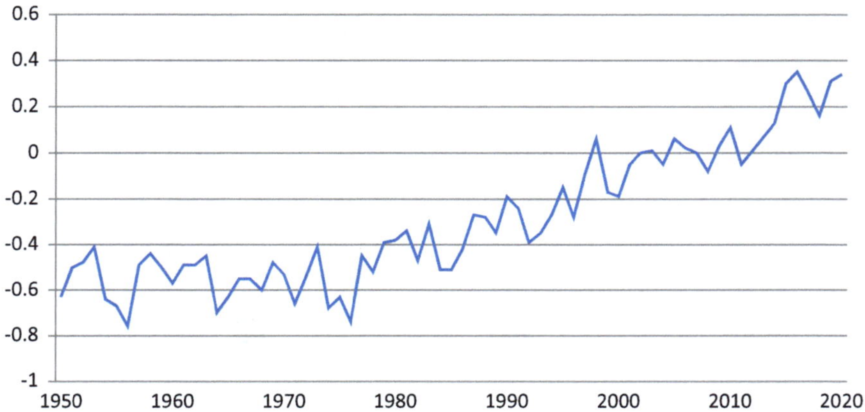

■ **Fig. 9.1** Changes in global temperature (°C) in 1991–2020 in terms of the difference from the average (Japan Meteorological Agency 2025)

3 Other GHs include nitrous dioxide, perfluorocarbons, and sulfur hexafluoride.

If global temperatures rise, Antarctic ice and the perpetual snow on high mountains will melt, causing sea levels to rise. Should this occur, low-lying areas at or near sea level, as well as islands with minimal elevation, will be submerged. The inhabitants of these regions are often among the world's poorest populations. Additionally, the damage from storm surges and tsunamis is expected to become more severe. Furthermore, global warming will likely exacerbate the spread of infectious diseases and increase crop losses due to pests and diseases. Even in temperate regions, a significant rise in temperature could make the emergence of malaria plausible.

Previously, the term *global warming* was commonly used, but now *climate change* has become the preferred terminology. This shift reflects the expectation that not only will temperatures rise, but extreme weather events will also become more frequent. In East Asia, there is a heightened risk of powerful typhoons; in South Asia, cyclones with even stronger winds and rainfall than typhoons; and in North America, large-scale hurricanes. In Africa, where rainfall is scarce, droughts may become increasingly common. For these reasons, the term climate change is now used instead of global warming. Personally, I feel that *deterioration* might be a more appropriate term than simply change, but in extremely cold regions such as Siberia and northern Canada, rising temperatures may actually be beneficial.

As illustrated by the bathtub water analogy in ◘ Fig. 9.2, the volume of GHG emissions, converted to CO_2 equivalents, far exceeds the amount that the Earth

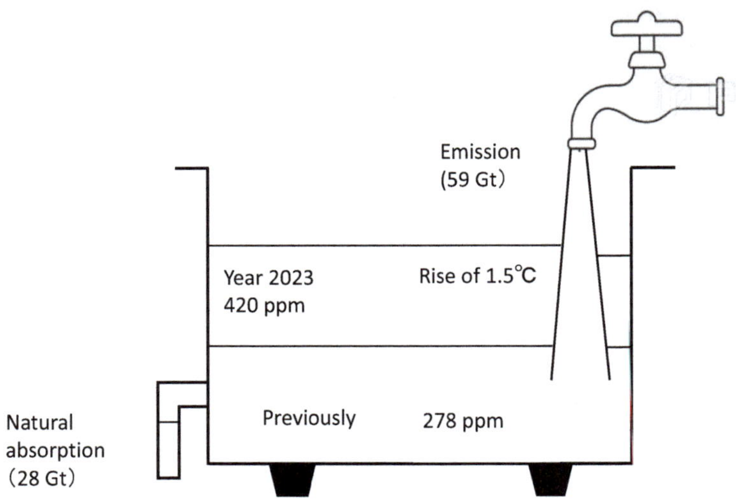

◘ **Fig. 9.2** Illustrated structure of climate change: Emission of greenhouse gas and accumulation of CO_2 in the atmosphere (Gt means gigaton or billion tons in CO_2 equivalence) (IPCC AR6 Synthesis Report: Climate Change 2023)

Table 9.3 Prediction of increase in average temperature on Earth in the late twenty-first century (2081–2100) compared with the 1850–1900 period (IPCC AR6 Synthesis Report: Climate Change 2923)

Scenarios	Efforts for mitigation	Average increase (°C)	Range of expected increases (°C)
SSP1–1.9	Maximum	+1.4	1.0~1.8
SSP1–2.6	Strong	+1.8	1.3~2.4
SSP2–4.5	Moderate	+2.7	2.1~3.5
SSP3–7.0	Modest	+3.6	2.8~4.6
SSP5–8.5	None	+4.4	3.3~5.7

SSP means shared socioeconomic pathways

can naturally absorb.[4] The difference between these two quantities represents the net increase in GHGs.[5] Consequently, the atmospheric concentration of CO_2, measured in parts per million (ppm), is steadily rising, much like the water level in a bathtub. As of 2012, the concentration had already surpassed 390 ppm, and by 2023, it had reached 420 ppm. At this rate, it is considered virtually inevitable that the concentration will exceed 450 ppm, regardless of mitigation efforts. Should this occur, the average global temperature in 2050 is projected to be more than 2 °C higher than current levels.

Table 9.3 presents future projections from the IPCC's Sixth Assessment Report (2023). According to these projections, under a scenario with no restrictions on GHG emissions (Shared Socioeconomic Pathways [SSP5–8.5]), the global temperature could rise by approximately 4.4 °C by the end of this century. In contrast, under a scenario in which emissions are reduced to zero by the end of the century (SSP1–1.9), the temperature increase can be limited to 1.4 °C. Achieving net-zero emissions is an extremely ambitious target, but it is not considered unattainable. Nevertheless, without extraordinary efforts, it is a reality that a temperature increase of around 2 °C is unavoidable.

Developing countries argue that, since developed countries emitted the majority of GHGs, the responsibility for reducing emissions should rest with them. This is a reasonable argument (World Bank 2009); however, as will be shown later, the current total GHG emissions from developing countries are now roughly equal to those of developed countries. Therefore, unless developing countries also engage in emission reduction efforts, halving global emissions will be impossible. If differentiated responsibilities are adopted—for example, developed countries reduce emissions by 80% and developing countries by 20%—then global GHG emissions would be halved. Assuming technology remains constant,

4 I am grateful to Professor Emeritus Shuzo Nishioka of Keio University for his assistance in preparing this figure. Note that GHG emissions are sometimes expressed in terms of CO_2 equivalent and sometimes in terms of carbon (C) equivalent. The former is 3.67 times the latter.

5 According to the latest Sixth Assessment Report of the IPCC, net emissions have reached 31 Gt.

developed countries would have to reduce their energy consumption by as much as 80%. Nevertheless, the European Union (EU) has set a goal of achieving net-zero greenhouse gas emissions by 2050. This demonstrates a commitment to the development of groundbreaking energy-saving technologies and significant advances in the efficiency of renewable energy utilization. Without such progress, it will not be possible to halt climate change (Stern 2006; World Bank 2009).

There are many uncertainties in these climate change projections. For example, not only is it impossible to accurately predict the extent of temperature increases, but also the frequency of extreme weather events. The occurrence of pests and diseases due to global warming, the proportion of children suffering from malnutrition, and the rise in sea levels are all extremely difficult to forecast. Nevertheless, if the predictions regarding climate change are accurate, what scale of damage can we expect? The renowned British economist Stern (2006) estimates that, if humanity fails to make efforts to reduce GHGs, per capita consumption would have to be cut by about 20%. This is equivalent to a long-term decline in income of 20%. According to Rosegrant et al. (2024) of the International Food Policy Research Institute (IFPRI), global grain production is projected to increase by 38% between 2020 and 2050. However, demand is expected to rise even further due to population growth and higher incomes, resulting in an estimated 20% increase in grain prices. The latest study by Sundiang et al. (2025), which compares ten economic models worldwide, predicts that even without climate change mitigation measures, grain production will increase by 37% by 2050 and grain prices will rise by about 4%. The fact that grain prices hardly increase suggests that supply and demand are nearly balanced; nevertheless, it is still expected that about one in ten people worldwide will face hunger. Their model even predicts that, if productivity increases are assumed, grain prices could actually decline. These projections differ remarkably from the earlier estimates by Nelson et al. (2010), who predicted that, without productivity gains, grain prices would rise by 60% to 80%. As noted in ▶ Chapter 4 of this book, none of the above models account for the possibility that small-scale agriculture in Asia may experience declining production efficiency as economies develop. Therefore, the credibility of these forecasts is questionable, but it is certain that if the global environment deteriorates significantly, the damage will be immense. Moreover, the uncertainty regarding the scale of such damage only adds to the sense of foreboding.

9.4 The Environmental Kuznets Curve Is Not Relevant for Climate Change

One of the leading figures in development economics, Kuznets (1966), argued that in the early stages of economic development, income distribution worsens as per capita income increases; however, once a certain income threshold is reached, income distribution improves. In other words, if income is plotted on the hori-

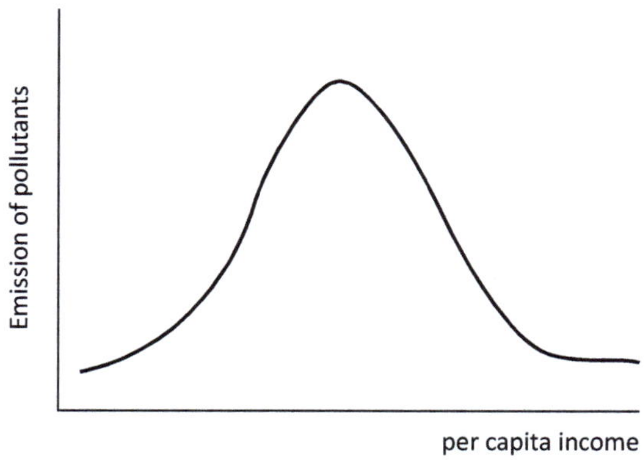

Fig. 9.3 Illustrated environmental Kuznets curve

zontal axis and income inequality on the vertical axis, the trajectory forms an inverted U-shape, resembling a bell curve. Although it is difficult to obtain long-term data to prove this, the claim is generally considered to be valid.[6]

The application of this inverted U-shape concept to environmental issues is known as the *environmental Kuznets curve* (see Fig. 9.3). At low-income levels, environmental degradation increases with rising income, as poorer populations prioritize material satisfaction over environmental concerns, and because the development of pollution-intensive chemical industries and energy-intensive heavy industries gradually progresses. However, as income rises further, public awareness of environmental issues increases, energy sources shift from highly polluting fuels such as coal to relatively cleaner fuels like crude oil and, eventually, to natural gas, which is even cleaner. Additionally, the industrial structure shifts toward less polluting service industries, resulting in reduced pollution. If this theory holds true, environmental problems may be resolved once the economy has developed sufficiently. It appears that a considerable number of environmental researchers from the natural sciences hold such expectations.

To examine the validity of the Environmental Kuznets Curve, Fig. 9.4 presents the trends in sulfur dioxide (SO_2) concentrations, continuously measured at 17 locations across Japan. According to these data, pollution from sulfur dioxides follows a pattern resembling the right side of an inverted U-shape. The absence of data before 1965 likely reflects the fact that air pollution was not yet considered a serious issue by the authorities. From the immediate postwar period to 1965, manufacturing gradually developed, and the number of automobiles steadily increased; therefore, air pollution must have become increasingly severe during this time. If data from this period were available, the upward-sloping portion of the curve would be visible, and the overall trend would form an inverted U-shape. Although the horizontal axis in Fig. 9.4 represents calendar years rather than per

6 There are various possible causes, such as the gradual migration of poor rural populations to urban areas, but these will not be discussed here.

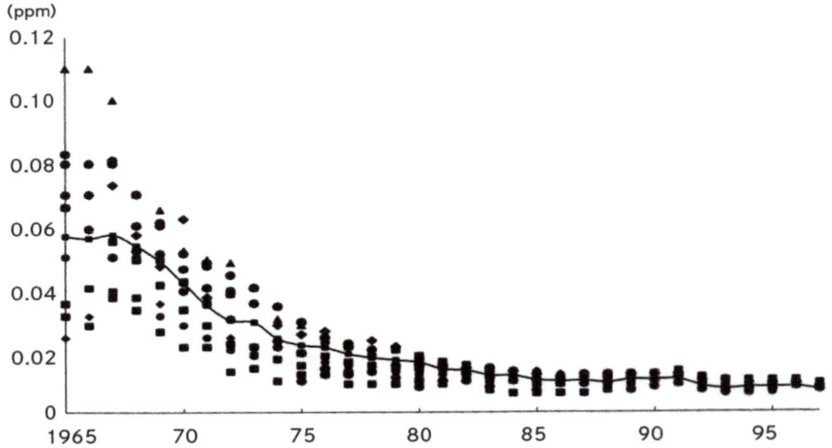

Fig. 9.4 Changing pollution of sulfur dioxide in Japan (Ministry of the Environment of Japan, Nippon no Taiki osen Jokyo [Air pollution in Japan] various years)

capita income, the trend would likely be the same if income were used instead. These findings support the applicability of the environmental Kuznets curve to sulfur dioxide emissions in Japan. Numerous related studies have also reported that air and river pollution follow an inverted U-shaped trajectory.

It is important to emphasize here that, while the environmental Kuznets curve may apply to so-called local pollution, the emission of greenhouse gases—a global negative externality—is a different matter. When large amounts of sulfur dioxides or nitrogen dioxides are released into the atmosphere, local residents are directly affected. As a result, complaints from residents lead to policies aimed at curbing these emissions. In contrast, even if large quantities of CO_2 are emitted into the atmosphere, we do not immediately experience any tangible harm. Therefore, there are no complaints when a nearby factory emits CO_2. This is a fundamental difference between local pollution and climate change. Consequently, without international agreement, there is no guarantee that GHG emissions will decrease with rising income as the environmental Kuznets curve suggests. This issue will be further discussed in ► Box 9.1.

Box 9.1 Pollution and Climate Change Are Different

Japan experienced numerous pollution problems during its process of economic development, such as *Minamata* disease, *Itai-itai* (sore-sore) disease, and severe asthma due to air pollution, widely known as Yokkaichi asthma. In this sense, Japan was a forerunner in pollution issues. I myself remember, as a child, that even during the day, the sky over central Tokyo was darkened by exhaust fumes, making it dim and gloomy. This was in the late 1950s. While it may be insensitive to use the word resolved, given that some people still suffer physical or psychological pain, mercury contamination, air pollution, and river pollution have at least been significantly reduced. This pattern is exactly as described by the environmental Kuznets curve.

Pollution progresses up to a certain point, after which it begins to improve. The reason is that those affected by the damage voiced their grievances. As a result, the authorities were compelled to take action to control pollution. Politicians who were indifferent to pollution issues likely found it difficult to win elections. Thus, to a considerable extent, pollution could be addressed through the will of the local population. The key point is that, in order to control pollution, the government regulated free economic activity and "forcibly" reduced pollutant emissions.

However, climate change is a different story. No matter how much carbon dioxide is emitted, local residents do not feel any pain, discomfort, or distress. Therefore, residents do not protest. This is happening all over the world. As a result, greenhouse gases accumulate in the atmosphere, global climate change begins to occur, and damage is being observed in various regions.

Local negative externalities can be addressed locally, but global negative externalities cannot be resolved without global cooperation. This is the fundamental difference between pollution, which is a local issue, and climate change, which is a global issue. In addition, climate change presents the problem that GHG emissions by the current generation will worsen the environment for future generations. Because the voices of future generations cannot be heard, the current generation does not make earnest efforts to reduce emissions.

Solving global climate change is only possible when countries around the world are committed to finding solutions and show concern for future generations. While it is relatively easy for people in a neighborhood with shared interests to unite, in the case of climate change, national interests often conflict, making consensus difficult to achieve. Those who hope that greenhouse gas emissions will decline as economies develop, as suggested by the environmental Kuznets curve, and who are waiting for developing countries to achieve economic growth, are likely to be disappointed.

The Paris Agreement, a multilateral international framework for mitigating climate change, set the goal of limiting the rise in global average temperature to less than 2 °C above pre-industrial levels, and ideally to less than 1.5 °C. To achieve this, as with pollution control, it is necessary to regulate free economic activity and *compulsorily* reduce emissions of pollutants—in this case, greenhouse gases. However, under the 2015 Paris Agreement, each country is allowed to set its own greenhouse gas emission reduction targets. Surprisingly, countries are not even obligated to achieve these targets. Unless countries act altruistically and consider the interests of others, as long as they remain self-interested, it is virtually impossible to keep the average temperature increase below 2 °C. The fundamental reason why it is not possible to impose strict emission reduction targets compulsorily is that each country prioritizes its own national interests. In this context, the EU's commitment to achieving net-zero greenhouse gas emissions by 2050 is highly commendable. In reality, as shown in ◘ Fig. 9.5, greenhouse gas emissions continue to rise, with no sign of a downward trend.

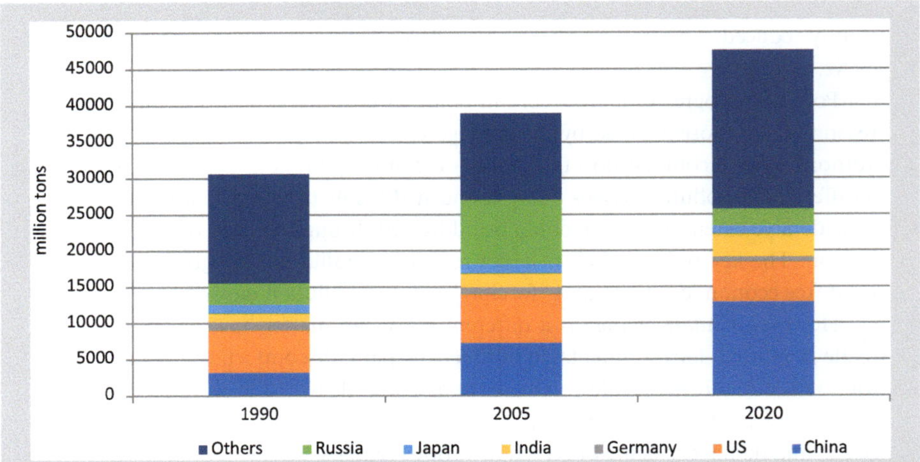

Fig. 9.5 Emission of greenhouse gas by country in 1990, 2005, and 2020 (International energy agency CO_2 emission statistics 2020)

9

Let us now use Table 9.4 to examine the differences and changes in SO_2 and CO_2 emissions in China and Japan. This table reveals several important facts. First, the amount of SO_2 emissions from the industrial sector, shown in the first row, does not necessarily change in proportion to the industrial energy consumption shown in the second row. In China, for example, while energy consumption increased more than fourfold between 1990 and 2020, SO_2 emissions actually decreased. In Japan, energy consumption fell by about 25% from 1990 to 2020, but SO_2 emissions declined even more significantly. In particular, compared to 1980, the reduction in SO_2 emissions is remarkable. To clarify this point, the SO_2 emission coefficient was calculated by dividing SO_2 emissions by energy consumption (see row [e]). The lower this value, the less SO_2 is emitted relative to energy consumption. This shows that Japan's emission coefficient is significantly lower than China's. This is likely due to the use of desulfurization equipment to control SO_2 emissions, as well as the increased use of cleaner fuels such as natural gas. In Japan, the decline in the emission coefficient has been especially pronounced since 1975. In China, too, it is said that domestically produced desulfurization equipment spread rapidly after 2000, resulting in a substantial decrease in the SO_2 emission coefficient. In other words, both countries, to varying degrees, have implemented effective measures to address air pollution caused by SO_2 emissions.

Rows [c] and [d] show the changes in total CO_2 emissions and energy consumption for the entire economy. These trends differ significantly from those observed for SO_2. In China, both CO_2 emissions and energy consumption have increased rapidly. In Japan, however, there has been little change in either CO_2 emissions or energy consumption between 1980 and 2020. This indicates a fairly proportional relationship between the two. To confirm this, let us examine the CO_2 emission coefficient (row [f]). In Japan, the CO_2 emission coefficient remained almost constant from 1980 to 2020. In contrast, in China, this coefficient in-

Table 9.4 Comparison of emission of sulfur dioxide (SO_2) and carbon dioxide (CO_2) and energy use between China and Japan (China Statistical Bureau, China Statistical Yearbook various years; Japan Environmental Agency, Comprehensive Survey of Air Pollution various years; International Energy Agency, World Energy Balance various years)

	China					Japan				
	1980	1990	2000	2010	2020	1980	1990	2000	2010	2020
[a] Emission of SO_2 from industrial production (million tons)	n/a[a]	14.90	16.20	18.60	11.03[b]	2.34	0.62[c]	0.46[c]	0.32[c]	0.41
[b] Use of energy in industrial production (million tons in oil equivalence)	181	234	302	924	1,068	91.2	108	103	91.7	76.1
[c] Emission of CO_2 in the economy (million tons)	1,430	2,195	3,209	8,110	10,068	907	1,056	1,161	1,137	991
[d] Use of energy in the economy (million tons in oil equivalence)	487	658	781	1,645	2,180	236	290	336	314	264
[e] Ratio of SO_2 emission to energy use in industries [a] ÷ [b]	n/a[a]	6.37	5.36	2.01	1.03	2.57	0.57	0.45	0.35	0.54
[f] Ratio of CO_2 emission to energy use in the economy [c] ÷ [d]	2.94	3.34	4.11	4.93	4.62	3.84	3.64	3.46	3.62	3.75

[a] n/a means data is not available
[b] Emission from all economic activities
[c] In Japan, data in 1990 is actually from 1989, in 2000 from 1999, and in 2010 from 2011

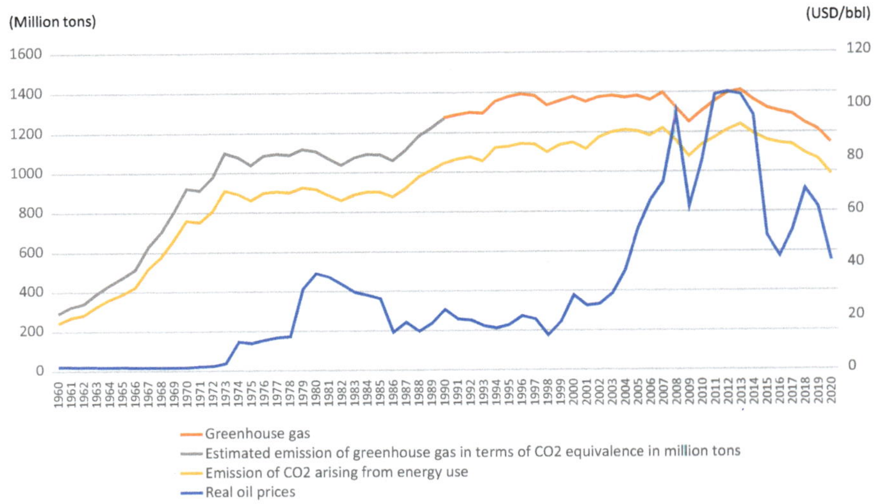

Fig. 9.6 Comparison of the emission of carbon dioxide and greenhouse gases (left-hand axis) and changes in real oil prices (right-hand axis) in Japan (The Institute of Energy Economics, Japan, EDMC Energy and Economy Statistical Yearbook [2024]; World Bank's World Development Indicators various years)

9

creased considerably over the same period. Moreover, China's emission coefficient is higher than Japan's, reflecting China's heavy reliance on coal, which emits more CO_2 per unit of energy consumed. According to the Chinese government, coal accounts for approximately 76% of the country's CO_2 emissions. However, compared to SO_2, the difference in CO_2 emission coefficient between Japan and China is smaller. This suggests that it is technically difficult to reduce CO_2 emissions. In other words, under current technologies, reducing CO_2 emissions requires not only cutting back on coal use but also reducing overall energy consumption.

Unfortunately, the inverted U-shaped relationship posited by the environmental Kuznets curve does not seem to apply to CO_2 emissions. The most important finding from this analysis is that, without the implementation of mandatory emission reduction measures, it will not be possible to achieve a significant reduction in total CO_2 emissions.

Interestingly, Japan has not continuously increased its CO_2 emissions throughout its postwar economic development. As shown in Fig. 9.6, during the period of rapid economic growth in the 1960s, CO_2 emissions—which account for about 80% of greenhouse gas emissions—increased sharply, but stagnated in the 1970s and have only risen slightly since then.[7] The main reason for this appears to be changes in crude oil prices. When oil prices rose during the two oil shocks of

7 For the period prior to 1990, there are no official statistics on GHG emissions. Here, I present estimated emission values kindly provided by Mr. Shigeru Suehiro of the Institute of Energy Economics, Japan.

the 1970s, the entire economy made efforts to conserve energy, resulting in suppressed CO_2 emissions. However, when oil prices fell in the 1980s, CO_2 emissions increased again, and after 1990, rising oil prices and economic stagnation once more led to reduced emissions. Not only in Japan, but in many advanced economies, CO_2 emissions reached their lowest levels during the oil shocks.

What does this imply? As the theory of induced technological progress suggests, rising prices prompt efforts to reduce the use of the affected resource. Judging from Japan's experience, the quantitative impact of this effect appears to be quite significant. This is valuable information when considering global GHG reduction strategies. In other words, higher energy prices have a strong effect in promoting energy conservation.

9.5 The Main Cause of Climate Change

What are the direct sources of GHG emissions? ◘ Fig. 9.7 shows the sources of GHG emissions in 2021.[8] By far the most important source is energy production using fossil fuels, which accounts for 76% of total GHG emissions. The majority of these emissions occur in advanced economies. Somewhat unexpectedly, agriculture is also a major source of GHG emissions, particularly in developing countries. The main reason is methane emissions from rice paddies and livestock. When rice is cultivated in continuously flooded fields using nitrogen fertilizers, methane gas is released. Other sources include emissions of fluorocarbons from factories and GHGs released from waste, but their overall significance is much lower.

Deforestation accounts for only 3.7% of greenhouse gas emissions; however, the burning and decomposition of trees associated with deforestation continue, and tree-covered forest areas have been in continuous decline, predominantly in developing countries. While emissions from deforestation are currently low in developed countries, it is certain that, during their historical economic development process, these nations released significant amounts of GHGs through forest destruction. Trees absorb CO_2 as they grow, but when they are burned or decomposed, they release an equivalent amount of CO_2 back into the atmosphere. Therefore, if trees are planted and subsequently used, for example, to make disposable chopsticks, the amount of atmospheric CO_2 remains unchanged, representing a perfect recycling process without any net GHG emission. In mature forests such as the Amazon, the total biomass remains constant, so there is no net absorption of CO_2. In other words, when forest area and tree biomass increase, CO_2 is absorbed; conversely, when tree biomass decreases due to deforestation or other causes, CO_2 is released from the trees. Thus, while the existence of the Amazon forests does not reduce atmospheric CO_2, their destruction would release the large quantities of CO_2 stored within the trees into the atmosphere.

8 I attempted to reproduce ◘ Fig. 9.6 using recent data. Unfortunately, I was unable to obtain data disaggregated by developing and developed countries. However, it is likely that the current situation does not differ significantly from the past.

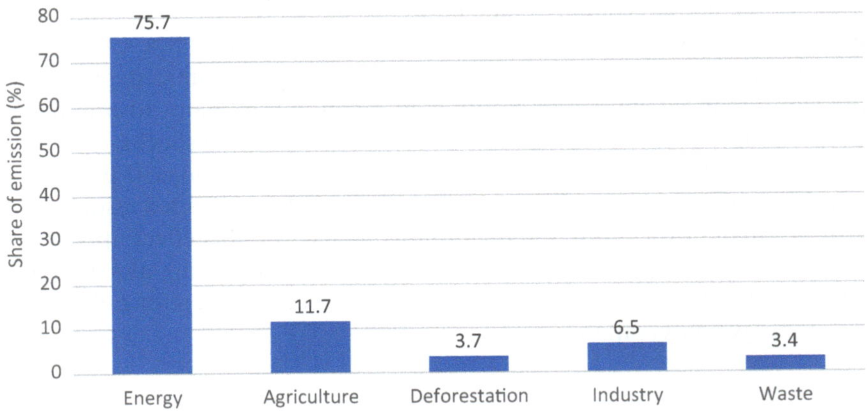

Fig. 9.7 Sources of greenhouse gas emission in 2021 (IPCC AR6 Synthesis report: Climate change 2023)

9

It is important to emphasize that, as of around 2007, GHG emissions from developing countries had already reached nearly 40% of the global total. Historically, developed countries were responsible for the overwhelming majority of GHG emissions, but the current reality is that developing countries are now also major emitters.

This trend is illustrated even more clearly in Fig. 9.5. Between 1990 and 2020, global GHG emissions increased by more than 50%. This is a significant problem, particularly because emissions from China and other countries—most of which are developing nations—have risen sharply. China has now surpassed the United States to become the world's largest emitter of GHGs. The rapid increase in emissions from India is also a major concern. Furthermore, the total emissions from developing countries have slightly exceeded 50% of the global total. Therefore, unless all countries, including developing nations, make efforts to reduce GHG emissions, it will be impossible to achieve a substantial reduction in global emissions.

Without efforts by developing countries to reduce GHG emissions, attempts to prevent or mitigate climate change will remain purely theoretical. While there is consensus that developing countries should also make some effort to reduce emissions, their commitment has not been proactive. Although the principle of "differentiated responsibilities" should be respected, the reality is that, unless the entire world—including developing countries—makes a concerted effort, it will be impossible to halt climate change.

9.6 Developing Countries Must Actively Participate in the Global Framework

For a long time, developing countries have argued that, since developed countries caused climate change by emitting GHGs, only developed countries should be responsible for curbing emissions. This argument is reasonable, and, naturally, developed countries should bear a greater share of responsibility through *differentiated reductions*. According to the World Bank (2009), developed countries, which account for one-sixth of the world's population, have emitted two-thirds of the GHGs accumulated in the atmosphere. However, it is a major problem that developing countries themselves have been reluctant to accept the proposal from developed countries that they, too, should reduce GHG emissions. The first issue is that China, the world's largest emitter, has not committed to significant emission reductions. Under China's leadership, other developing countries have also aligned themselves in minimizing their commitments to emission reductions. In addition, the United States, the second-largest emitter, withdrew from the Kyoto Protocol, which called for developed countries to reduce GHG emissions by an average of 5% from 1990 to 2010, and later withdrew from the 2015 Paris Agreement, which aimed for much more substantial reductions. The current Trump administration does not even acknowledge the worsening of climate change. Given that the two largest emitters, the United States and China, are reluctant to make significant reductions, it is unsurprising that efforts to mitigate climate change have yielded limited results. However, it is encouraging that, more recently, some island nations among developing countries—those threatened by sea level rise—have begun to take a more proactive stance on GHG emission reductions.

There are several reasons why developing countries should take more proactive measures to prevent climate change. First, as Stern (2006) points out, the countries and people most severely affected by worsening climate conditions are the poorest in poor countries. The impacts of global warming are most serious in tropical developing countries, which already experience high temperatures, rather than in developed countries. The World Bank (2009) predicts that 75%–80% of the damage caused by climate change will be borne by developing countries. Furthermore, whether it is global warming or extreme weather events, wealthy individuals can protect themselves through air conditioning and various other measures, thereby avoiding much of the harm. In contrast, poor populations are directly exposed to the adverse effects of climate change. Second, if developing countries do not commit to reducing GHG emissions, energy-intensive industries from developed countries may relocate to these regions and continue emitting GHGs. This would undermine the emission reduction efforts of developed countries.

Additionally, energy conservation in developed countries tends to lower international energy prices, which could lead to increased energy consumption in developing countries if left unchecked. In other words, efforts by developed countries alone cannot be expected to achieve significant reductions in global GHG emissions. Third, the total GHG emissions from developing countries, including China, now account for approximately half of the global total. This clearly indicates that developing countries are also responsible for exacerbating climate change. Under these circumstances, if only developed countries work to reduce GHG emissions, halving global GHG emissions becomes unattainable. In short, without the participation of developing countries, substantial mitigation of climate change is impossible.

The responsibility of developing countries cannot be disregarded, however. A particularly important issue is China's future environmental policy. The Chinese government is fully aware that China is the world's largest emitter of CO_2, accounting for 31% of global emissions—far surpassing the United States, which is in second place at 13%. As previously mentioned, the primary causes are coal consumption and the prominence of coal-intensive industries such as steel and cement. To address this, the Chinese government aims to achieve carbon neutrality by 2060 through increased use of electricity as an alternative to fossil fuels, improvements in energy efficiency, expansion of renewable energy, and industrial restructuring. If China succeeds, it will not only enhance its own international standing but also significantly influence the attitudes of developing countries toward environmental issues. However, there is some concern that the Chinese government is strongly focused on reducing the *ratio* of CO_2 emissions to GDP. If GDP continues to grow, the amount of emissions could still increase even if the ratio declines. As a policy objective, it would be preferable to set a clearer target for reducing the *absolute amount* of energy derived from fossil fuels.

Fourth, there is the issue of utilizing the Clean Development Mechanism (CDM). The CDM allows emission reductions achieved by developed countries in developing countries to be counted toward the developed countries' own GHG reduction targets. Since energy use efficiency in developing countries is generally low, it is relatively easy to improve it through technology transfer from developed countries. Actively leveraging this mechanism to enable developed countries to achieve greater GHG reductions is desirable for climate change mitigation. However, recent international negotiations have become contentious, with some arguing that a portion of the GHG reductions achieved in developing countries should be counted toward their own reduction commitments. In any case, improving energy efficiency also reduces pollution, which is a significant benefit for developing countries that are beginning to suffer from environmental degradation.[9]

Fifth, developing countries will need technological innovations such as the development of crop varieties resistant to heat, drought, and flooding, as well as new infrastructure investments for climate change adaptation, including the construction of seawalls, dams, and levees.[10] Therefore, developing countries will inevitably require additional assistance from developed nations. While maintaining the principle of differentiated responsibilities, it is now more important than ever for developing countries to also commit to reducing GHG emissions and to cooperating with developed countries in both emission reductions and mitigation of climate change impacts. Nevertheless, when observing the Conference of the Parties (COP) discussing GHG emission reductions, it appears that not only developing countries but also developed countries such as the United States, Japan,

9 While writing this chapter, I had the opportunity to travel to Delhi and Beijing, and in both major cities, air pollution was extremely severe.

10 Modern rice varieties are early-maturing and can be harvested in a short period, making it easier to avoid droughts and floods. For further details, see Tsusaka and Otsuka (2013).

and China are primarily focused on their own national interests. As a result, discussions have reached an impasse, falling into a "prisoner's dilemma" (see ► Box 9.2). It is crucial to understand the nature of climate change, recognize the decisive importance of global cooperation, and for the entire world—including developing countries—to determine bold and feasible GHG reduction targets. Without a strong commitment to such decisions, humanity will inevitably suffer enormous losses due to climate change.

Box 9.2 A Typical Prisoner's Dilemma Scenario

Two close friends, both in financial trouble, decided to commit a theft. Before carrying out the crime, they made a firm promise to each other: leave no evidence behind, and if caught by the police, remain silent to secure an acquittal. The theft itself went smoothly, but unfortunately, their suspicious behavior led to both being arrested by the police. However, there was no evidence of the theft. Therefore, if both kept silent as promised, they could be acquitted.

The two were interrogated separately. The investigator said, "Your partner is being questioned in another room. If you confess to the theft before your partner does, your sentence will be lighter. However, if your partner confesses before you, your punishment will be much more severe." The man thought, "If he confesses first, I'll get a heavy sentence. But if I confess first and he stays silent, my sentence will be lighter. In that case, it's better for me to confess." Thus, the man broke his promise and confessed to the theft. His partner, unable to resist the same temptation, also confessed. As a result, both became prisoners, receiving rather severe sentences. Although neither intended to betray the other, and there was no evidence against them, they should have exercised their right to remain silent. Had they done so, both would have been acquitted. Why did both end up confessing? The reason lies in their failure to consider the negative impact their confession would have on their partner.

Former US President George W. Bush's approach to climate change closely resembles that of the thief in this scenario, in that he ignored the interests of his partners (other countries). President Bush stated, "We will decide whether to participate in the Kyoto Protocol based on whether restricting greenhouse gas (GHG) emissions is beneficial to our country." The answer was obvious: the United States withdrew from the Kyoto Protocol. For the US to restrict GHG emissions would require sacrifices from the American people, with the benefit being the improvement of the global environment, including for Americans. Weighing these factors, President Bush declared non-participation. What was overlooked here is that if the US reduces GHG emissions, partners around the world—not just Americans—stand to benefit. Just like the thief in the interrogation room, President Bush ignored the impact of America's decision on its global partners.

Nor was President Bush alone in this regard. President Trump's actions were even more extreme. Under the banner of "America First," the United States withdrew from the Paris Agreement. If President Trump were a true patriot, he should have actively participated in the Paris Agreement and contributed to the improvement of the global climate, including that of the United States. Without such action, few would consider America a truly "great" nation. The Japanese government's response has been nothing short of embarrassing. In the aftermath of the Great East Japan Earthquake, Japan found it increasingly difficult to rely on nuclear power, leading to a rise in coal-fired power plants, which emit large amounts of carbon dioxide. However, disregarding the global environmental impact and continuing to emit carbon dioxide is simply unacceptable. Moreover, Japan has even provided financing for the construction of coal-fired power plants in developing countries. Listening to the statements of the relevant ministers, it is clear that Japan is acting just like that prisoner who thinks only of his own interests.

Observing international negotiations on GHG reduction, it seems that, except for the EU and island nations threatened by rising sea levels, most countries focused solely on their own interests. Yet, such an approach will neither reduce GHG emissions nor prevent climate change. Unless world leaders begin to consider mutual interests beyond their own national gains, they will all ultimately suffer, just like the two thieves in the classic dilemma. If the world as a whole cooperates, it is possible to mitigate climate change, enabling people everywhere to enjoy a more comfortable life. I sincerely hope that world leaders—and indeed, people everywhere—will adopt this kind of global perspective.

At the 2015 United Nations Climate Change Conference (COP21) held in Paris in December, all countries, including the United States and China, agreed to set "voluntary targets" for GHG emissions after 2020. But what exactly are voluntary targets? If every world leader sets voluntary reduction targets based solely on national interest, all countries will inevitably fall into a prisoner's dilemma.

9.7 Conclusion: A Blueprint for Sustainable Development

In this section, I will summarize both this chapter and all other chapters by referring to ◘ Fig. 9.8. At the bottom of the figure, it is shown that the success of an industrialization strategy leads to industrialization and urbanization, while the success of an agricultural development strategy leads to agricultural development. The overarching goal is poverty reduction, as indicated by the arrows pointing from the two boxes on the left (Industrialization and Urbanization, Agricultural Development) toward the poverty symbol. In short, Chapters 1 through 7 have explained how industrialization and agricultural development contribute to poverty reduction. Although not depicted here, agriculture and industry are also interconnected through population movements and the exchange of goods and services.[11]

However, industrialization and urbanization have negative impacts on the global environment through the emission of GHGs. Similarly, agricultural de-

11 Although not previously discussed, it is also important to note that urbanization and industrialization increase demand for water, which in turn leads to competition with agricultural water use.

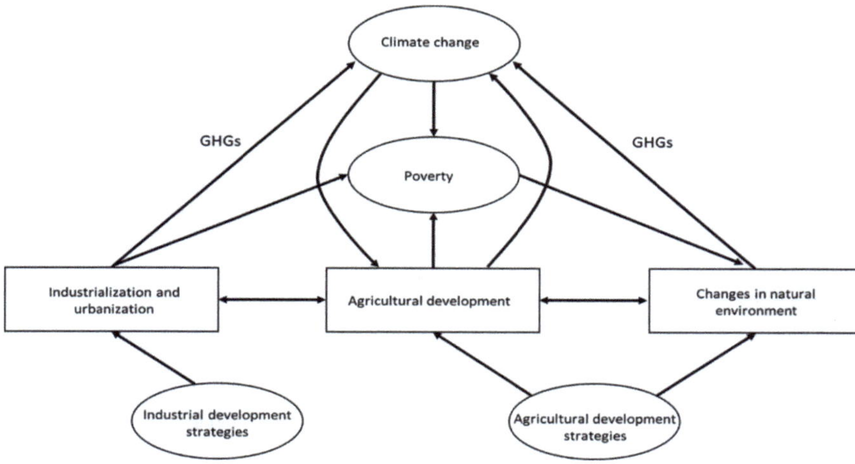

Fig. 9.8 Relationships among climate change, poverty reduction, and development strategies

velopment—especially the expansion of rice and livestock farming—worsens the global environment through the release of methane, one of the GHGs. While the likelihood is not high, if sufficient food production can be achieved, it may be possible to reduce environmental burdens by using crops such as sugarcane and palm oil as biofuels.[12]

On the other hand, the failure of agricultural development leads to environmental degradation, such as deforestation for the expansion of farmland. In particular, impoverished people who cannot find work in non-agricultural sectors may resort to clearing forests to create new farmland. Deforestation negatively affects the global environment through the release of CO_2. Additionally, poor people may overgraze livestock to secure their current food needs, which is a major cause of desertification.

Climate change directly impacts human life through rising sea levels and the spread of infectious diseases, and it also adversely affects agricultural production through higher temperatures and increased weather-related disasters.

Although not shown in Fig. 9.8, the reduction of GHG emissions itself may have adverse effects on agriculture. In order to reduce emissions, it is necessary to decrease the use of fossil fuels. From the perspective of companies producing chemical fertilizers, this is essentially equivalent to an increase in energy prices. The concern is that as energy prices rise, the cost of producing fertilizers increases, leading to higher fertilizer prices. As a result, fertilizer application may decrease, causing a decline in agricultural production. As illustrated in Fig. 9.9, when grain prices surged in 2009, crude oil prices also rose sharply. Therefore, the

12 The use of plant-based fuels, including firewood and charcoal, releases the same amount of carbon dioxide as is absorbed during growth, so in principle, the net environmental impact is zero. Moreover, the fact that fossil fuels are not used has a positive effect on the environment.

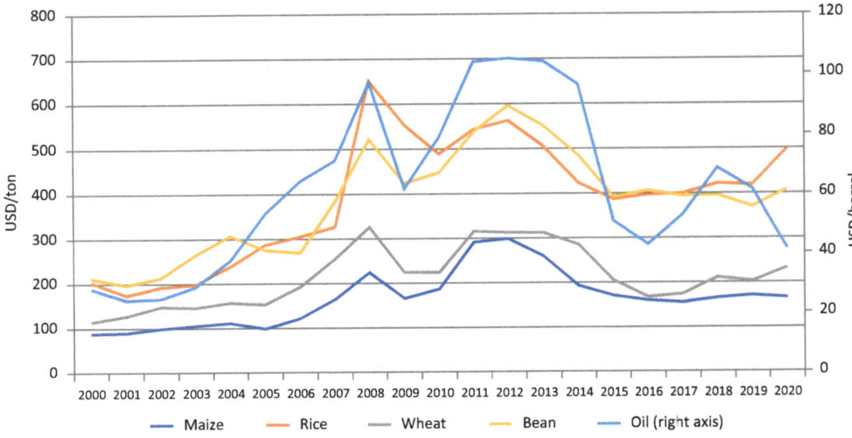

Fig. 9.9 Relationship between oil price and food prices in recent years (World Bank's World Development Indicators various years)

9

relationship between reduced energy consumption, fertilizer prices, and grain production is an issue that requires careful attention. It will likely become necessary to develop more efficient methods of fertilizer use than those currently employed. The existence of climate change does not justify relaxing efforts toward industrialization and agricultural development. On the contrary, these efforts should be vigorously promoted to reduce poverty. In particular, failure in agricultural development and poverty reduction could also lead to environmental degradation.

To reduce GHG emissions, the first priority should be to curb emissions generated by industrialization and urbanization. This requires artificially limiting the total amount of fossil fuels used by each country. An effective way to achieve this is to increase the cost of using energy produced from fossil fuels. This could be accomplished through a carbon tax or by artificially restricting the total consumption of fossil fuels. As a result, the prices of gasoline, electricity from thermal power plants, and city gas would rise significantly.

As energy costs increase, consumers and businesses will be incentivized to conserve energy and to purchase energy-efficient appliances and equipment. Japan's efforts to reduce energy consumption and curb CO_2 emissions during the oil shocks are emblematic in this regard. In the long term, as demand for energy-efficient products is anticipated to increase, companies will intensify their efforts to develop energy-saving technologies. In response, universities and research institutes will also invest substantial resources in developing such technologies. Significant research efforts will undoubtedly be directed toward improving the efficiency of renewable energy sources such as solar and wind power.

In this way, raising the cost of energy derived from fossil fuels is an absolute prerequisite for *induced technological progress* globally. This will serve as the "mother" of technological innovation (see ► Box 9.3 for further discussion).

Box 9.3 What Is the Mother of Invention?

People rise to the challenge when faced with difficulties. This is the essence of the theory of induced technological progress, which has been repeatedly discussed in this book. We are troubled when energy prices rise. Paradoxically, however, we would be in even greater trouble if energy prices did not rise.

For example, what would happen if the prices of crude oil, electricity, natural gas, and gasoline were to triple? Our daily lives would be seriously affected, but this would also create business opportunities. Manufacturers of insulation materials that can drastically reduce heating and cooling costs would be driven to improve their products, as demand for such materials would surge. Automobile manufacturers would be compelled to develop fuel-efficient hybrid cars, electric vehicles, and fuel cell vehicles, as consumers would seek cars that save more gasoline than ever before. Electronics manufacturers would devote their corporate resources to developing energy-saving appliances. In addition, many private companies and public research institutions would undoubtedly compete to develop energy-saving technologies. Research and development would also lead to dramatic improvements in the efficiency of renewable energy utilization. Although the output of renewable energy depends on natural conditions, if electricity can be stored in lithium-ion batteries, the utilization efficiency will increase significantly. The sharp rise in energy prices, combined with advancements in lithium-ion batteries, would serve as a powerful catalyst for technological innovation on an unprecedented scale.

Necessity is the mother of invention, but much of the background behind that necessity is rising prices. As previously discussed, Japan achieved significant energy conservation in a short period during the oil shock era. I am firmly convinced that, if we are to reduce greenhouse gas emissions through technological means, rising energy prices are the most effective remedy. For technological development to alleviate human suffering in the long term, humanity must endure some hardship in the short term. To curb global climate change, the most effective approach is to artificially raise the cost of using fossil fuels, thereby restricting their use. I have no doubt that the true "mother" of invention is rising prices. If we hesitate to allow prices to rise, the global environment will continue to deteriorate for decades, or even centuries.

However, it is insufficient for only developed countries to reduce fossil fuel consumption. When developed countries decrease their use of fossil fuels, global demand falls, leading to a decrease in global fossil fuel prices. As a result, consumers and businesses in developing countries will increase their fossil fuel consumption, thereby raising GHG emissions. Moreover, energy-intensive industries in developed countries may relocate their production bases to developing countries where fossil fuel prices are lower. If this occurs, all efforts will be in vain. Developing countries must recognize that they are the greatest victims of climate change and must act to prevent such outcomes. To this end, developing countries must participate more actively in international efforts to reduce GHG emissions, establish emission caps, and strive to reduce their emissions.

In agriculture, methane emissions from rice paddies and livestock are a significant issue. It is well known that emissions from rice paddies can be greatly reduced by intermittently flooding and draining the paddies, rather than keeping them continuously flooded. A key challenge is how to monitor these practices and use incentives (rewards for reducing methane emissions) and penalties (fines for emitting methane) to motivate farmers to cut methane emissions. Additionally, since increased tree cover absorbs CO_2, a system that rewards forest conservation and reforestation, and penalizes deforestation, would greatly contribute to mitigating global climate change. Here too, the ability to monitor tree growth and deforestation and to impose appropriate incentives and penalties is crucial to success.

The problem of global climate change can only be solved through global cooperation. The mindset of "What losses and benefits will our country incur if we reduce GHG emissions, say, by 20 gigatonne (Gt)?" will not lead to meaningful reductions. Instead, we should consider, "If our country reduces GHG emissions by 20 Gt, and all other countries also reduce by 20 Gt, what benefits will accrue to our country when the world as a whole committed to achieving a promised reduction of GHG emission?" If we approach international negotiations with this perspective and make bold decisions to reduce GHG emissions, it will be possible to mitigate climate change. Furthermore, if this can be achieved, advances in science and technology will be induced to greatly alleviate climate change. This is the only way to simultaneously achieve poverty reduction and global environmental protection. I believe that the only option left to us is this path.

Questions

1. Is it possible to achieve economic development and improve the global climate simultaneously?
2. Why do developing countries suffer more severely from climate change than developed countries?
3. What is the role of energy prices in mitigating climate change?
4. Since the global climate has deteriorated primarily due to the economic activities of developed countries in the past, should it be developed countries, not developing countries, that reduce GHG emissions?
5. What is the difference between the prisoner's dilemma story and the international agreement on GHG emissions?

References

China Statistical Bureau. (various years). *China Statistical Yearbook*.

Intergovernmental Panel on Climate Change (IPCC). (2023). *IPCC AR6 Synthesis Report: Climate Change*.

International Energy Agency. (2020). *CO_2Emission Statistics*.

Japan, Environmental Agency. (various years). *Comprehensive Survey of Air Pollution*.

Japan, Institute of Energy Economics. (2024). *EDMC Energy and Economy Statistical Yearbook*.

Japan, International Energy Agency. (various years). *World Energy Balance*.
Japan, Meteorological Agency. (2025). ► https://www.data.jma.go.jp/cpdinfo/temp/list/an_wld.html.
Japan, Ministry of the Environment. (various years). *Nippon no taiki osen jokyo [Air pollution in Japan]*.
Kuznets, S. (1966). *Modern economic growth: Rate, structure, and spread*. New Haven and Yale University Press.
Nelson, G.C., Rosegrant, M.W., Palazzo, A., Gray, I., Ingersoll, C., Robertson, R., Tokgoz, S., Zhu, T., Sulser, T.B., Ringler, C., Msangi, S., You, L. (2010). *Food security, farming, and climate change to 2050*. International Food Policy Research Institute.
Rosegrant, M.R., Sulser, T.B., Dunston, S., Mishra, A., Cenacchi, N., Gebretsadik, Y., Robertson, R., Thomas, T., & Wiebe, K. (2024). Food and nutrition security under changing climate and socioeconomic conditions. *Global Food Security*, *41*, 100755.
Stern, N. (2006*). The economics of climate change*. The Office of Climate Change, UK Government.
Sundiang, M., Oliveira, T.D., Masoan-D'Croz, D., Gibson, M., Beier, F., Benavidez, L., Bordirsky, B.L., Bos, A., Chepelief, M., Chen, D.M.C., de Lange, T., Doelman, J., Dunston, S., Frank, S., Fujimori, S., Hasegawa, T., Havlik, P., Hristov, J., Jägermeyr, J., Kozicka, M., Kuiper, M., Kyle, P., Lotze-Campen, H., Luchtenbelt, H., Mishra, A., Muller, C., Nelson, G., Palazzo, A., Domínguez, I.O., Popp, A., Sands, R., Springmann, M., Stehfest, E., Sulser, T., Takahash, K., Tassinari, G., Thom, F., Thornton, P., Tsuchiya, K., van Zeist, W.J., van Meijl, van der Mensbrugghe, D., Vuuren, D.V., van Zanten, H.H.E., Weindl, I., Wiebe, K., Zhao, X., Harrero, M. (2025, forthcoming). *Bundling of actions can unlock the potential for food systems transformation*. EAT Lancet Commission on Food, Planet, Health,
Tsusaka, T., & Otsuka, K. (2013). The changes in the effects of temperature rainfall on cereal crop yields in sub-Saharan Africa: A country level panel data study. *Environmental Economics, 4*(2), 70–80.
United Nations. (2025). *2000–2015, Millennium Development Goals*. ► https://research.un.org/en/docs/dev/2000-2015
World Bank. (2009). *World Development Report 2010: Development and Climate Change*. World Bank.
World Bank. (various years). *World Development Indicators*. World Bank.

Supplementary Information

K. Otsuka, *A Primer on Development Economics*, Classroom Companion: Economics,
https://doi.org/10.1007/978-981-95-5397-6

Index

N

O

P

Q

R

S

T

W

Z

MIX
Papier aus verantwortungsvollen Quellen
Paper from responsible sources
FSC® C105338

If you have any concerns about our products,
you can contact us on
ProductSafety@springernature.com

In case Publisher is established outside the EU,
the EU authorized representative is:
Springer Nature Customer Service Center GmbH
Europaplatz 3, 69115 Heidelberg, Germany

Printed by Libri Plureos GmbH
in Hamburg, Germany